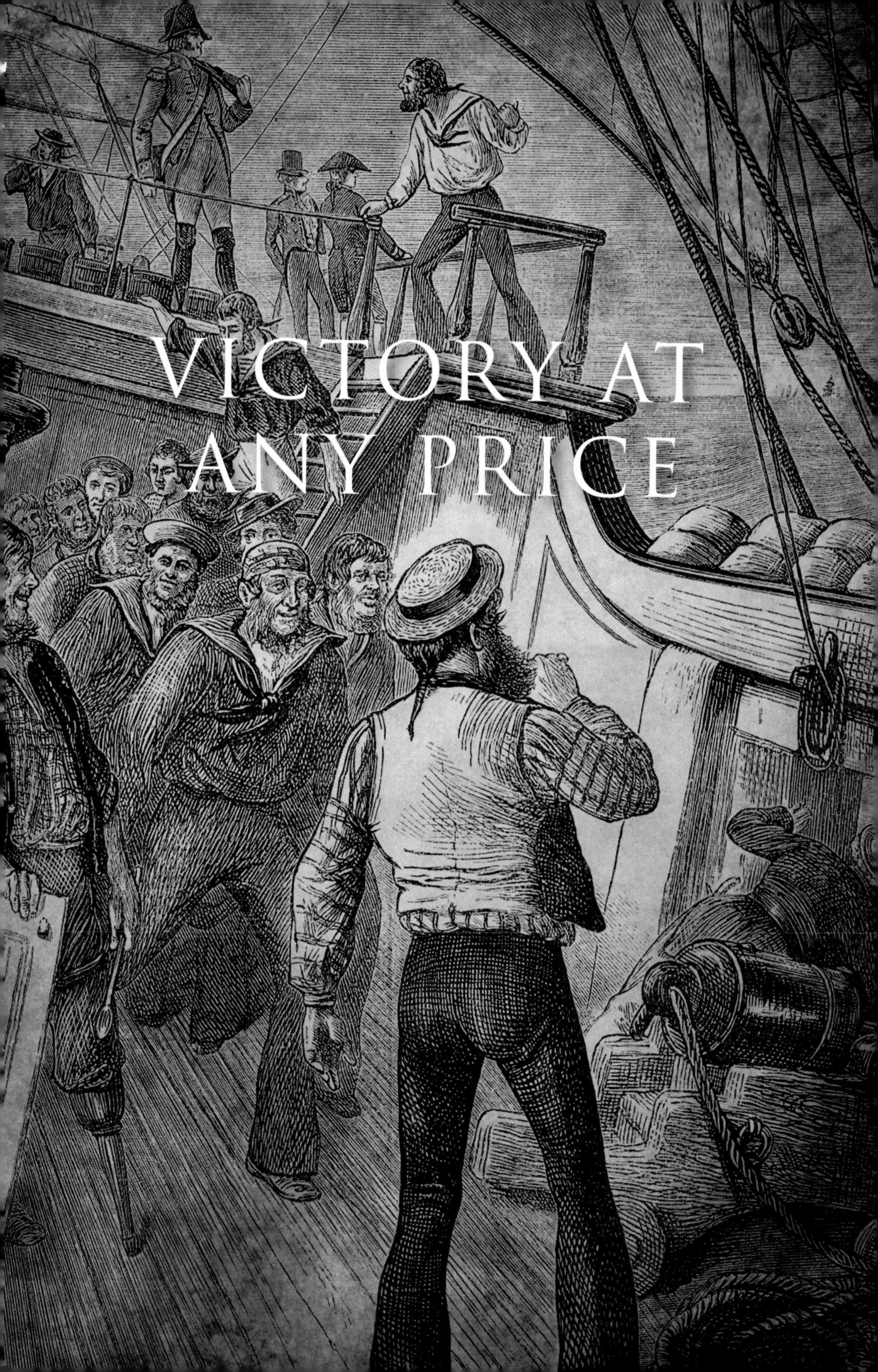
VICTORY AT
ANY PRICE

First published in Great Britain in 2009 by
Jonathan Bowman

A CIP Catalogue of this book is available from
the British Library

ISBN 978-0-9563823-0-6

Typeset in Caslon 11½ pt by
Chandler Book Design
www.chandlerbookdesign.co.uk

Printed and bound in Great Britain by
Ashford Colour Press

Limited Edition

Certificate

I certify that this edition is limited to one thousand copies

EDITION NO. 728

AUTHOR'S SIGNATURE:

...AT ANY PRICE

CONTENTS

PART ONE MAKING PASSAGE

PART TWO FLAGSHIP PROJECT

CONTENTS

DEDICATION

This book is dedicated to the memory of three men who made the project possible:

Nick Varley, whose intuition and creativity brought this opportunity to light and set it on its path; Mick Lock for whom the words 'it can't be done' did not exist; and to my business partner John Morgan, one of 'The Sons of Zebedee' and a true son of thunder.

ACKNOWLEDGEMENTS:

I would like to thank all those who took part in our attempt to create a lasting commemorative tribute to Lord Nelson and the victory at Trafalgar, in particular:

Rear Admiral Sir Peter Spencer KCB ADC

Lieutenant Commander Frank Nowosielski MBE RN

Alan Aberg, Chairman of the Society for Nautical Research

Sym Taylor, Chief Executive of The Disposal Services Agency, MOD

International Craft and Hobby Fair Ltd

Trek Highway Services Ltd

Mid-Norfolk Canopies and Trailers Ltd

David Burton and Caroline Richmond

Finch Seaman Enfield Ltd

Brookside Metals Ltd

Pussers Rum

Woodforde's Norfolk Ales

Purina Pet Food Division of Nestlé

Musto Ltd

The Bell Inn, Houghton-on-the-Hill, Essex

Tripstamp Ltd

The Sons of Zebedee

My daughter Amy who provided much needed help with design

… and of course, my wife Janet – acting unpaid Packing and Despatch Manager and all-round powder monkey.

AUTHOR'S NOTE

I WROTE this book with three things in mind. First, to provide some kind of provenance and reference source for the use of *HMS Victory*'s arisings, including The 1805 Collection and other projects, for the benefit of future collectors or other interested parties. Secondly, I offer it as a light and unacademic account of starting a small business. Those concerned with doing such a thing might find something in here of use, and those involved in studying small businesses may find in it some elements for discussion, debate or critique. It is very plain to me with the benefit of hindsight that there are many things that could have been done differently or better, or that an entirely different outcome may have been achieved with a longer term or otherwise alternative base strategy. The third reason was just to tell a story about people and events linked together by an historical milestone event. In truth, the writing of it has been a cathartic exercise for me, finally drawing a line under the project.

The exercise of getting the book published has been a learning experience in itself. This is clearly something of a niche product, unsuited to any of the literary genres that are appealing to publishers, and unlikely to push Harry Potter off the shelves of Heathrow Airport's bookshops. However, since the project needed a record, I decided to venture into the world of what is known by the more sniffy literati as 'vanity publishing', encountering one or two sharks in the process. The upshot was that I decided to go it alone, having received valuable advice from many valued sources – to whom many thanks. It seemed fitting to echo much of the project by offering the book as a limited edition of 1,000.

JC Bowman 2009

PROLOGUE

WHEN people ask me: "How did you become the owner of 34 tons of reclaimed oak and 10 tons of copper from *HMS Victory*?" I usually give a wry smile and say: "I guess I wasn't paying attention at the time". It is, of course, a fair and frequently asked question; getting to the real reason is an exercise I have put myself through countless times. The ensuing project, which is described in this book, was the result of an impulse. It was a time of learning and humour, of stress and frustration, but most of all of personal relationships. It was at the same time bizarre, rewarding and enlightening.

I should perhaps have heard some faint alarm bell ring when, one bright, crisp February Sunday morning, I received a bizarre phone call from a complete stranger who said his name was Boddy, and would I be interested in running his woodland burial site? The answer was an unequivocal "no". Not because it was not a worthwhile project, but because I had just spent 11 years running a good sized company and did not want to do the managing director thing again. Nonetheless, the conversation was intriguing enough that I agreed to drive the five miles to his home and the site of the proposed burial ground in order to meet this unusual man who later became the link to Victory and a partner in the venture.

So, back to the question of how, or perhaps why? Certainly, the infectious enthusiasm and interminable optimism of James Boddy was a factor. I, however, was conventional Corporate Management Man… business school, blue chip companies with multi-million pound turnovers and legions of employees. Mr Entrepreneur I was not. But in there somewhere was the little voice that had tried to be heard over the years saying: "Do your own thing; create something of your own instead of implementing other people's visions."

On the wall next to the door into my office is a framed print of a Chinese junk given to me by an old friend at university. We had been discussing careers and

I had expounded somewhat bombastically a philosophy that the true businessman should break new ground, do the unusual, create new paradigms. When challenged for an example, I suggested travelling to the Far East, buying a Chinese junk, sailing it back to England, mooring it in the Thames and turning it into a restaurant. It was a daft notion for all sorts of reasons and meant really to illustrate a point – 'do different', as they say in Norfolk. Nevertheless, when I graduated my friend presented me with the print (purchased ironically from the National Maritime Museum, home of the largest Nelsonia gallery in the world) as a reminder of our conversation. I had it framed, hung it on the wall and effectively forgot about the philosophy. Or did I?

HMS Victory is no Chinese junk, though 44 tons of her salvage was unquestionably junk in the eyes of some friends and acquaintances. The decision to buy it was not carefully thought out, but rather an impulse, a gamble. With hindsight, it really was the first step on that trip to China.

FOREWORD

WHEN I joined the Royal Navy in 1972 as a Seaman Radar Operator I could never have imagined that my naval career would culminate with being the Commanding Officer of *HMS Victory* the oldest commissioned warship in the world. I held this position for just under eight years from April 1998 to March 2006 and currently stand as the ship's longest serving Commanding Officer in its 250 year history. It was truly a remarkable experience and great privilege to step foot onboard each day and have the opportunity to influence and assist in the ship's on-going restoration and maintenance, whilst presenting the ship as the Flagship of the Second Sea Lord and Commander in Chief Naval Home Command as well as opening the ship to the general public each day.

Maintaining *HMS Victory* in a manner that befits her iconic status to the Royal Navy and to the British public is both a costly and a sensitive operation. The decision by the Ministry of Defence to sell into private hands the "arisings" created by her restoration raised concerns in some quarters that there was a real risk that insensitive commercialisation could demean her and put her reputation at risk. Equally, it was plain that the sale of the materials and royalties from their use could make a real contribution to restoration funds at a time when they were most needed.

When I was asked to put my name to Provenance Certificates for the project outlined in this book that risk suddenly became personal. I met the new owners and listened to their plans. It became apparent that James, John and Jonathan had recognised the concerns about maintaining dignity and respect for Victory, and that there were very good commercial reasons for promoting her reputation and not degrading her. I judged that the "arisings" were in trustworthy hands and decided that supporting the project would not only strengthen its prospects of success but also give me some degree of influence if I felt they were being misused. It was also clear from the outset that the materials were going to be used by professional crafts people for the production of high quality items that befit their status and history.

I feel a combined sense of relief and satisfaction that the project turned out well for all those involved in it. Only by reading this book have I realised just how much went into it from so many people. The funds the project created for the ongoing upkeep of *Hms Victory* will help ensure that she remains a proud reminder of our naval heritage and a truly extraordinary visitor experience.

Lieutenant Commander Frank Nowosielski MBE RN
Commanding Officer, Hms Victory 1998 to 2006

PART ONE

MAKING PASSAGE

1

HMS VICTORY AFTER TRAFALGAR

HMS VICTORY was a middle-aged lady at the time of her greatest triumph as flagship to the flamboyant Lord Nelson at the battle of Trafalgar. At 40 years of age, and with one complete refit already undertaken, this 100 gun ship of the line led the windward van column into the 'pel-mel battle' much loved by Nelson against a much superior force. Small wonder then that she suffered significant topside damage, limping back to Gibraltar after the action in the teeth of a fearsome storm wearing only a jury-rigged foretopsail as her main sail and a handkerchief of foresail. Artist Dr Mike Haywood painted a splendid and technically accurate depiction of *HMS Victory in the Storm after the Battle of Trafalgar* especially for The 1805 Collection with limited edition prints mounted with oak and copper fragments from the ship.

A major refit at Chatham in 1806 followed by more smaller repairs and modifications allowed her to continue service, though latterly as a 'second-rater' with reduced armament and crew and little in the way of serious engagements.

There followed a series of refits, repairs and modifications in her role as flagship, among others for the Port Admiral during the late 1880s. The amount of money expended on her maintenance dwindled during this period, and her deteriorating state was considerably worsened by an incident in 1903 when she was struck at anchor by another ship that had broken loose from a towline. Efforts were made to tidy her up for the centenary celebrations of the Battle of Trafalgar in 1905, but there was clearly a level of public indignation at this time that this icon of British naval power had been allowed to deteriorate so much.

In 1910 she was modified to act as a troop carrier and the onset of war in 1914 delayed any further move to restore the ship. It was not until 1922 that *HMS Victory* through the good offices of the Society for Nautical Research, was finally dry-docked in Portsmouth and major works commenced to bring her back to the magnificence we see in Number 2 dock, Portsmouth, today.[1]

In simple terms, the work undertaken had three objectives: first, to make her sound; second, to return her to her Trafalgar configuration, recognising that she had undergone a number of changes in the meantime; and third, more recently, to make her safe for visitors in compliance with health and safety regulations. However, the prime task of making her sound was complicated by the fact that she was now sitting on concrete and not on a cushion of water. Her great weight threatened to cause serious collapse, so it became a matter of priority to take weight out of her wherever possible, replacing parts with strong but lighter materials. One obvious opportunity was to remove the copper sheathing from the bottom of the hull. This alone weighed in excess of 12 tons. Once removed, a clearer and more daunting picture of the state of hull beneath was revealed.

The works carried out to achieve the three objectives lasted for 80 years and *HMS Victory* was complete for the bicentenary celebrations in 2005. In true navy fashion, none of the material removed was wasted, being stored in Portsmouth dockyard in case good use could be made of it as the project progressed. Only timber that was seriously infected by woodworm or death watch beetle was burned. It was this salvaged material that gave life to The 1805 Collection.

Today *HMS Victory* is still in commission as the flagship of the Second Sea Lord and Commander in Chief, Naval Home Command. As such she is the oldest commissioned warship in the world. She is open to the public, restored to her full Trafalgar glory, and is a truly remarkable visitor experience.

1 For full details see *HMS Victory. Her Construction, Career and Restoration* by Alan McGowan, published by Caxton Editions.

2

TEA AND SALVAGE

ONLY in England could a life-altering episode commence with a cup of tea. It was a warm June afternoon in 1999 at an open day organised by James Boddy to share plans for his woodland burial ground that I first met Nick Varley. As we sipped tea on the terrace Nick told me the story of his involvement with the 'arisings', as the Navy call them, of Nelson's great flagship.

Nick was a skilled clockmaker or horologist, apprenticed as a young man to the company that built the clock in the Houses of Parliament, famous for its Big Ben bell. He ran his own company using these skills to make and repair clocks and similar intricate mechanisms. About three years before our conversation on the terrace Nick had been approached by a well-known American company called The Franklin Mint to make for them a limited edition of famous ships' compasses. As part of that project he had travelled down to Portsmouth and was standing on the deck of *HMS Victory* talking to her Commanding Officer when he noticed a large skip on the dockside with smoke coming from it. On enquiring what was happening, he was told that the ship was in an ongoing state of repair and that some of the timber removed was being burned. His immediate response was one of incredulity that historic material was being destroyed in this manner. His mind was soon put at rest, however when it was explained that they only burned timber that was so badly infested with death-watch beetle or woodworm that this was the only safe course. All sound material, he was told, was stored in warehouses within the dockyard and had been accumulating there since the work commenced in 1922.

The knowledge that there was so much heritage material being stored and apparently not used played on Nick's mind. He could think of all sorts of interesting things he could do with it if he could get his hands on it. Eventually he contacted the Ministry of Defence (MOD) and asked if he could purchase some.

They asked him to put forward a proposal that would seem appropriate for the use of this historically important asset, and this he duly did. Negotiations and exchanges of correspondence began.

At this point, when Nick had every reason to think he was making progress, disaster struck. He became ill and was diagnosed as having cancer at an advanced stage. Doctors told him he might have as little as four months left to live. Then began hospitalisation, treatment and the fight back. In the months that followed he wound up his business, put his affairs in order and concentrated on proving the doctors wrong. Astonishingly, nearly two years later, the condition seemed to be in remission and Nick started to think tentatively about getting on with his life. It was at this time that the MOD, apparently needing the space in the naval dockyard, decided to put the arisings from *HMS Victory* up for public tender. It seemed they had not forgotten the discussions with Nick and realised that there might be some real value to be had from its sale, particularly with the bicentenary of the battle of Trafalgar only a handful of years away.

"The MOD had the courtesy to tell me about the tender," Nick said. "But I felt both anger and frustration that my ideas had somehow created an opportunity for others to do what I had planned to do."

In the circumstances, he felt compelled to put in a bid for the material through his now dormant company Varley and Dyke Ltd. Much to his amazement, his bid won the tender.

"The trouble is, I now have just three weeks to come up with the money or I will have lost the tender," he told me. "And I don't have any money! I don't even own a car anymore – my son brought me here today. I have been ill for the thick end of two years and have not worked in that time."[2]

This was the point when my normal reserve and common sense deserted me. Perhaps I could take it on or somehow get involved.

"Look, Nick," I ventured. "It sounds as though you need some cash, while I need a challenge. Would you consider selling the opportunity?"

We explored various mechanisms that might meet his need for funds and my need for a business opportunity. We also talked about how much money it would take to pay the MOD and to give Nick a reasonable return on his sale of the project. It was very tempting. Could I afford it? Well, yes… but this was a high-risk project and the thought of taking it on by myself was a lonely one. The prudent thing would be to share the risk with others and at the same time bring in some additional business and creative skills. Our host, James Boddy, would certainly be up for something unusual like this, and when I broached it with him it turned out that he was a huge fan of Nelson. No problem there, then. The two of us decided to approach a third person, John Morgan, whom we both knew to

[2] Sadly, Nick lost his battle with cancer the following November.

be interested in small business investment and whom I had known for a number of years.

"Sounds like an interesting punt," was John Morgan's comment, and so the three of us stitched together a deal with Nick.

We purchased his company Varley and Dyke Ltd, whose only asset was the tender from the MOD, and paid over the contract amount to the Disposal Services Agency of the Ministry of Defence.

I did not fully appreciate it at the time, but I had just made the decision to crown my business career by becoming a scrap merchant.

3

BRASS TACKS

"EXPERIENCE is something you always acquire just after you really needed it," so the aphorism tells us. The full magnitude of what we had taken on did not really register, even when we went down to Portsmouth to inspect our purchase. For me, this did not happen until all the materials were fully relocated to my barn in Norfolk. Even then, I would take a daily reality check by walking into the barn and surveying its contents with a mixture of awe, respect and dread that this time I had really blown it.

Before we signed off on the contract, the shareholders thought it prudent to visit Portsmouth and inspect the materials. The Commanding Officer of *HMS Victory,* Lt Cdr Frank Nowosielski, welcomed us to his office aboard the historic ship. The meeting did not get off to the best of starts when John, being handed the CO's card, said:

"Nowosielski? What kind of name is that for an officer in the Royal Navy?"

It was intended as an icebreaker, and typical of John's rather provocative sense of humour, but it grated. I winced, wondering how much work we would now need to do to bring onside someone who was clearly going to be key to the success of our project. Happily, Frank took it in good part, and later I was able to establish a positive and friendly relationship with him. He turned out to be most supportive and helpful throughout the life of The 1805 Collection. We were fortunate that, in view of the looming bicentenary celebrations in 2005, Frank was asked by the Navy to remain in that post until the event was over. This meant an unusually long stint in what is normally a posting of about three years and he was awarded the MBE for his services.

After an informal chat in his office, during which Frank voiced the hope that the owners of this heritage material would use it in a suitably respectful and tasteful manner, he took us into the part of the dockyard where the timber and copper were stored. The accumulated salvage of 80 years lay in heaps in three different locations. The bulk of it was in a cellar, down worn brick steps. It did not occur to me at the time that simply getting that volume of material out of this place would be a challenge in itself. The timbers were piled willy-nilly in two enormous heaps, and it was impossible to see the character of most of them since they were buried beneath the top layer.

The sizes, shapes and general condition were such that no two pieces were the same. Some timbers had clearly been sawn out, others ripped out. Some showed evidence of rot and woodworm in parts (usually just the edge), while others had steel bolts or copper rivets protruding from them. Others yet had holes through them where bolts or rivets had been or had wooden dowels or 'tree nails' in them. Some had the distinctive yellow paint seen on the outside of the ship and others had white paint from the interior. The paint was generally layer upon layer upon layer. Most had no paint at all. The vast majority of it was oak, but in time we found some quantities of teak, pitch pine, iroco (a relatively modern addition) and even some walnut. Sizes varied from pieces no larger than a child's fist to four hanging knees, believed to be from the lower gun deck that weighed some 200-250 kgs each. It was essentially lengths or sections of beams, and not what might be described as planks. Many of our customers would ask us if we had deck planks, but anyone who has visited the ship will know that her size is such that all timbers on the ship were of significant thickness, and the decks are not made of the sort of timber one associates with domestic flooring.

The other two locations were ground level warehouse type buildings, but characterised by the same haphazard heaps of material. There had never been any method in the storage, and you could hear the supervisor saying "OK lads, chuck it over there!" Importantly, however, the material had all been stored dry and with sufficient ventilation, even in the cellar, to keep the timbers in suitable condition for re-working.

The copper came in two forms. The greatest bulk was in sheets that had been the copper-bottom cladding of the ship. Around 3,500 sheets with a measurement of 14 inches wide by 48 inches long had been used, each with an individual weight of over 3kgs and a total weight of around 12 tons or more. Only part of that material remained and was sold in the tender, and for the most part this was sheathing that was replaced in the 1830s or the 1880 refit. It was covered in the green patina found on all copper exposed to the elements, and was about 1mm thick. All around the edges were nail holes, and in some cases the bronze or brass nails were still attached. There were holes in most, often where the maker's mark had been cut out for cataloguing or collection, but many were also very worn with the copper having a lace-like look to it. Some of the sheets had been cut to smaller sizes – presumably as patches – and some had just deteriorated so much that they fell into smaller pieces. They were, by virtue of the green dust, extremely dirty. A chemical analysis carried out later in the project identified this material as particularly pure copper, but with small traces of arsenic. I later learned that much of this copper had been mined in Amlwch in Anglesey. Its old port and mine are undergoing restoration as a tourist attraction and site of historic interest. When I contacted them they were very excited to know of the existence of some of their material with such a noble provenance and they duly acquired some for their exhibition.

King's Mark

The remaining copper (and indeed some bronze) came in the form of rivets. These were solid copper rods, usually mushroomed over at one end where they had been bludgeoned into place, in varying diameters and lengths. The largest were about 35mm in diameter, and there were lengths from a few centimetres up to well over a metre. The latter were extremely heavy. We had a visit from a shipwright and Victory enthusiast who told me that these large rivets were knocked in by attaching chains to opposite sides of a heavy duty canon ball, and then two men, one on the end of each chain, would swing it like a huge skipping rope, crashing the iron ball onto the end of the rivet. Such was the length and size of these copper fasteners that it was impossible to drive them with any hammer that one man could wield. Smaller diameters of 20mm and 25mm came in an equally random set of lengths, generally having been sawn off to extract the timbers that they had been fastening. There were also a number of smaller, pointed pins of a heavy copper alloy that typically had lengths of 200 to 300mm and a diameter of around 15mm. They had domed heads and were really just large nails. These proved of great interest to collectors, and we sold out of them quite quickly.

One interesting feature of all the copper was the presence of the King's Mark, Pusser's Arrow or even Devil's Clawmark. This is the arrowhead symbol that used to be seen in the old black and white films on prisoners' uniforms. It indicates that the item is the property of the Crown. Use of copper as sheathing and fastening in Nelson's navy had become mandatory. The copper sheathing protected the oak hull from attack by the teredo worm that was highly destructive and costly. It had the added benefit of acting as an anti-fouling device, thus enabling the ship to sail faster. The term 'copper-bottomed' derives from this nautical association, and although the French navy used the same technique with their ships, it was nonetheless one of the features that gave advantage to the British navy as a world sea power at that time. Copper was, as today, a costly, valuable and highly marketable commodity. Quantities of it would disappear from shipyards and be sold on the black market, so it was deemed necessary to identify this copper as belonging to the Crown. On many of the rivets the arrows were to be found over the entire length at distances of no more than an inch apart. The expression 'pinching an inch' meant that you could not pinch, or steal, more than an inch of this material without including a mark. It had nothing to do with losing weight. The use of copper fasteners became the norm for all fastening below the waterline following early disasters with the sheathing. The first time that copper plates were fixed to our ships' hulls, ordinary iron nails were used. The chemical interaction of iron with copper and salt water meant that the nails quickly disintegrated and the copper sheets fell off. Great news if you supply the copper sheets, but bad news for the Admiralty. Somewhere beneath all the patination on both sheathing and rivets, the King's Mark was generally to be found.

During our initial inspection of this material I noticed in the cellar that there were two buckets of the small bronze or brass nails that were used to hold the copper sheathing in place. Unfortunately these disappeared before the salvage was delivered to us. Sadly, nothing changes in dockyards!

4

THE DEAL

AS NICK VARLEY had already created the deal that formed the basis of the contract with the Ministry of Defence, we, the new owners of Varley and Dyke Ltd, had no opportunity to change it. The key features of the contract were:

- We were the sole owners of all oak and copper salvaged from *HMS Victory* to date, and we would have first refusal on any subsequent salvage of this sort. The monopoly nature of the deal was critical as it would have been impossible to control the provenance of anything claiming to be from the ship if it was in the hands of multiple owners. It would also have been impossible to set and sustain a value for it if we were competing with others. Additionally, we would have found it difficult to engage with artists and craftspeople if they thought their own competitors could source *HMS Victory* materials elsewhere.

- The material was sold on the basis of £ per ton, at a higher rate for copper than for timber. The amount was estimated roughly to be 50 tons of oak and 15 tons of copper, but would be charged according to the weigh bills as it was removed from the Portsmouth dockyard. In fact there were 34 tons of timber and 10 tons of copper.

- Royalties would be paid on the sales value of all materials and of products made for Varley and Dyke Ltd for resale. These royalties were: 1% to the Save the Victory Fund and 9.5% paid to the Ministry of Defence, Disposal Services Agency (DSA). I was given assurances by the Chief Executive of the DSA that this 9.5% would also find its way back to *HMS Victory* for ongoing refurbishment and maintenance. This clause, though placing a burden on the end price of the material, meant that our project could take on an important fund-raising role for the historic ship and allow our customers to feel that by supporting it they were contributing to the future of this great naval treasure. It also put us in a relationship with both the Society for Nautical Research (that administered the Save the Victory Fund), as well as with the Ministry of Defence, making it possible to call on their support in making a success of the venture.

- All materials had to be removed from the dockyard in Portsmouth at our expense and within a short period of time. This created our first real challenge.

We subsequently discovered that there had been relatively few bidders for the tender, but not surprisingly we ended up working closely with two of them. These were the Royal Navy Museum in Portsmouth and Nauticalia Ltd.

5

THE SONS OF ZEBEDEE

"And James the son of Zebedee and John the brother of James; and He surnamed them Boanerges, which is The Sons of Thunder". Mark 3:17

PARTNERSHIP is the creature of necessity, generally inspired by shared goals or passions. It is also frequently the optimistic genesis of doomed business ventures. I had known John for many years in a business context, and James for considerably less. Nonetheless we three had worked together for about 12 frenetic months prior to the Victory project trying to put together an ambitious, groundbreaking internet business, only to be brought up short just prior to launch by the collapse of the then burgeoning internet bubble. We were all sufficiently different from each other, both temperamentally and business-wise, to feel that we would generate synergy and contribute a mix of skills that could only benefit our endeavour. The big question for me was whether the Sons of Zebedee, as I liked to think of them, would turn out to be the Sons of Thunder.

John Morgan was almost a caricature of the thrusting, successful businessman. A chemical engineer by training, he led the management buy out in the 1980s of a company called Porvair and then went on to take it public on the London Stock Exchange. He drove it as Chairman and Chief Executive to become one of Norfolk's leading manufacturing companies, based in King's Lynn. He was a tall, spare, energetic Welshman, tough, outspoken and intensely competitive. His genial bonhomie could change rapidly to a steely, uncompromising stubbornness if challenged or crossed. I think he was aware that this characteristic could sometimes make him difficult to deal with as he once said to me:

"Jonathan, if I'm being too executive about things at any time, don't hesitate to tell me."

I am happy to say that I never did have to tell him so, even though mildly tempted once or twice.

James Boddy could not really be called a caricature of anything, and is undoubtedly one of nature's one-offs. Educated at Paston College, Nelson's school, he spent some time at sea in the merchant navy, both of which surely are responsible for him being an enormous fan of the hero of Trafalgar. James made his money in the financial services industry, mainly involved with providing second mortgages, giving himself the flexibility to become something of a business buccaneer. Indeed, his business ventures liken him in my mind more to the eccentric bouncing character of Zebedee in The Magic Roundabout than to the faithful, if ambitious disciple James. He brought an immense passion for Nelson to this venture, together with a highly developed imagination and an inexhaustible supply of optimism.

My own profile, as the third member of the partnership, seems perhaps more prosaic than the two other rather extreme characters. I had a firm business grounding, acquiring an American MBA in the late 1960s when they were just becoming fashionable, and working in an international sales and marketing environment for a small handful of blue chip manufacturing companies. I came to Norfolk in 1987 to take on the role of Managing Director of the leading writing instrument manufacturer Berol Ltd in King's Lynn. I held this post for 11 years until we sold it to the American company that subsequently acquired pen maker Parker. Berol was moved shortly afterwards into the Parker establishment on the south coast of England. At the same time that I was running this Victory project, I was also non-executive Chairman of the East of England Tourist Board.

On the face of it, the three of us pulled together a useful mix of business skills and personal characteristics. The question was, would it work? All three of us might have thought harder about that question at the outset if we had had a clearer vision of what we were getting into. The truth was though, that in the first instance our involvement was simply as joint investors in a unique asset. At that stage, I had no plans to run a business myself, having had plenty of that already. We all shared the view that this material had potential for making money, given the Trafalgar bicentenary that was just five years away. We probably all thought that we would find a third party to turn it into a business and that we would just be non-executive directors together, jointly working for an optimal return on our investment. That common cause was simple enough to make us feel comfortable about joining forces.

The way it unfolded (and about which, more later) I found myself single-handedly running what became a complex business, with James and John as non-executive directors and investors. It was this change in the relationship mix that made the partnership chemistry more of an issue. The bottom line is that overall it worked out pretty well. There was no great falling out, no seriously unwanted interference or any major difference of views that can so often scupper business partnerships. As the man at the coalface, I undoubtedly was more sensitive to the role and attitudes of my partners, both of whom had other fish to fry and were happy to let me get on with it. But could it have been better, or indeed, worse?

James, the Nelson fan, was really engaged with the whole project. To an extent, this occasionally gave me grounds for fearing a conflict of interest and me possibly being forced down a path I did not want to take the business. However, as it turned out, this fear was without grounds.

James would say: "We have the Crown Jewels here. The value of this stuff is immense. We need to be taking it much more up-market."

It was typical of James that he wanted to aim for the stars, to create exquisite and rare objects that would dominate the antique auction houses in decades to come. Certainly there was appeal in that, but there were practical constraints to it for me. First, we had over 40 tons to shift, so we had to find the right balance between volume and value if we were to optimise our returns. Secondly, the market for such extravagant pieces is small and difficult to identify. Making that a priority would have soaked up my time and our resources at an alarming rate. In the end, James set up his own company called Remember Nelson in order to address that top end market. His company purchased Victory oak and copper from me for use in expensive furniture and tableware. Reference to this collection is made in Part 3.

Typical of James's creativity and enthusiastic vision was Victory silver. He arrived one day bubbling over with exuberance.

"We can turn all the copper into silver," he proclaimed. I suspected some kind of alchemy. "In Nelson's time there was a limited amount of Britannia standard silver minted, and it is very collectable. Britannia silver has 5% copper in it, unlike Sterling silver, which has 7.5%," he explained. "We can get the Royal Mint to turn all our copper into Britannia silver and grant us an exclusive hallmark..."

I started to do the mental arithmetic: we had ten tons of copper which would represent 5% of this new silver, so we would end up with 200 tons of silver!

"Hang on, James, what on earth are we going to do with 200 tons of silver? Who is going to buy it? How much will it cost to make?"

In due course some common sense re-entered the conversation.

"OK," said James, "sell me 65 kilos of copper and I will get the Royal Mint to turn that into silver for me."

"But that is still over a ton of silver. Are you sure you can handle that?"

Nothing daunted James. He bought the aforementioned quantity of copper and duly had some of it made into silver. A number of splendid silver items were produced, some of which were sold through The 1805 Collection and the rest were sold by his company called Remember Nelson.

John was quite the opposite. He had no interest in Nelson, Trafalgar or the history of *HMS Victory*. For him it was a simple investment decision. He would phone me periodically to ask how it was going and to lend me support and encouragement, and I was grateful for that. Running a business single-handed is a lonely undertaking. On the few occasions that he visited an exhibition of The 1805 Collection he would opine that most of it was not to his taste and that there were very few items he would consider buying himself. This did not worry me since John was clearly not the target market, but there were times when I could have used more positive feedback.

When we finally wound the company up and ended the partnership, the three of us remained both solvent and friends, so we had successfully negotiated the great partnership minefield. The greatest test of the relationship came at the end when, as agreed, I gave up running the company at the end of 2005 and we sold the remaining material to Nauticalia Ltd. This was the investors' moment of truth, when our financial returns were in the melting pot. At John's insistence we had some expensive audited accounting done mid year so that he could "get a handle on the real value of the business which I will need to negotiate the sale." The fact was there was only one party interested in buying it, and they were already good customers of ours. They were not buying the business, but just the stock of wood and copper. The value, I argued, was what they would give us for it, and no amount of audited accounts was likely to alter that. In the end, John prevailed. This is the way things are done in major business transactions, and it made him comfortable to do it. It gave me a good deal of extra work and headache and made absolutely no difference to the deal we finally concluded. But you have to give and take in partnerships, and with his significant share of the business he had every right to have that done.

The project certainly achieved my own financial objectives, and the return to shareholders was in excess of 400% over an active trading period of about three and a half years. This is far in excess of stock market performance, property growth or any other investment I am aware of.

John died in January 2009. I lost a friend and a business inspiration.

6

BRINGING HMS VICTORY TO NORFOLK

THE excitement of taking on the project evaporated swiftly when we realised we had little more than a month to find somewhere suitable to store the reclaimed material and to move it out. Failure to do so would incur penalties under the contract.

I live in an old farmhouse with a large barn, quite capable of housing all the salvaged material. It would need clearing of the multitude of junk that had been stored there, and then fitted out with appropriate racking. In the neighbouring village there was a small industrial park with a 2,500 square ft unit for rent, and I visited this both to see how that might work as an alternative and to establish the rental value of that much space. It was a useful exercise in that it convinced me that there would be all sorts of risks in storing this heritage material in a publicly accessible location. Notably several tons of copper would be a great temptation to thieves. The idea of having to get in the car and travel a mile each way every time I needed access to it was also a deterrent. I suggested to my partners that the best solution would be for the company to rent my barn at the commercial rate, and that I hire someone to clear the barn, erect the racking and undertake the business of loading and transporting the salvage from Portsmouth to Norfolk. I knew just the man.

Mick Lock was a skilled joiner and builder whom I had known for many years. He had undertaken the re-roofing and re-cladding of our 17th century barn, as well as converting the old cow byres into a cottage. We shared a passion for sailing and had become good friends. Mick was one of those people who could turn his hand to any practical task, large or small, and the more unusual the better. He immediately grasped the nettle and set about helping me to empty the barn and scavenged for good second-hand racking. Within a couple of weeks the space was cleared and fully racked out with rows each side of the barn and one down the middle. The bays were one and a quarter metres deep and just under a metre high, in three tiers to a total of 32.5 linear metres. These turned out to be only just sufficient. The centre racks only reached half way down the length, and the rest of the centre space was made up of some ten steel mesh stillages containing the copper sheets and rivets.

With the space ready to receive our new treasure, Mick took on two men who had laboured for him over the years, Les Whitwood and Alan Bunn, and set off for Portsmouth dockyard where they sorted out the necessary security clearances to allow them to come and go and remove the material. They booked into a nearby pub for an indefinite stay. None of them really knew what they were facing, and in the end they spent some seven days without a break carrying each piece from the cellar up the worn brick steps and loading them onto pallets. They borrowed a forklift truck from the dockyard and loaded the pallets onto 40 foot articulated lorries contracted from Turner's Transport in Soham. They filled two of these behemoths before all the oak was cleared. The remaining oak together with the stillages of copper were loaded on to seven ton curtain sided trucks which Mick drove back to Norfolk himself, making the trip three times. Each load was taken on to the dockyard weighbridge, and the net weights from this were used as the basis for the final reckoning on payment to the Ministry of Defence.

It was a wet December evening when the first 40-footer arrived. The turning space from the country road into my drive was too small for it to negotiate. This had not been anticipated. Nothing daunted, Mick drove immediately to one of our neighbouring farmers who had a tractor with forks. The lorry was pulled as tightly as possible into the edge of the road, leaving just enough room for other traffic to pass with great care. I took up traffic direction duties while our tractor driver started unloading the pallets and taking them the 100 yards up the drive to the barn. It took a couple of hours to unload the pallets and allow the truck to depart. This happened twice, of course, and it seemed remarkable to me that this congestion and activity could happen in a small rural community without a single person asking us what we were up to. I was particularly glad of this, as I did not want it becoming common knowledge that all this heritage material was under my roof.

Once the pallets had been unloaded the contents had to be manhandled onto the racks in the barn, just as the loads from the seven tonners had been. It was a sobering thought that every piece of timber had been manhandled twice – once out of the dockyard and on to pallets, and once off the pallets onto the racks, meaning that three men had lifted and carried 68 tons of timber completing this phase of the project. That was not counting the copper, much of which had also to be stacked into the stillages in Portsmouth. The physical effort involved was not helped by the dust and dirt harboured by this ancient salvage. It had been a mammoth undertaking, and I dread to think how much it would have cost if I had contracted it out to a specialist firm. The project owes a real debt of gratitude to Mick and his two amazing assistants.[3] I would also like to record our thanks to the dockyard personnel who proved most helpful during this difficult operation.

[3] Mick Lock used his skills making components for The 1805 Collection, including the Trafalgar Cross. Sadly, he died suddenly in December 2006.

7

SWINGING THE LEAD

IT IS curious how the old naval practice of 'swinging the lead', which actually means 'taking soundings' has come to mean skiving or doing nothing of value. Once the oak and copper were safely stored in Norfolk, very little happened with it for over a year, and at times I wondered whether perhaps we were 'swinging it' a bit. However, the time was used to take soundings and to reflect on how best to use this extraordinary asset. Almost daily I would venture into the barn, contemplate the stacked racks of old bits of wood and copper and think, "What on earth have we done? What are we going to do with this stuff?" Depending on the weather and my own moods I would feel depressed, overwhelmed or inspired. The barn had developed a real atmosphere, largely due to the signature smell of seasoned oak and pitch that greets you when you go aboard *HMS Victory*. Some visitors said they could almost sense Nelson's presence there. Sometimes I would talk to him.

"OK, Horatio, have you got any ideas about this? You were a man with an eye (no offence) to the main chance. What do you reckon I should do with it?"

I like to think that maybe he answered. Within two or three months of us taking on the project, the name Victory Ltd became available at Companies' House due to the demise of the previous business that traded under that name. We snapped it up for about £60 and changed the name of our company from Varley and Dyke Ltd to Victory Ltd. I felt this was a good omen.

The fact that this material was now under my guardianship inevitably left me with a sense of responsibility for doing something with it. I was not being paid to work, but clearly somebody had to do something if we were ever to realise any value from our investment. The first thing I did, therefore, was to build a simple website. When we set up the company the three of us put up enough capital to buy the contract and shell company from Nick Varley and to pay off the Ministry of Defence for the contract. We then negotiated a working capital loan from Barclays Bank for a similar amount. There were funds available to work with. I approached a local IT company called System Solutions Ltd with whom I had had satisfactory dealings in the past, and created the rough artwork and template for a website. This was designed to advise people that the material was now available to anyone who wanted it, and would serve as an initial 'plumb line' to gauge interest. It had the facility for anyone visiting the site to fill in their details, indicate the nature of their interest and trigger an email with all that data to our new domain – www.nelsonsvictory.com.

Much to my surprise (for I had never run a website myself before this) we started to get expressions of interest from all sorts of places around the world. It was highly encouraging, and made me realise that the next task was to sort out the whole business of authenticity. We knew from the outset that provenance and authentication were at the heart of the value of this material. The things that secured this for us were enshrined in the MOD contract – namely that we were the sole and exclusive owner of all *HMS Victory* 'arisings', that sale of them would generate funds for her ongoing support; and that the Disposal Services Agency of the Ministry of Defence was a partner with us in the venture. In other words, we had common cause with the Royal Navy and the MOD. Personal relationships would need to be established between those two key players and ourselves, and we would need to convince them that our conduct in regard to the material was beyond reproach. They would also only put their support to a programme that was deemed appropriate to the stature and importance of Nelson's flagship, particularly going in to the high profile bicentenary celebrations.

What we needed was a certificate of authenticity, carrying an appropriate signature that could be used for either pieces of the material or products made using it. Nick Varley had already addressed this issue in his plans and the artwork he created was among the papers we acquired with his company. It gave me a good idea of the general sentiment and wording, and I gave this to a designer to rework the graphics. The brief was to produce two certificates, one for products and one for materials, both of which would allow for description, unique reference codes, limited edition numbering (for use with products), the date and name of purchaser. Armed with the completed artwork, I arranged to visit the Commanding Officer of *HMS Victory* Lt. Commander Frank Nowosielski.

PRODUCT CERTIFICATE

This collection is dedicated to the
OFFICERS AND MEN
Who fought at the
BATTLE OF TRAFALGAR

Certificate of Provenance

"I hereby certify that this item is made from original material removed from HMS VICTORY during her restoration, and that a royalty resulting from its sale will go to the 'Save The Victory Fund' to assist in returning the ship to her configuration at Trafalgar 21st October 1805."

Product........................ Limited Edition of........................
Edition Number........................ Collectors Name........................
Original Material Provenance reference........................ Date........................

Horatio Nelson

Signed F. Nowosielski
Lt Cmdr.Frank Nowosielski MBE RN
Commanding Officer, HMS VICTORY

England Expects
Every MAN to
do his DUTY.

MATERIAL CERTIFICATE

Certificate of Provenance

"I hereby certify that this is original material removed from HMS VICTORY during her restoration, and that a royalty resulting from its sale will go to the 'Save The Victory Fund' to assist in returning the ship to her configuration at Trafalgar 21st October 1805."

Material........................ Purchaser........................
Approximate Dimensions........................ Weight........................
Original Material Provenance reference........................ Date........................

Horatio Nelson

Signed F. Nowosielski
Lt Cmdr.Frank Nowosielski MBE RN
Commanding Officer, HMS VICTORY

England Expects
Every MAN to
do his DUTY.

Frank was, as ever, very supportive and helpful and agreed to lend his printed signature to these two certificates. He took the opportunity once again to reiterate the need for both our products and our conduct with regard to the sale of materials to be appropriate, recorded and auditable. These exigencies were also stated in the MOD contract, and I assured Frank that it was in the interests of Victory Ltd to guard these values well since credibility was at the heart of the value equation in this project. We discussed the issue of possible duplicity and misrepresentation. In broad terms it boiled down to two simple reasons why it was not in our interest to be anything other than totally honest with the material.

The first had to do with the quantity and nature of the timber in particular. There was just so much of it that the idea of augmenting it with other old timber was just a non-starter. We would have enough trouble shifting the tonnage we had.[4] Also, it was a requirement of the contract that we had to report quarterly to the MOD on the quantities of material sold. Our books and stock were open to inspection, and it would soon have become apparent if we had sold more than we had purchased! Secondly, the slightest inkling that the project was anything but totally genuine would render all the material valueless, as well as exposing the directors to charges of fraud. We were religious in weighing and recording every piece of material that left our premises, noting its destination. It was only in doing this that I felt able to defend both our own integrity and the integrity of the project.

Armed with proper certification, I was now able to start selling. The first sale was of oak to a customer called Out of the Woods on 15th May 2000 when the price charged was £7.50 per kg. The issue of how much to charge was a real puzzler. Basic economics looks at two essential questions – first, how does supply match up with demand, and how elastic would the demand be if prices were stretched; and second, given the costs incurred, how much would we need to sell and at what price in order to make a satisfactory return? Unfortunately classical economic theory and standard business models were no help. I knew exactly how big the supply was but had no idea what the demand would be or at what price we would shift most volume. There was no precedent or past history to call on. At the same time, it was clear to me that we needed to present the material as having intrinsic value. If we under-priced it, people would assume it had little value; we needed to make a statement about its rarity and singularity. I had no choice but to 'suck it and see'.

For the rest of that year, just selling from the website, I sold a little over £15,500 worth of material before VAT, weighing just over two tons. It was not a lot, but it was important psychologically. It brought me into contact with people who were interested in it, and from them came thoughts and ideas for the future.

---

[4] At the time of writing there is an estimated eight tons left, much of it in small pieces.

By the end of the year 2000 I was persuaded that we had the foundations of a business, but equally that it could not be achieved on this sort of hobby basis. At the same time, I thought we needed to know more about the market and the opportunities before we could make serious plans. I also had realised that in 2000 there was as yet no public consciousness about the bicentenary coming in 2005. Timing was going to be important if we were not to squander our meagre resources. I determined, therefore, to get another 12 months of trading experience before creating any serious plans.

8

LEARNING THE ROPES

I ALWAYS viewed October 21st 2005 as the climax of the project and the point at which I would want to be looking for ways to move on. John saw this project as an opportunity to establish a company with unique expertise in converting historic salvage, to build a long-term business making money from old ships, trains, rockets, buildings or whatever became available. I could appreciate the logic, but lacked the hunger. I could see myself becoming a relic before my time just working through Nelson's particular piece of history. Anyway, whatever we did over the next four years, it would not circumscribe John's vision. I wanted to use the next 12 months for experimenting with the various bits of the business mix.

There were lots of things I needed to know. How good was the timber for making things? I had heard comments that it would be too hard to work, or that there would be so much hidden metal in it (nails and bolts, not musket balls) that woodworking tools would be damaged. What could we do with the copper? Could it be cast or beaten into products? How much would people be prepared to pay for a piece of naval history? How do we find the people who would pay anything for it? What products could be made, and by whom? What would be the best so-called 'routes to market'? Retail shops, perhaps, or direct mail or was the internet going to turn out the golden pathway that everyone predicted? As ever, the only way to find out was to 'try it on the dog'.

Nick Varley had been of the opinion that the best idea would be to cut all the timber up into standard sized planks and that there would result a simple inventory of lumber that makers of all sorts could buy. Sadly, this was just not realistic. To begin with, the sheer quantity of pieces ran into the thousands, and every one was different. The cost of doing it would have been prohibitive. We would have ended up with a huge quantity of waste. It seemed to me that there were more unusable surfaces for manufacturing purposes than there was good timber inside.

It reminded me of a tale my father-in-law told me about his grandfather who had run away to sea as a boy and become a cabin boy on a schooner. The captain and first mate would eat together, with the boy serving and then having what was left himself. The captain's wife had sent her husband away with a handsome home cooked plum duff which the boy was about to serve.

"Do you like duff ends, boy?" the captain asked.

"No sir," said the boy honestly.

"Well, me and the mate do," said the captain, whereupon he cut the plum duff in half, giving half to the mate and taking the other half himself. I could see a lot of duff ends if we had adopted that plan.

I needed to get people making things with it who could then tell me what could and could not be done with it. My own knowledge of timber and woodworking stretched little further than sharpening a pencil. I started drawing up a list of suitable products that would have a high-perceived value if made from or with salvaged materials from *HMS Victory*, with a view to finding people who could make them. It was not long, however, before I learned that the best route was to find skilled woodworkers and then to ask them what they would like to make with it. This way the woodworker had more of a sense of ownership, and tended to make things he knew how to make. If he already made such items out of ordinary timber, the chances were he would also know where and how to sell them. With that in mind, I drafted some editorial copy and sent it off to some of the woodworking magazines. This started the ball rolling, and by the end of 2001 I had contact with a number of makers. My conversations with them gave rise to a much fuller understanding of the limitations and possibilities afforded me by our stock of timber.

That, at least, gave me a steer on the product capability of our timber. Next, I started to think about the routes to our marketplace – whatever that might be. It seemed likely that if I could interest others in taking raw material or products to sell, then this would in turn indicate who the consumer might be. Before that, I could tackle the obvious group myself. I joined the Nelson Society. With several hundred members and a scholarly quarterly magazine, this society attracted the largest group of aficionados of the great man and his history both in the UK and overseas. The 1805 Club was much smaller, but also of great interest. I took a full-page advertisement in the *Nelson Despatch*, the Society's publication, advising of the existence and purpose of Victory Ltd and the availability of the Victory arisings. From this I made contact with several of the most active members, including those who had a particular interest in the ship and its history. It generated a modest amount of sales, but was helpful in the wider context of spreading the word. It became clear to me that there was disapproval among some elements of the Nelson fan club that were unhappy about this historic material being sold off into the vulgar world of commerce. No doubt they were concerned that it was going to be prostituted for private gain and at the expense of the 'immortal memory'. It was an understandable concern and one I was keen to repudiate. The best method of doing so would be to use the project as a means of generating funds for the ongoing upkeep of *HMS Victory*. This was to be an important plank in the underlying strategy of the business going forward. The rather depressing learning from this first attempt at direct marketing of the Victory materials was that the cognoscenti were not a significant market sector for the quantity we had to sell, and that identifying the target market would be far harder than originally thought.

The next route to the market was retail. What shops might be interested in items made from Victory oak and copper? The most obvious was the Victory Shop in the Naval Dockyard, Portsmouth, right next to the ship, and the inevitable destination of all those who visited the ship and the attendant museum. Curiously, the Royal Naval Museum, which owned the shop, had been one of the unsuccessful bidders for the material when it was put up for tender. I was later advised by the Director that there had been some members of the Board who felt that the museum should own this material and that it should not be allowed to pass into the hands of private business. The Director was not persuaded that the museum was the proper owner, or that their organisation had the skills or resources to make best use of it – a view with which I entirely agreed. In order to show willing, a low bid was entered but it was something of a relief when that bid failed.

This background was explained to me on my first visit to the ship and the museum, and the shop manager had at that time also waxed lyrical about the market for the oak in the shop.

"Just cut it up into small pieces, put it into a box with a label saying what it is and we will sell it by the ton. We already do this now, but now that you own it we cannot continue unless you supply it," he told me.

With this conversation in mind, I called him to discuss pricing and presentation. I duly made notes, sourced some sample clear Perspex boxes as instructed, cut up some small pieces and sent them, together with a price based upon the formula agreed on the phone. Silence. No response at all. When I finally got him on the phone he was dismissive to the point of rudeness and asked me how I dared tell him how to price his products in his shop? And did I seriously think people would pay that price for a piece of wood in a box? I was flummoxed. I had the notes from our original conversation in front of me. The consumer price was as agreed, the shop would make 55% gross margin as is normal (he had told me so and I had spent 11 years running a consumer goods manufacturing company, so pricing for retail distribution was not a mystery to me). Of course, he now had to pay for the timber, whereas before it was free. Maybe he did not like the idea that we were making some money, too. I bit my tongue and took my best shot at an orderly and dignified retreat. I would fight another day.

The best course seemed to be to find some way of adding more value to a small piece of timber sold at pocket money prices to museum shop customers. I commissioned a marketing agency in Norwich to design a suitably attractive certificate that would support a fragment of oak on the front, and on the back we would have some information about the restoration of *HMS Victory* written and signed-off by the Society for Nautical Research (SNR) that is responsible for that activity. The SNR was most helpful and came up with just the right thing. It also drew attention to the fact that a proportion of the sale value would go to the Save the Victory Fund, and each certificate had its own unique reference number. At postcard size, it would fit into any off-the-shelf photo frame. The resulting certificate, complete with a fragment of oak, was contained within a clear plastic envelope, and 50 such certificates were placed in a specially designed counter-top box with flip-top lid and cut out section to merchandise the product. The Victory Shop manager agreed to trial them. We had our first retail product. This approach would not work for the copper sheathing, however. I tracked down a company near Huntingdon that produced a wide range of trophies using acrylic encapsulation. Together we agreed a simple design for a desk ornament or paperweight in which a piece of the copper sheathing was suspended in clear acrylic, and the words 'Copper from the hull of *HMS Victory*' laser etched on the front. We did a similar one with a piece of oak. The quality was good, but the price was rather high. Without sending the materials abroad I could not find anywhere that could better the offering. I was reluctant to send material away to where I had no control over what came back. We went with it, and once again the Victory Shop agreed to stock it. We now had a small retail range with which to test the market. I am pleased to say that the relationship with the Victory Shop developed well over the next two or three years, and they mounted a substantial exhibition of The 1805 Collection which generated good business for us both.

At this point we were taking soundings in the retail, direct marketing and internet sales channels. Then one day I met David Burton and he introduced me to the world of craft shows, and a lot more besides.

9

PLOTTING THE COURSE

ANYONE who had walked into the barn in those early days would have come to the conclusion that the only way to shift its contents would be to find people who could make things with it. Otherwise, with the exception of the few that would like to own a piece just for its own sake, this was so much firewood. I needed 'makers,' and preferably commercial makers rather than hobbyists. It was this early realisation that had led to submitting editorial copy to the woodworking media. It was just such editorial that brought David Burton to Victory Ltd. He phoned one day in early November and introduced himself as a maker of leather-topped tables. He had some ideas he would like to discuss. Would I by any chance be planning to visit the forthcoming Crafts for Christmas Show at the NEC in Birmingham since he would be exhibiting there and I could see what he made? It occurred to me that I would also meet other prospective makers at this show so I agreed to come and meet him.

Joining the throng of people pushing through the aisles of this popular show, I eventually came to a small shell stand at the rear of the hall. It was stacked from floor to ceiling with a variety of coffee and occasional tables, all covered in hand tooled leather and bearing colourful paintings of birds, trees, flowers and other exotic designs. Standing in the middle was a man who looked for all the world as though he had just escaped from the set of Brigadoon. At five foot six, with a well trimmed goatee beard and twinkling eyes, and dressed in a colourful brocade waistcoat, he was delivering the good-humoured patter of one well accustomed to shows and market stalls. He had a firm handshake that foretold a firm conviction that he had in his own skills and abilities. David turned out to be a strong influence on the future direction of the business, as well as a good friend.

He had been selling leather-topped tables at craft shows for some time but sales were declining. He saw an opportunity to add a whole new dimension to his work by producing some tables featuring pictures of *HMS Victory*, and possibly Nelson, and incorporating into them some Victory oak or copper. David had served in the Royal Navy as a chef and as a diver and, like most naval men, had real admiration for Nelson and his legendary victories. I sensed that this man could bring some useful skills and a lot of energy to our project. I was happy to provide the oak and copper, as well as product certificates, to allow him to produce a range of tables. We went off to get some lunch and discuss the Victory project. The more we talked about it the more David's excitement grew. Thoughts and ideas came thick and fast, some interesting and some completely off the wall. It was to be like that for the duration of our business together. He suggested I walk around the show and see what other craftspeople might be able to join the project, as had been my intention. He knew many of the exhibitors well since they saw each other regularly on the circuit, and suggested some who he thought to be suitable. I spent a useful, if exhausting, afternoon meeting a variety of characters who created a colourful patchwork of products and stories in the ensuing four years.

It was at this point that I learned my next crucial lesson about the future direction of the business: David, like nearly all craftspeople, was skill rich and cash poor. If I wanted to sell Victory oak at an appropriately high price, I was not going to get it by selling it to craftspeople. Furthermore, it was not just cash shortage that afflicted the craft industry – it was also the absence of a good platform for them to sell their wares in any volume. Craft fairs, as I was to discover, are hard work and very competitive.

As 2001 drew to a close I had tested the water for products, makers and routes to market, and had a pretty good feel for how a proper business might be developed. Thus far I had been doing this on an unpaid basis, and it was high time the project was taken forward in a more professional way. I set up a meeting with the Sons of Zebedee to discuss the way forward.

"We need a person to run the business," I declared, and there was no dissent. We spent a while discussing how much we would need to pay for the right person, and then cast around for people we might know that could handle the task. No one came readily to mind.

"Let's put an advertisement in the jobs' page of the *Eastern Daily Press*," suggested James. That was agreed.

"Jonathan, why don't you draw up a job specification and a personal profile for us all to agree and then draft the ad?" suggested John.

Why me? I wondered. Hadn't I already done more than my share? Still, I was the one who had the feel for it by now, I reasoned.

"OK," I said, "I'll see what I can do".

Over the next couple of days I sat with a pad and scribbled notes, trying to draw a picture of the kind of person who could grasp this unusual challenge and make something of it. A person with a marketing background, experience of running a business, able to manage money, good at forming relationships with other small business people, practical, entrepreneurial, visionary and trustworthy… No chance – not on the sort of salary the three of us had agreed upon. The more I thought about it, the more I reckoned it would have to be me. Not that I was a particularly good fit for the profile, I hasten to say, but because it was doubtful if anyone with those qualities would have been insane enough to consider it at the budget salary. But did I want to do it? What's more, would James and John want me to do it? I weighed up my own position. I did not want to retire until I was 60, and that would be at the end of 2005 – ideal for the main lifespan of the project. That meant I needed to generate enough income during the period in question to allow my pension fund to remain untouched and to carry on growing. With my other non-executive directorships the salary level discussed would provide sufficient income to achieve that goal, so a tick in the financial box. But what about the personal interest box, could I put a tick in that? It was so different from anything I had done before that I convinced myself. Tick.

"Right," I said at the next meeting of the shareholders, "I reckon I'm going to have to do it".

I explained my rationale. We talked about it for a while.

"Fine," said John crisply. He always said, "fine" crisply whenever he was going to nail someone to the wall. "If you think you can do it why don't you prepare a business plan for us to consider, and if we like it you can have the job!"

He grinned. James did too.

"Bollocks," I said, and meant it.

They were right, though. We needed to have a good plan of where we were going, and it would have to be made, or at least approved by the person that was going to carry it out. I had it all in my head, and it would take another year for someone else to get up to speed on this. It was another reason why I should do it. The three of us adjourned to the pub.

10

COOKING UP A PLAN

OBJECTIVE: Victory at any price – to make this historic material available to anyone who wants it, at a price they can afford and in a form they would find appealing.

The Recipe

INGREDIENTS:

- 34 tons of old oak that is unsuitable for mass production
- 10 tons of highly patinated and distressed copper sheet and rod
- A talented range of artists and craftspeople who cannot afford to pay an economic price for the raw material
- An unquantifiable market with few identifying features
- No clear, well-established routes to market
- Potentially crippling pricing burdens (royalties, VAT, distribution margins)
- The promise of a national celebration in four years' time
- An opportunity to raise funds to support a national heritage asset
- Modest working capital

STARTER

CRUDITÉS

Choice pieces of Victory oak and copper, fully certified

MAIN COURSE

THE 1805 COLLECTION

A wide selection of hand-made, limited edition pieces using Victory oak and copper, complete with a Deed of Provenance

DESSERT

Choose from our retail range of affordable mementos featuring Victory oak and copper

METHOD:

The first principle must be that Victory Ltd, which is the owner of the Victory material, should concentrate on selling just the material and any retail products that feature in the 'Dessert Menu'. This first phase will simply require rolling out the work that has already started. The company will not hold inventory of anything other than the original materials, and any retail products will be batch made against orders received. The reasons for this are:

1. The company is VAT registered (this was done at the outset in order to recover the VAT paid on the contract materials), and pricing and accounting for these items will be straightforward.

2. Royalties are payable on all sales of material or products made for the company from the material. Accounting for these will be straightforward.

3. Working capital requirements will be minimal.

The second phase will address the main course – The 1805 Collection. To implement this, we will form a new company called Victory Marketing Partners Ltd (VMP). Its purpose will be to act as a sales and marketing agency business for individuals and companies that make products for The Collection. It will seek out makers, agree products and pricing with them, and market The 1805 Collection.

Victory Ltd will allocate stock of Victory material to them as required at a price of £25 per kg, and the maker will pay Victory Ltd for this material only when the products are sold. All products will be made to order, and all orders will be accompanied by full payment, except in the case where products are highly priced and/or will take longer than four weeks to produce, in which case a deposit will accompany them. Deposits will always be sufficient to cover the value of the Victory materials. In this way, makers never have to purchase stocks of material. The transaction takes place between the customer and the maker, with VMP simply acting as the maker's agent.

The pricing structure for the product will include a margin for VMP of 30% when VMP generates the order, and 15% when the maker generates the order (the maker taking the other 15% to reward his sales effort). The maker will produce an artist's proof to determine how much Victory material is required and how much money is required to make the item. The artist's proof will be exhibited at shows from which orders will be generated. To determine the consumer price, the maker's price is added to the price of the Victory material, and the total is multiplied by 1.43 in order to include the 30% margin. The resulting number is rounded to the most appropriate price point. Control of the process will be maintained by VMP through the issue of accompanying Deeds of Provenance, and by VMP collecting payment for the products on the maker's behalf. When an order is taken, the payment will be banked by VMP who will then prepare the Deed of Provenance for the item and send it, together with the maker's fee (plus 15% if he has generated the order) to the maker. They will then produce the item and send it to the customer. Postage will be added to the order and included in the payment sent to the maker. VMP will then pay Victory Ltd for the Victory materials used. Since the majority of makers are not VAT registered the product will not carry VAT on its selling price.

The benefits of this approach are first that skilled craftspeople can participate in the project without having to take any financial risk. Secondly, no one has to make stock and the transactions are always characterised by positive cash flow. Finally VAT does not burden end pricing except where makers are VAT registered, nor are royalties levied on the products. Once VMP reaches a certain size VAT will have to be added to its commission within the overall pricing structure, but this is still preferable to adding VAT to the full price.

The final phase (dessert) will involve working with retailers to identify suitable low cost items that can be mass-produced, particularly by casting with the copper. This will be most appropriate when the bicentenary celebrations are coming into the public consciousness, hopefully in 2004. Early indications have not been very encouraging, with only museum type shops showing any interest.

11

LAUNCHING THE 1805 COLLECTION

JAMES and John liked the menu and bought the plan, accompanied by lots more detail, including budgets and projections. Like all such exercises, the forecasts were mythology; there was simply no evidence on which to base meaningful predictions. I ran it on a tight cost-control model with the objective of paying off our working capital overdraft as soon as possible, and then recouping our initial investment. I did not want to be working for the bank any longer than absolutely necessary, and I figured we could achieve this point in a couple of years. Once we were making money rather than paying it back we could revisit the strategy. It looked as though I was back to being Mr. Managing Director, albeit with a workforce of one. My wife signed on as acting unpaid Packing and Despatch Manager.

I set up Victory Marketing Partners Ltd and acquired a PO Box number for both companies from the Post Office. I did not want to advertise the physical location of our valuable inventory. The immediate need was for an identity and a brochure explaining what VMP and The 1805 Collection was all about. I had heard about a new small design company in Attleborough, Norfolk called Created Images, combining the talents of former RAF photographer Rod Scott with the graphic arts skills of Martin Miller. They were both hungry and enthusiastic, and took on the task of creating a logo for The 1805 Collection while I drafted the text of a suitable prospectus that would set out our philosophy, goals and ambitions.[5] I was well pleased with the results, and used their creativity for other work later in the project. Once again, the qualities of legitimacy and prestige were central to the status and success of the project, so I was highly delighted when the Second Sea Lord, Vice Admiral Sir Peter Spencer, whose flagship was *HMS Victory*, graciously agreed to act as Patron to The Collection.

[5] See Appendix 1

One other essential piece of documentation required to get us up and sailing was a Deed of Provenance. I put Created Images on the job, and they came up with a high quality, folded A5 size leaflet on similar textured stock as that used for the prospectus. The front cover carried the logo of The 1805 Collection, and on the inside front page was a list acknowledging our official supporters and headed by our Patron. It is interesting to note that in those early days, anticipating the magnitude of the 2005 bicentenary celebrations, a committee was formed of all interested parties, including the National Maritime Museum, The Royal Naval Museum, the Nelson Museum in Monmouth, the Sea Cadets, *HMS Victory*, the Royal Navy and others. It was called the Official Nelson Commemoration Committee (ONCC) and took upon itself the role of prospective organiser, or at least advisor to the event with pretensions to authorise and monitor the sale of commemorative items. The committee gave its approval to our project, but in the end there was no such quality approval role for the ONCC and it is unclear whether this body actually did anything. I suspect it suffered the fate of all well-meaning committees comprising a wide range of interests and agendas and little or no funding or authority, and ended up navel gazing. The epithet seemed appropriate. Horatio would have chuckled.

The facing page was a Certificate, naming the product, its edition size and number, the purchaser and date. It carried the printed signatures of the Commanding Officer, *HMS Victory*, the Chief Executive of the Disposal Services Agency of the MOD, and the Managing Director of Victory Ltd. Generally, this Deed of Provenance was very well received and conferred real value and authority to the products it supported (see Appendix II). Nevertheless, there was one unbelievably pompous man from the South Coast of England who ordered a Quoin (a scale replica of the graded wedges used by naval gunners to elevate the cannons for range). This was a hand carved and engraved item made entirely of Victory oak by a craftsman based in his locality. He had seen the artist's original and waxed lyrical about it on the phone to me when ordering it. It was duly made and despatched, together with the Deed of Provenance. I was dumbfounded some days later to receive a ranting and rambling phone call from the customer complaining that the signatures were all printed, and what is more…

"all done with the same pen if you ask me. This is clearly a swindle, a rip-off. You must take me for a right mug. I demand my money back at once."

I had no hesitation in refunding it. I tried to explain that it was totally impractical in a project of this size to have every Deed signed by hand, particularly when two of the signatories were extremely busy, high ranking individuals. I added that they would have been after my blood if I had been forging their signatures, and that the printed signatures were reduced to a common size for aesthetic reasons. He just ranted some more. He must have been having a bad day.

There was, regrettably, one aspect to this part of the project that was not a success. Sponsorship. It seemed to me that there was a further opportunity here to raise funds for the Save the Victory Fund by getting sponsors for each item in The 1805 Collection. The proposal was that a sponsor would pay for the artist's proof of an edition of their choice, plus the printing costs of adding four centre pages to the Deed of Provenance for that particular edition. One page would be narrative about the Battle of Trafalgar; one page would be about the product, one page about the maker and one page about the sponsor. At the end of the project, all sponsored artist's proofs would be auctioned and the entire proceeds donated to the Fund. Sponsorship costs would be small; for example, if sponsoring a £200 item with an edition size of 150 pieces, the cost would be printing at around £250 (full colour, short run) plus the item cost to a total of £450. The sponsor would also be entitled to edition number 1, and a discount of 15% on all purchases of his chosen edition. Unfortunately we only managed to secure a handful of sponsors. The main problem was the time involved in trying to find and persuade sponsors. I spent many hours approaching companies whose brand or product range might have been relevant to a particular product (e.g. Price's Candles Ltd for the candlestick, or the Post Office for Nelson's Last Letter) but with little success. I put this down to my own limited powers of persuasion, a lack of awareness or interest in the Trafalgar bicentenary generally, and the ironic fact that the amount of money was too small to be taken seriously by marketing departments of large companies. There is nothing more demoralising when you are fired up with crusading zeal than to have rejection after rejection. As the project built, I had less and less time to give to this aspect of it. I tried to engage the help of the Society for Nautical Research, *HMS Victory* and the Royal Naval Museum, but they were also working with limited resources and were unable to provide any practical assistance. In the event, the few sponsors we found were those provided by the makers themselves through personal or business links. I would like to extend my appreciation to those few businesses that did take up this opportunity.

And so we had the structural framework for The 1805 Collection. All that remained was to find affordable, cost-effective routes to take it to market, particularly by finding makers who would be good at selling it themselves. By this time I was little further ahead with identifying a typical market profile. There was the Nelson Society and The 1805 Club, but I knew this was limited in size and scope. The next obvious sector was the navy – particularly the Royal Navy, but also the merchant navy and some foreign navies for whom Nelson was an icon. The Royal Marines, too, were highly relevant since marines played a critical role in the Battle of Trafalgar and more widely in Nelson's navy, but I was quickly made aware of the dangers of lumping the Royal Marines in with the Royal Navy!

Each service very much has its own traditions, priorities and perceptions of their illustrious pasts. The big unknown was how the man in the street perceived Nelson and Trafalgar. Were there many fans or enthusiasts, other than in the sectors already mentioned? If so, what kind of people were they, how numerous were they and how could I reach them?

CJ at Sunshine Foods (from the 1970s TV comedy *The Fall and Rise of Reginald Perrin*) would probably have recommended "running it up the flagpole and seeing who salutes it," and with no other business guru to hand (at least, not on my budget) it seemed as good an approach as any. I duly beefed up the website, using a database system that would enable me to upload new products, change pricing when necessary, add news stories and generally keep it up-to-date myself without having to pester my service provider every other day. Next, I engaged the services of a small PR agency in North Norfolk, and we set about issuing press releases to all and sundry. I was particularly pleased to be asked to do a live interview on BBC Radio Four's *Today* programme. They sent a taxi to pick me up at 7am one morning and took me to the BBC Radio Norfolk studios in Norwich. I was shown into a small cubicle with a desk with a microphone on it and told to put on the headphones. I listened to the end of the piece ahead of me and suddenly heard the familiar voice of John Humphries introducing the story.

"So, Mr Bowman," he boomed without even a warning shot across the bows, "Thirty four tons of oak and ten tons of copper removed from *HMS Victory*. Is there anything left of the wretched ship?"

There is nothing like a rolling broadside to get an engagement off to a rollicking start. However, I must have weathered it, and he went on to ask me about the project and what sort of products we had to offer. It was over in a flash and I left somewhat dazed to the waiting taxi.

Meanwhile, David Burton had been working out some plans that would help him to become a major player in The 1805 Collection, which he saw as a unique opportunity to lift his craft show business out of the doldrums. The largest organiser of good quality craft fairs in Britain is International Craft and Hobby Fairs Ltd (ICHF). David had been a customer of theirs for many years and knew the owner David Bennett and his son-in law Simon pretty well. He suggested to them that the presence of this growing and unique collection at their fairs in the lead up to 2005 could be a significant point of differentiation for their shows, as well as being an additional attraction for visitors. Moreover, there was the prospect that many of his customers – the craftspeople who exhibited at his shows – could also benefit by becoming makers for The 1805 collection. Everyone would win. David Burton generated real interest, and he and I worked out a proposition that would harness this particular route to market. ICHF generously agreed to give free stand space to The Collection at their shows, in a prime location, for the whole of 2002 and 2005. In the interim years we would have it at a much-reduced rate.

The author with Lt. Cmdr. Frank Nowosielski MBE RN

They also agreed to sponsor one of David's tables in The Collection. For his part, David would manage the stand completely in exchange for 15% of the orders received at the shows. VMP would pay petrol and accommodation for David and his partner Caroline at these events. All parties were happy with the deal.

Our first show was at Penshurst Place in Kent in May 2002 and was a great success. On the strength of that we decided that we should plan an official launch for The 1805 Collection at the NEC in Birmingham that November. This was exactly 12 months after my first meeting with David Burton, and was the biggest of the ICHF shows, lasting for five days. The Commanding Officer of *HMS Victory* , Lt. Cdr. Frank Nowosielski agreed to come and officiate at the launch. I had been in discussion with the owners of the old traditional navy rum brand, Pussers Rum, to sponsor our two Victory oak rum tubs. They kindly agreed to support the launch by sending up a former Royal Navy boson who would pipe 'Up Spirits' and hand out tots of Pussers Rum from a traditional navy grog tub at the launch to all who wanted some. There was no shortage of takers, though we had to advise people to water it down, as it is extremely strong. Not surprisingly, we had a record day of sales. Frank made a speech in which he welcomed the project and offered his ongoing support. I made a small speech of thanks and presented Frank and his wife with one of our Capstan Pepper Mills. BBC TV promised to cover the event but sadly did not turn up – as something more headline grabbing came up at the last minute, as is so often the case. Nonetheless we had radio and press coverage, and we considered The 1805 Collection duly launched.

David Burton, Janet Bowman, Caroline Richmond, Lt. Cmdr. Frank Nowosielski, Jonathan Bowman and our Bos'un at the launch of The 1805 Collection

12

SITTING WITH NELLY

WHAT is now known in management circles as 'on-the-job training' used to be known before the advent of management-speak as 'sitting with Nelly'. History was never my strong suit. Like many of my generation I spent tedious hours bombarded with names, dates and events about which I could not care less, and all to do with the Tudors and Stewarts. The Napoleonic wars never cropped up, and even if they had, it is likely they would have bored me to tears. When I took on this project I knew little about Nelson and even less about Trafalgar. My mind was, therefore, a blank sheet onto which all manner of new information could be written. This whole episode of British history is very well documented and there are many learned minds that can impart fact, deduction and hypothesis about it. My purpose here is not to add to that body of knowledge but to record the things I learned along the way about our most momentous sea battle and its hero, which fascinated me. There will probably be some readers who will see this as superficial and shallow, but I make no apology for it. Maybe it will strike a chord with those who, like me, find history best digested in small mouthfuls.

THE BATTLE OF TRAFALGAR

- The original Battle of Britain was fought off the coast of Cadiz in South West Spain against the combined fleets of France and Spain on October 21st 1805. Napoleon was poised to invade England, but first had to secure the English Channel. The only thing that stood in his way was Nelson's Mediterranean fleet that was significantly smaller than its enemy. Nelson's decisive victory at this battle not only destroyed the French fleet but more importantly gave Britain uncontested control of the seas for more than 100 years. It was this supremacy that enabled the growth of the British Empire, the development of trade and the high standard of living we enjoy in Britain today.

- The French and Spanish Combined Fleet numbered 33 ships, including the largest warship afloat at that time, plus five frigates and two brigs. It was superior to the British Fleet, which numbered only 27 ships, by 474 cannons and 8,124 men.

- Nelson's famous flag signal to his fleet: "England expects that every man will do his duty" was originally ordered as "England confides that…" but the signals' officer was unable to make 'confides' and so it was changed. The last signal sent was: "Engage the enemy more closely", and this remained flying until destroyed by cannon fire at the height of the engagement.

- Casualties were high. Although not one single British ship was lost, nonetheless 450 of her men, including Lord Nelson, died and over 1,200 were wounded. The enemy fleet lost over 4,500 men with a further 2,400 wounded and some 7,000 taken prisoner. In a 'rolling broadside' where Vice Admiral Collingwood's ship *HMS Royal Sovereign* sailed close across the stern of the Spanish ship *Santa-Ana* firing its cannon loaded with double shot one after the other down the length of the gun decks of its doomed adversary, some 400 seamen were killed or wounded."

- Nelson's tactics were unconventional, though this was not the first time that he split his column in two. In the face of unequal odds he preferred a 'pell-mell' battle – his word for organised chaos – in which the superior gunnery and close-quarters action at which his navy excelled could be deployed. Conventional sea battles of the time had one fleet sailing parallel to its opponent, broadside to broadside, until the stronger won. Nelson split his smaller fleet into two squadrons, one led by himself on *HMS Victory* and the other leeward column led by his friend Lord Collingwood on *HMS Royal Sovereign*. The two columns bore down on the extended line of the Combined Fleet, cutting through it in two places. The enemy front section was instantly out of action because of the wind direction, and so the odds for Nelson were considerably improved. The ensuing battle was devastating and close fought, but the outcome an overwhelming victory for Nelson.

- The battle lasted from noon until 5.45pm. *HMS Victory* took incoming fire for ten minutes from the centre of the enemy line before being able to engage her own guns.

- Nelson was shot by a marksman from the rigging of the *Redoubtable* and died at 4.30pm knowing the battle was now won.

- Rather than hoist a flag signal, which would let the enemy know that Nelson had died, a man was despatched from *HMS Victory* in a small boat to advise Collingwood that he was now in command of the fleet.

- After the battle, a ferocious storm blew up from which the losses were enormous and some of the prize ships were lost with all hands. *HMS Victory* limped back to Gibraltar under a jury-rigged foretopsail.

- One of the more bizarre aspects of sea battles of the time, and Trafalgar was no exception, related to livestock. Ships would have animals on board to provide fresh meat, but when the decks were cleared for action at a serious engagement, there was no place for loose beasts. They went overboard (as did loose furniture). With 60 ships engaged in battle, it must have looked as though the first sinking was Noah's Ark.

LORD HORATIO NELSON

- Born on September 29th 1758, Horatio Nelson was the son of a Norfolk clergyman and proud of his Norfolk roots. He declared: "I myself am a Norfolk man and rejoice in being so". In 2005, after much lobbying, Norfolk County Council agreed to amend the county road signs to read 'Norfolk, Nelson's County'. When I first proposed this to the Chief Executive in 2003 she replied: "Why not Rider Haggard's County"? Probably for the same reason that the principle landmark in London is not called Solomon's Mines' Square.

- Horatio was just 12 years old when he joined his first ship as a midshipman. She was a 64-gun warship, the *Raisonable*, under the command of his uncle Edmund Suckling.

- He would not fit today's physical profile of a Hollywood

super-hero. He stood just 5 feet 6 inches, and never enjoyed robust health. His right arm was shattered by a musket ball in Tenerife in 1797 and had to be amputated, and he lost the use of his right eye from rock splinters fired by a ricochet during a battle at Calvi in Corsica. Vanity, of which he had an abundance, stopped him from wearing an eye patch, although he did have his famous hat modified by the addition of a small peak above that eye.

- An early indication of his fearlessness was when, still only a young midshipman, he ventured onto the ice off Greenland to kill a polar bear. His musket misfired, so Nelson decided to attack the animal with the butt of his musket rather than lose it. Fortunately a warning shot fired from the ship frightened the bear way, so avoiding disaster.

- Although married to Fanny Nisbit whom he met at her father's house in Nevis in the West Indies, the great love of Nelson's life was Emma Hamilton. Emma came from a humble background but had great beauty and grace – assets that she used to become first the mistress and then the wife of Sir William Hamilton. During his stay in Naples Nelson became besotted with her, and she with him, apparently with the tacit approval of her husband. Emma bore Nelson two children, and Fanny bore him none. Before he died, Nelson's wish was that Emma be taken care of by the nation that he had served so well. In spite of Nelson's immense stature and popularity in England, his dying wish was ignored and Emma died in poverty in France some years later.

- Nelson's four great naval triumphs, each of which feature on a bronze relief on the four sides of the base of Nelson's Column in London, were Cape St Vincent, Copenhagen, The Nile and Trafalgar. Each was marked by his inimitable strategic flair, outstanding leadership and fearless courage. The famous incident when Nelson 'turned a blind eye' took place at the Battle of Copenhagen when he ignored a signal to disengage from what his Commander-in-Chief saw as a highly perilous situation for Nelson. Knowing he could win through, he chose to ignore the signal. He put the telescope to his blind eye and said, "I really do not see the signal". His persistence led to a famous victory.

- He was a vain man, and craved recognition and reward. He wore his many decorations at any opportunity, and this was probably his downfall at Trafalgar when he refused to remove his coat while pacing the deck in the thick of battle. He was too easy a target for the French sharpshooters to ignore. Nonetheless, after being felled by a sniper's musket ball, he required that his face and identity be hidden from his crew when he was carried below decks, so as not to damage morale.

- Nelson was a hugely popular leader amongst his men at a time when life on a Royal Navy warship was harsh and when many captains evoked fear rather than respect from their men. This adulation stemmed from many factors. First, Nelson was successful and won considerable prize money from vanquished ships and their cargos. By tradition such prize wealth was shared among the crew, so Nelson's crew did well. Secondly, Nelson understood the need to look after his men, feeding them as well as was possible in all circumstances, and being fair with grievances. Notwithstanding, he was tough with his men when the situation required it to be so. He was also a great believer in training his men well, and the standard of gunnery in particular in his Navy was exceptionally high. Finally, he had charisma and invariably led from the front.

- When Nelson had to have his right arm amputated on board ship, he declared that the worst part of the experience was the coldness of the saw's steel. He ordered that in future all blades used in surgery should be warmed, an exercise which coincidentally helped sterilisation of the instrument.

- It is hard to exaggerate Nelson's popularity, not just with those who served under him, but also among the ordinary people of Britain. It is important to understand why this is so and why to this day we allow his image to have so dominant a position in our nation's capital. The fact is that Britain at that time was locked in a war with France under the leadership of Napoleon – a man whose dreams of European conquest were as real and as frightening as those of Adolph Hitler nearly two centuries later. The threat of a French invasion of England was very real, and fear of Napoleon and his French army was at the front of everyone's mind, particularly in the south of England. Hatred for the French amounted almost to mass hysteria. Nelson's several triumphs over the French fleet, therefore, propelled him to fame and adulation, achieved as it was with so much style and courage. It is interesting to note, however, that he was not always valued so highly in political circles – partly because of his high profile affair with Emma Hamilton and partly because he was frequently outspoken in ways that offended some in power. Perhaps the best example of this situation is the fact that Nelson's Column was erected through donations from a grateful populace, and not as an act of the Government.

- Finally, Nelson's funeral drew even greater mass attention, in relative terms, than did the funeral of Diana, Princess of Wales. A massive flotilla of vessels of every kind escorted the barge bearing his body up the river Thames. At the nation's insistence, he was given a State funeral, hitherto only the privilege of monarchs, and was buried in St Paul's Cathedral where his tomb has a dominant place today.

- As a footnote I have to report and debunk two outrageously amusing claims made to me by different people about Nelson. The first relates to his Chalenk which is the diamond encrusted turban ornament presented to him by the Sultan of Turkey and which he wore on the front of his hat. No, it really was not clockwork, and never did rotate. The second concerns the return of his body from the Battle of Trafalgar. It is a matter of fact that his corpse was placed in a barrel of brandy to preserve it on its journey back to Gibraltar and then on to England. In Gibraltar the cask was unloaded and two marines stood guard over it night and day. It is not true, however, in spite of the insistence of one businessman with whom I had dealings, that two musket balls were found in his body. The idea that the gases in his body built up until they were too much for the cask to withstand, and that the body was propelled out of it with such force that one of the marines shot it in mid flight like a clay pigeon is the stuff of schoolboy farce. I still chuckle at the image.

- The building of *HMS Victory* commenced in 1759 at Chatham Dockyard in response to the Admiralty's need for a First Rate 100 gun ship of the line. She was launched in 1765. This was 40 years before her triumphant role at Trafalgar.

- She was one of the largest warships afloat at the time, but not the largest. This distinction went to the Spanish flagship ranged against her at Trafalgar, the *Santissima Trinidad*. *HMS Victory* has a length of 69 metres, (which is also the height of Nelson's Column in Trafalgar Square) and a width at the widest point of 16 metres. She displaced 3,500 tons. Her main mast stands 62 metres high and she carries overall 37 sails that could produce a maximum speed of 12 knots. Her rigging, if laid end to end, would stretch some 25 miles.

- She was built almost entirely of oak, using up around 3,000 trees, most of them home grown and the rest coming from the Baltic. Britain's navy or 'wall of oak' used so much timber that conservation and planting was a major issue at the time. Nelson's friend and second in command at Trafalgar, Admiral Lord Collingwood, used to carry acorns in his pockets to plant wherever possible for the fleets of the future. Some teak was used, but was very unpopular with sailors. Flying splinters caused most injuries in battle, and teak's oily splinters would almost invariably go septic while oak was much cleaner.

- Fastenings were oak or beech dowels or 'treenails', which could be as much as three feet long, Wrought–iron bolts up to 12 feet long or spikes, were also used[6]. Later, brass and copper were used, particularly below the waterline and in the powder magazines where the danger of sparks had to be eliminated.

- At Trafalgar *HMS Victory* carried a total of 104 guns consisting of: 32-pounders located on the lower gun deck (30 in total); 24-pounders on the middle gun deck (28 in total); and 12-pounders on the upper, forecastle and quarter

[6] Full details of *HMS Victory's construction and restoration*, complete with detailed drawings, can be found in Alan McGowan's excellent book *HMS Victory, her Construction, Career and Restoration*, published by Caxton Editions

decks (44 in total). There were also two 68-pound carronades on the forecastle deck. The poundage relates to the weight of the shot or ball.

- Her full complement was 850 men. Of these about 250 were volunteers, about half were recruited by the press gangs and the rest either foreigners or 'rogues and debtors'. There were probably around 60 boys, some as young as 12 years of age, many of whom were 'powder monkeys', feeding the gun crews with gunpowder during the battle. Sleeping accommodation for the crew was provided by hammocks slung on the gun decks, with just 16 inches width per man, enhanced by a wool mattress and a pillow.

- Surgery was performed on the orlop deck, below the waterline. The floor in this area was painted red so that blood would be less noticeable.

- Her first battle was the engagement at Ushant in 1778, and she saw action frequently in the Mediterranean against the French during the 1790s, including Nelson's famous victory at Cape St Vincent. She spent a period as a hospital ship moored in the Medway at the end of that century but had a major refit between 1800 and 1803 when she sailed to Malta to become Nelson's flagship and spent much time shadowing and pursuing the French Fleet until her crowning role at Trafalgar.

- One of the most frequently asked questions about the 'arisings' used in The 1805 Collection was, 'Is the oak (or copper) original?' Our answer was always that the only claim we could make about it was that it came from *HMS Victory*. This was not evasion, so much as a recognition that not only was the salvage of the material over an 80 year period not documented on a piece-by-piece basis, but also that the term 'original' is not easily defined. It could mean 'from the original build' or could it have been at Trafalgar. We simply did not know. Some would have been in the original build, and yet more would probably have seen the great battle, but how much and which pieces are a complete unknown. It must be remembered that she was an old lady of 40 years at Trafalgar and had had that major refit between 1800 and 1803. It is also the case that running repairs were made at sea by the carpenters on board from materials they had with them – no more so than in the period from 1803 to 1805 when she was almost continually at sea. She was badly damaged at Trafalgar, and major repairs were carried out following the battle. Other refits, repairs and modifications were carried out before she was dry-docked in 1922. The materials purchased from the MOD could have become integral to the ship at any time. However, in spite of all the refits over the years, she is not, as one man suggested to me at one of the shows at Birmingham's NEC, 'like the original Brummagem broom' that has had three new heads and six new handles.

13

RUNNING THE BUSINESS

THE first sale was exciting, even though the amount was not great. It had made me think about the practicalities of handling transactions. The immediate need was to go out and purchase our first (of very few) pieces of equipment – a weighing machine. I had some knowledge of the scale trade having worked as Marketing Director for Salter Industrial Measurement Ltd whose hanging and counter scales can be seen in shops, post offices and supermarkets around the country. I was on familiar territory, and secured an electronic bench scale with a capacity of 300kg and a resolution of 10grams for £300. It turned out to be an excellent machine, and very good value. Our whole stock control programme, as well as the quarterly report to the MOD required us to weigh each piece, and sales values were also to be weight-related. A few months later I acquired a good size band saw for cutting the oak. These two items, plus a digital camera and a computer were all the equipment we purchased.

The next issue was recording each transaction and collecting data for accounts purposes. For Victory Ltd, this was a very simple matter. A spreadsheet would do that – noting date, customer details, material type with weight and measurements and finally the price and date paid. It was always cash with order or at the point of sale, so no credit risk attended this simple business of gradually disposing of our stockpile. The interest and the hassle came, as always, from the customers.

In the main, people preferred not to travel to Norfolk to select their material, but I tried hard to persuade them. If they were serious craftspeople who wanted to turn or cabinet make, I generally insisted. Having stuff returned because the grain went the wrong way or there was a hole in the wrong place just added cost and frustration. Serious makers quickly understood that and preferred to come and select the pieces that suited them. I was quite happy, though, to find pieces for those who just wanted an interesting looking piece for its own sake. Mostly we would have a conversation on the phone, I would get them to give me a budget price and an idea of what they would like and then go and search one or two examples that fitted the profile. When possible, I would take a digital photo and email it so that the customer could make the final choice. They would send me a cheque – or from 2002, give me their credit card details – and we would wrap and despatch the item complete with Certificate of Provenance. Quite often the customer would just trust me to find something suitable, and we never had anything other than thanks and enthusiasm for their purchase. Jan would wrap and take the parcels to our village post office. We were keen to put as much business as possible through this fantastic but threatened rural service. Sometimes the parcels were too big for the amount of weights they had for their 'bump scale' and we would have to pass 1kg bags of sugar from the shop shelves through the hatch to make up the appropriate balancing weight. Once, when a large piece had to be despatched urgently on a Wednesday afternoon when the village post office was closed, Jan put a sack trolley in the car with the parcel and then pulled it through the streets of our nearest market town and stood in line with the pensioners at the larger post office and shop to make sure it got away on time.

The difficulty I had experienced early in the project of identifying our market was explained somewhat by the eclectic mix of people who visited to select their own pieces. The only constant was their reaction when they first walked into the barn – mostly "Wow!" or maybe some Anglo-Saxon variation. Anglia Television did a piece on The 1805 Collection and the presenter described it as "an Aladdin's Cave for nautical history enthusiasts". It always gave me a buzz to see people's eyes light up as they wandered round. Frequently the original idea they had for buying some of it changed as they sifted through the dusty stacks. It had the ability to inspire anyone with a creative streak, and the man who, for example, had come to find a piece of oak to make a mount for the model of *HMS Victory* that he was building would leave with not only that but some more to make a model cannon or even a beam to use as a bressummer above his fireplace. We sold three or four for this purpose. I had one visitor who was a landscape gardener and was interested in the possibility of using a large beam to be built into a stone framed bench in the Prince of Wales's garden at Highgrove House. I particularly recall the long-distance truck driver from the North of England. He was a large, muscular man with tattoos and a ponytail and what I would describe as a very positive manner. He spent over two hours climbing all over the bays like a monkey, pulling pieces out and getting more excited by the minute.

"My wife will kill me when she finds out how much I have spent" he muttered, picking up a brass stanchion that had somehow found its way into the copper rivet cage. He added that to the growing pile. There were no reports of dead long-distance truck drivers over the next few weeks, so no doubt he won her over.

Jan soon hit on the idea of selecting interesting shaped pieces of oak, cleaning, polishing and mounting them, adding a brass plate stating: 'Oak from

HMS Victory' with a unique reference number and selling them as sculptures. We sold over a hundred pieces in this way. Most notable among these customers was a lady whose son was in California and starring in the Hollywood movie and Nelson period drama *Master and Commander*. So well accepted was the gift that she immediately ordered a further six for other members of the cast and crew, including one for Russell Crowe who was alleged to be delighted with it, as was the historical advisor to the film who, I was assured, slept with his next to his bed!

It was the creation of The 1805 Collection and Victory Marketing Partners Ltd that changed everything. To this point, it had been a nice, simple semi-retirement or hobby business. The second company, with its close interactivity with Victory Ltd, added levels of complexity that I had not anticipated. On the face of it, the two businesses would work together in harmony. I needed to set up a standard sales ledger format, once again on a spreadsheet, for each of the limited edition items that were made and sold. I did this for each one as they came on stream. Every time we made a sale I would fill in the 'edition sales ledger' with all the appropriate information, give it a sequential invoice number for Victory Marketing Partners Ltd (VMP01 etc), then copy that transaction entry and paste it into a general sales ledger for VMP. Then I would enter the Victory material value from that product into the Victory Ltd sales ledger. That way we had a rolling ledger for all transactions made by VMP including a discreet ledger for each edition, and the Victory Ltd sales ledger was updated. Simple. But it became far from simple.

First, there were commissions to consider. If the item was sold by the maker it would carry a 15% commission in addition to their price; if it were sold by David Burton at one of the shows it would also carry a commission to him – 15% the first year (when we paid any other costs) and 17.5% the following years (when he paid the other costs). Then there was part payment. On more expensive items such as the Victory stool, or those with a longer lead-time, the customer would pay a deposit on ordering with the balance paid before despatch. These had to be carefully tracked. Sometimes the maker sold the item and also took payment, so we had to collect our commission and payment for the Victory material before despatching the Deed of Provenance to the customer. This was our ultimate protection against payment default – no payment, no deed. Then there was VAT which can always be guaranteed to screw up any complex transaction. Most of the makers were not VAT registered, but one or two, including the Victory Stool which was one of our most successful products, carried VAT, so the invoices from Victory Ltd and VMP to the makers of these products had to satisfy the VAT requirements. By the second year of trading, VMP had passed the VAT threshold and so had to register for VAT. This meant that 17.5% VAT had to be added to the commission element which was VMP's revenue. The upshot of this was that all prices had to be changed, VAT tracked, pricing equations explained to bewildered makers for whom VAT was a land somewhere beyond the Mountains of Mordor for many. And two sets of VAT returns had to be completed every quarter. On top of this, there were the shows. At the end of a three or four day show David would send in a pile of orders and a mixture of cash, cheques and credit card slips. These had to be recorded, balanced and understood. Frequently there would be notes written on the order form with special requests from the customer about what to write on the Deed of Provenance, or mailing requirements like could we ask the postman to leave it with the neighbour because they worked, or special dates were critical for delivery. For overseas orders there were customs forms, and different countries have different needs. Australia, for example, gets highly excited about importing foreign timber. It soon became a nightmare, with me spending endless hours in front of the computer trying to get it all done. It was not what I wanted to do.

It was clear that a good, simple, foolproof order processing system was required that would cater for all these permutations, as well as the inter-company trading between Victory Ltd and VMP. I had a meeting with our accountants to discuss this. Their initial proposal was that we installed a popular small business accounting software package called Sage. I investigated, and discovered two things; first, it could not really handle the particular peculiarities of my businesses, and secondly that it would have been like buying a combine harvester to cut the rectory lawn. I looked at a number of off-the-shelf small business accounting packages, but failed to find one that could work for a sales agency company like VMP. They all seemed to work on a model where you either made products or sold them or purchased products and sold them. Seemingly only business deviants got other people to make things and then sold them on their behalf.

The solution (as I thought) appeared from an unexpected quarter. I own a small cottage on my property that I rent out. When I took on the incumbent tenants, I had shown it to another couple that were very keen to have it but were second in line. They asked me to contact them when it next became vacant. At the point when I was quite prepared to throw the computer overboard and abandon ship the tenants in the cottage gave notice to leave, so as promised I phoned this couple. It turned out they were now well suited with their new home, but the husband Gary asked how the Victory project was going. That was akin to asking Captain Bligh of *HMS Bounty* fame whether he enjoyed the row to Pitcairn Island. He listened patiently to my ranting and suggested he might be able to help. It turned out that he was not working at the time but enjoyed creating computer systems and had created and run such a system for a landscape gardening company in Scotland a few years ago. I suggested we meet to discuss this further.

The upshot was that Gary agreed to build a system for me that would address my particular needs. It would be based on the Access database software and offer a menu driven process for recording orders, creating invoices and generating VAT ledgers. It would also provide the usual database search facility for products, customers, orders, invoices as well as sales ledger information. This was indeed the

Promised Land. The cost? £500, and ready in six to eight weeks. Done. What is more, he would also come and run it for me for four days a week at five hours per day. The Sons of Zebedee agreed to this major hike in our overheads and Gary started work in the summer of 2004. Victory Ltd had staff.

The two of us got along fine and my life was transformed. This was the time to be planning for the all-important Trafalgar bicentenary celebrations just a year away. Gary adapted to the rather feast-or-famine nature of our order intake and consistently produced the paperwork, making occasional modifications to the programme as he became more familiar with the demands of our unusual business. I got on with developing some retail products, extending the range of The 1805 Collection and attempting to generate publicity. I took on a small PR agency in Holt who adopted the project with enthusiasm, generating press releases with gusto and firing them off to all manner of media the length and breadth of the land. Sadly, most of them went into the editors' bins, but we did get coverage from local media who always like home grown stories, and from specialist areas such as the navy news and woodworking magazines.

The agency's major triumph was in persuading a well-established art gallery in Holt to hold a ten-day exhibition of The 1805 Collection. Picturecraft were great to deal with, and saw this as an opportunity to extend their customer base. We had an open day with wine and a finger buffet for invited guests (mostly drawn from the gallery's own customer list) and secured good coverage on radio and in the local press. I even met an aged relative I had not seen for years who came along to see what it was all about. The sales results were excellent, and made me wonder about using the same tactic with other galleries in different parts of the country. My efforts at bringing this off bore little fruit, however. Most art galleries I have ever been dragged into seem to me to be in serious need of business. When was the last time you were jostled in an art gallery or had to wait for ages in a queue to pay for your purchase? This, I thought, would be too good an opportunity for them to miss. I researched a list of galleries in likely locations (London, Portsmouth, major port towns etc) and created a mail shot. Created Images came up with an excellent A5 leaflet, and off we went. Stony ground. I phoned a few to follow up and see what the problem was. A mixture of things conspired to make this a non-starter. Art galleries know about art – paintings and sculpture. This is familiar territory to them, and they are reluctant to venture into the unknown. Perhaps they worried that exhibiting 'craft' rather than art would tarnish them. Maybe they paled at the thought of being invaded by hordes of bearded boaty types who would ask all manner of questions to which they did not know the answers. Undoubtedly, a major factor was that we were only offering a commission rate of 15% when their normal expectation would be 30-50%. The volume and risk equation cut no ice with them. In short, they were risk averse.

Even released from the day-to-day chore of order processing I was busy, and the business kept growing the nearer we got to the magic year 2005. I was devastated, therefore, when Gary advised me, only six months into the job, that he was leaving to become a crime analyst with the police. He left at the end of March 2005 with just seven months to go to Trafalgar Day, and nine months until I had agreed to quit the business. There was not much point in trying to recruit and train someone else up given the short time frame. By the time we had found someone and they had become competent it would be all over and I would have become a basket case. To my delight, and not a little concern, my wife Jan, hitherto acting unpaid Packing and Despatch Manager, volunteered to take it on. My concern was that Jan was a first rate wife, mother, physiotherapist (not now practising) and homemaker. Her feelings about computers though were much akin to Nelson's feelings for the French. It is to her eternal credit that she had recognised this antipathy as a potential problem to life in the 21st century and had been attending several computer courses available on Norwich's Adult Education programme. She could do word processing and mail merge, including creating tables, but knew nothing about spreadsheets or Access databases. In a competitive recruitment campaign she would not have got to the interview stage. She was just what I needed. Gary promised to help train both of us for a couple of weeks before he left, and we decided that one way or another we could muddle through.

In the weeks that followed we did wonder whether Gary's decision to abandon ship had anything to do with the system he had created. It was dreadful. My old spreadsheet system was tedious and had plenty of scope for making mistakes, but the flip side was that it was totally flexible and could be amended easily. Gary's system was both inflexible and complex. When demonstrated by its creator it seemed like logic and grace personified. Left alone with it, it turned into an intractable, unwieldy, incomprehensible leviathan. We contemplated abandoning it and reverting to the old system but decided there was too much information already on this system. Gary had put all 2004 transactions into it and we were now well into 2005. We just had to learn to work with it, and this Jan did, with occasional support from me. It was a source of considerable stress, only made bearable by the knowledge that the clock was ticking and that there was an end date in sight.

To those who think that running your own business is glamorous I would say, think twice. Those with a vocation expect the graft and accept it as the price they pay for whatever drives them. If you become a soldier because you like the uniform, or a chef because you like soufflés you are in for a shock. The two words to focus on in 'running a business' are 'running' and 'business'. You cannot stand still, stroll or even walk briskly; you run. It is highly competitive and it is a marathon. It is also business – serious, impersonal and unforgiving. You need to be clear going in what you expect from it, and rejoice if you achieve that. Anything else is a bonus.

14

"TO SHOW OUR SIMPLE SKILL..."

...that is the true beginning of our end." Shakespeare, A Midsummer Night's Dream.

THE shows were David Burton's thing. He introduced us to ICHF, he set the shows up and, with his partner Caroline, he ran them. Jan and I were not much more than willing hands and moral support, and with the passage of time the hands became less willing and, it can be said, less necessary. In many ways the shows epitomised the conflicts between vision and reality and underscored the need in business to let pragmatism override one's personal emotions.

I had done plenty of stand time during my career, both from the planning and manning perspectives. My experience, however, had been of trade shows with good size budgets used to hire stand contractors, and with professional marketing teams and squads of salesmen to handle the events. I had done my share of selling, marketing and designing in a professional trade environment. Craft shows were a very different game.

Success at craft shows requires energy, determination, an understanding of show politics, and the gift of the gab. David had all of these in full measure, and I was still reading the manual. This became clear from the outset when my wife Jan and I turned up on build-up day for our first show at Penshurst Place in Kent in May 2002. A friend had arranged to provide me with a good size four wheel van box trailer for use in shows[7], and David had filled it with exhibits, a stand structure, carpet, lighting, display boards, folding chairs, tools, kettle, cash box, receipt pads and other stationery and anything else he might need to fill a stand area of about 30ft x 15ft. Just loading it before leaving home was a day's work. We arrived to find we had been allocated a prime position in the entry marquee so that all visitors, having purchased their tickets, would have to pass our stand on their way through to all the other marquees and the rest of the show, and pass

[7] Kindly sponsored by Trek Highway Services Ltd and Mid Norfolk Canopies and Trailers Ltd.

it again on the way out. There were no other exhibitors but us in this important area. ICHF, the show organisers, gave us this position at all of their shows as the presence of The 1805 Collection was the main promotional feature of their shows right up until the bicentenary.

David and I had discussed my vision of our exhibit, and I had produced some storyboards telling of the project's genesis, the Trafalgar story and the history of *HMS Victory*. The rest was down to him. My initial excitement on arrival that first day was short lived. Our space was a large area of damp, uneven grass on a gentle slope, bordered on three sides by wind-buffeted canvas. The fleeting thought that there might have been some similarities to being on board *HMS Victory* under sail failed to inspire. The advent of rain that somehow managed to find its way through joins in the canvas, particularly when the wind gusted strongly did not help matters. David started to empty the contents of the trailer which was parked just outside the tent, and we all willingly carted it through. At this point I started to feel about as much use as a ballet dancer on a building site. Only David knew what kind of structure he was going to build with the assortment of props he had brought, and he would modify it several times before conceding that he had the optimum display space and visitor frontage. My own suggestions and efforts were politely considered and diplomatically modified or rejected. This was a man who knew what he was doing, and all I could do was marvel at the inventive use that could be made of assorted lengths of carpet, soft furnishing fabrics, racking, boards, clamps, cables, trestle tables, duct tape, wire and boxes. It was like being a spectator at The Krypton Factor. My contribution at this stage was limited to passing the tools and uttering encouragement. I was impressed by David's constant banter and good humour throughout this activity, particularly as we were all the time working against the clock. The entire stand had to be finished and the site vacated for Security to take over in the early evening.

When it came to merchandising, I felt I was on safer ground. Once the stand structure was to David's satisfaction we commenced unpacking the exhibits and placing them to best advantage. I would put out three or four pieces and then go to unpack some more, only to find on my return that they were not as I had put them. David, Caroline and Jan all joined in this phase of the operation, and before long we were all moving each other's efforts around when they weren't looking. Eventually David would take control and impose his view that we all conceded was based upon his many years of experience at craft shows. Mostly this exercise was good humoured, with plenty of joshing and joking and we would end up with something we were all pleased with.

The shows typified to me the 'curate's egg' syndrome that crops up all the time in running a small business. You start off with a vision of what you want to do, but find that circumstances and unexpected factors mean you have to modify the vision and compromise to find an acceptable balance. In the early days of the shows we had probably less than 50 limited edition items that were part of The 1805 Collection. Our four small retail products that were ideal for those who wanted a small souvenir bolstered the product offering. In addition we would bring a supply of raw pieces as removed from the ship, together with Certificates of Provenance for them. Jan's Victory oak sculptures sold well at the shows, and soon David produced his own version of these, differentiated by mounting them on a leather-covered base and referencing them with a VNS number (Victory Natural Sculpture). In addition to these, David would bring along items he had made himself from Victory oak he had purchased but which were not part of The 1805 Collection. Therein lay my dilemma.

The deal I made with David was that he would run the shows and I would pay him 15% of the sales value of all our items sold at the show, plus mileage and an accommodation allowance. Any of his own Victory products sold at the shows would yield a 10% commission only to VMP since he had already purchased the oak from Victory Ltd. As time progressed, David realised that he would make more money by selling his products than from selling the others, so gradually the stand featured a growing dominance of David's products in the display and merchandising, thus diminishing the impact of The 1805 Collection. In time the stand had all the appearances of a Soukh in Marrakech, with every square inch occupied by a bewildering array of artworks, turned bowls, sculptures and other artefacts bearing testament to the varied talents of both David and Caroline. Furthermore, very few of these items were made entirely of Victory materials, and often featured just a small fragment of oak or copper within leather and other woods. It was a far cry from my image of an elegant and tasteful display of a discreet number of high quality limited edition items representing the skills of leading British craftspeople. David and I danced around this issue a little. He knew that I knew what was happening, and vice versa. The relationship was too important to both of us to risk going head to head. The way I rationalised it was this: David knew the craft market and what people would buy; we had 34 tons of oak to shift, and every item sold made a dent in that and created revenue for my business; I could not do the craft shows without him and would never find anyone else to take this on – certainly not in such a cash-positive manner; we were getting exposure, and finding new makers for the Collection, many of whom came on board because they knew David. The bottom line was that the shows were becoming a significant driver within the total business and I was not prepared to jeopardise that.

The fact that David had been smart enough to not only engineer himself a free stand at all major shows for the next three years with ICHF but had also grabbed the opportunity to re-invent his business based on Victory material at a time when his leather top tables range was in decline was not lost on me or on ICHF. While I was able to accept that with grudging admiration, ICHF felt it only fair to limit our free stands to the introductory year of 2002 and the bicentenary year of 2005, and to charge us a peppercorn fee for the intermediate years. I accepted their argument that other makers were complaining that David (and Victory Ltd) was getting unfair advantage and that our success was to some extent at their expense. They argued that visitors attending the shows had a limited spending power and we were getting a disproportionate share of it. Fortunately, David had been on the craft show circuit for years, knew most of the other serious makers well and was able to defuse most of the resentment. Many of his acquaintances joined us in The 1805 Collection. Mostly, this worked well. There was one unfortunate and totally bizarre incident, however, when he asked a highly skilled turner of large bowls if he would like to do a 'one-off' for us. The man concerned accepted the offer willingly, and David gave him one of our large and interesting Victory oak beams that we had been using as part of the stand decoration. We heard nothing from him for months, despite David leaving messages to chase him up. Finally, he approached David on build-up day at one of the shows and handed him a bag containing 300 life-size turned acorns, and then asked for payment! David went into orbit, and I was not ecstatic myself when he told me what had happened. Instead of turning a particularly character-full beam into one of his highly collectable bowls, to be paid for when sold as agreed with all makers in the project, he reduced it to a pile of something we did not want and did not order. I left it to David to sort out which he did in his usual inventive manner. David created a new limited edition product called the Collingwood Bowl, each of which features an acorn. Happily the product proved a great success, so the acorns were eventually used, though the price paid for them was lower than demanded.

Stand duty was all in a day's work for David and Caroline who had been doing it for years. For Jan and me it was torture – literally, in my case, as prolonged standing did nothing for a serious lower back injury I had incurred some years earlier. Standing on a slope for any length of time gave us all a sense of having had too many gin and tonics without the attendant pleasures. It was not entirely without its redeeming moments, however. At our first show we were agreeably surprised by the unannounced arrival of friends of ours armed with a plate of homemade smoked salmon sandwiches and a bottle of white wine. Colin Brown and his wife Heather made this into a pleasant ritual at many of our larger shows and we looked forward to it. Colin was a retired Brigadier whom I had met during my previous working life and who had been intrigued by our project. He did some charity work in Portsmouth and made some useful introductions for me. In the early days I had arranged for us to meet Alan Aberg, the Chairman of the Society for Nautical Research for the first time. Alan invited us to meet him for lunch at the Royal Naval Yacht Club in Portsmouth. Jan and I met up with Colin and we followed him as he drove us to the venue. We parked our cars in the street opposite the club and were standing on the pavement waiting to cross the road when we received a cheery "hello" and a wave from a man on the other side who was heading for the front door of the club.

"That must be Alan," I said as we crossed to meet him.

"Welcome," the man said. "Come on in. I've just been appointed Commodore."

"You must be kept busy, then, with all this as well," I ventured, shaking his hand and introducing the three of us.

He signed us in, walked us up the staircase, telling us about all the redecorating that had just been done, and took us into the bar where he ordered drinks for us. We were getting on just fine, chatting about the history of the club and then moving on to talk about Nelson when a stranger came over to the group and enquired:

"Is one of you Jonathan Bowman?"

I owned up.

"Ah, sorry I'm late," he said. "I hoped I would find you in here. I'm Alan Aberg."

We never did explain the mistaken identity to our host the Commodore, but laughed about the incident as we ate our smoked salmon sandwiches.

One regular feature of all our ICHF shows was the presence of a harpist who took up station in the entrance opposite our stand and played suitably relaxing music all day, every day with just occasional breaks for lunch or a drink. He was a pleasant and very talented man and I would go over and chat to him when things were quiet to break the tedium. He had some electronic amplification gear for his harp, and a small pile of his CDs that were for sale. Whenever anyone wanted to buy one he would stand up, keep playing with one hand while taking money and talking to him or her. I would watch and marvel at his ability to do both things at once without breaking rhythm, and looked carefully to see if he was actually playing the harp equivalent of a pianolla or player piano – that is, not really playing it at all but just miming. However, he always seemed to have at least two fingers plucking away. David hated it and was constantly muttering about it because it made it difficult for him to eavesdrop on customers talking amongst themselves about the display.

"I don't know why he doesn't do the job properly and get completely pissed instead of ha' pissed, then we wouldn't have to listen to it."

There is a definite 'us and them' culture about these shows. Camaraderie between exhibitors is the result of shared experiences and emotions, and offers mutual support. Customers drift through the shows, often oblivious to the people manning the stands, simply studying the wares on show. Exhibitors, on the other hand, derive not just their living but also their entertainment from the individual characters that make up the crowds. I used to view them as a sort of Happy Families pack of cards, trying to identify the family into which they would fit. There was the bored husband, dragged along to the show by his more enthusiastic family, and quite often he was our best customer, finding something masculine in Nelson, Victory and Trafalgar that was absent on most craft stands. There was the harassed mother trying to herd and control excitable children intent upon picking up everything on a stand she would happily have passed swiftly by had her husband not irritatingly chosen to stop and indulge his own interest. There were the studious and serious minded types, both male and female, who came to learn as much as to buy, and would ask intelligent questions. There were the know-alls who liked to come onto the stand and regale you with their knowledge of just about anything they could think of to talk about. There were a surprising number of disabled and wheelchair-bound people who mostly enjoyed the experience and variety offered, and appreciated that the stand was wheechair-friendly. There were foreigners, many of who knew more about the Trafalgar story than the locals. In particular, there was one elderly French lady who came to one of the shows in 2003 and engaged me in conversation.

"I like what you are doing here," she said encouragingly, "Though I don't like your claims of a great victory over the French".

Fair enough, I thought.

"Of course, Trafalgar was a victory for us, you know," she said.

"Really?" I said, surprised. "How do you figure that out?"

Well," she said triumphantly, "we killed Nelson".

It was a point of view. She went on to say graciously how much she liked and admired Britain, but had to have the last word. As she walked away she turned and said: "… but your railways are atrocious!"

The following year the same lady came to the show and started the conversation again. I forestalled her.

"I know," I said. "This was a great French victory, wasn't it? You killed Nelson!"

She peered at me and smiled.

"I remember you from last time," she said, and then set about praising Britain for its many good features.

Once again, however, she was determined to leave with the controlling shot.

"Anyhow, we have just won ten gold medals in the Olympics and you only got eight!" she said over a departing shoulder.

I did not have the heart to tell her the story just related to me by an American visitor about the comment made by US General Schwarzkopf on being advised that France had declined to join the Coalition in the second Gulf War:

"Going to war without France as an ally is like going on a deer hunt without your accordion!"

The biggest problem encountered with the public was initial cynicism. We had some difficulty in communicating the message that what was on the stand was made from oak and copper salvaged from *HMS Victory*, in spite of the fact that we had a five metre long banner across the front of the stand proclaiming '*HMS Victory* oak', as well as story boards around the stand describing the project, not to mention the fact that the laminated product price tags alongside each exhibit also referred to Victory oak or copper. One of the golden rules of designing an exhibition stand is that it should be obvious from first glance what the stand is all about so that the consumer can react. In this case it proved elusive and tended to demonstrate that people see what they expect to see or hear what they expect to hear. This is the basis of illusionism. Perhaps the idea that so many things on display at a craft show could have been made from salvaged material from Nelson's famous flagship was too alien for people to grasp without having it drummed into them. I used to amuse myself at the shows by imagining Basil Fawlty explaining it all to a hapless Manuel.

Engaging potential customers in conversation on a stand at a consumer show can be an artful process. If you see someone stop and look and then approach them, the chances are they will move away, doubtless afraid that they are about to be sold something they do not want. They see a ruthless salesperson equipped with mesmeric powers of persuasion about to corner them and subject them to revelations and logic so cunning that they will part with all their savings and become owners of something they neither want nor need. On a large stand such as ours you have to stalk them like gillies stalking deer in the Highlands and then, having isolated them from the herd, you have to engage in another outdoor sporting metaphor and tickle them like trout. When you have spotted your prey the first rule is to avoid eye contact. That would cause the prey to prick up its ears, flare its nostrils and scan for an escape route. Once identified, the best thing is to saunter aimlessly in the opposite direction and then circle round behind them, allowing time for them to feel comfortable, unthreatened and unaware of your presence.

"It is made from oak salvaged from Nelson's flagship," you announce conversationally from slightly behind their shoulder. "Everything on the stand is, in fact."

This always produces a reaction. Some (usually women) glare at you as if you have just made an improper suggestion and scurry away before they are violated. More commonly, though, this is met with "Really?" and you take it from there. Sometimes the "Really?" is in a tone of genuine interest that allows you to then get into a conversation about the project and possibly about a particular exhibit. Frequently, however, it is more of an "Oh yeah? Pull the other one" and is followed by allusions to fragments of the True Cross sufficient to build a cathedral. This negative response is actually a very good launch pad for a discussion about Nelson, Trafalgar and more particularly the restoration of *HMS Victory*. Sometimes, generally with men, you would find that all of a sudden the hunter had become the hunted. The conversation would move at a gallop down a particular avenue of interest to the punter, and you would have to hear about his theories on the Napoleonic wars, or how the black and white cottages of landlocked Worcestershire are all made of reclaimed ship's timbers, or how he is making a scale replica of the *Cutty Sark* from toothpicks, or why the French are all villains… Mostly, these exchanges were interesting or informative, and I learned all sorts of thing about Nelson, Trafalgar and shipbuilding from stand visitors. Sometimes the conversations were plain tedious.

The scepticism was, for the most part, healthy and ultimately resolved. It allowed us to fulfil an important part of what I considered to be something of a mission – namely to educate the public about the exciting and hugely important part of our national history that was Trafalgar. "How did you come by this material?" was a common question. David was apt to reply that we went down to the dockyard at dead of night wearing Zorro masks and equipped with a chainsaw and a bottle of rum and helped ourselves. That would open a good-natured bantering exchange from which David's extensive knowledge of the subject would emerge. On one occasion a man was clearly fascinated by David's commentary and explanation about a shallow-dished bowl that David had turned from an interesting piece of oak, while his wife was becoming increasingly bored by the whole business.

"And that," she said sourly, pointing to the shallow depression of the bowl, "is no doubt where a cannon ball hit it!"

Comments like that were generally good-humoured, and helped involve others who were studying the display on the stand. Nevertheless, there were those who simply would not listen. Some became quite irate that *HMS Victory* had been tampered with and resolutely refused to listen to explanations of why timber structures needed restoration and how that was accomplished. Some thought we were responsible for completely destroying this national asset, and we had to reassure them that the great ship was indeed alive and well and living in Portsmouth. On one well-remembered occasion a woman whom David later described as 'a Greenham Common type – long unruly hair, tie-and-dye skirt and Doc Martin boots" – was berating David's partner Caroline.

"How dare you ruin *HMS Victory*?" she ranted, refusing to listen to explanations. "It says here that you are cutting up the ship," she railed. She became more and more irate and aggressive to the point where David felt he needed to step in. She would not listen to him either, and became all the more venomous. Eventually David lost it.

"Just give me one minute," he said, "and I can explain it to you, or else you can f*** off and be wrong for the rest of your life!"

She chose the latter course.

Shows were typified by periods of frenetic activity, often caused by the arrival of another coach-load of visitors, and times of total tedium. We would use the dull periods to tidy up the stand and resite the exhibits displaced by previous visitors. David would use his natural exuberance to keep us entertained, pretending to swallow the naval dirk or clasping Nelson's death mask like an Oscar and delivering a speech to a non-existent audience thanking his mother for his great success in life.

"Today, madam," he would call to a woman walking past, "with every purchase we are offering a free holiday with Tom Cruise. If you don't want to go with him you can put him on your charm bracelet!"

And so it went on. Latterly, David acquired a replica Nelson uniform and would give short lectures on the Trafalgar story to visitors at agreed times. On one occasion, two elderly ladies were sitting in the second row, knitting. They probably had sore feet and could not resist the rows of seats set out for the lecture. At the end, they approached David.

"I know who you are," one of them said.

David smiled. "Go on then, who am I?"

She hesitated, pointing at him with one finger and pulling her chin with her other hand.

"Um, oh, wait a minute, oh no, it has gone. Give me a clue."

"HMS Victory" said David.

"Yes, that's it" she said, "um, er… what's his name? Give me another clue!"

David pulled his right arm inside the sleeve of his jacket and brought the seemingly empty sleeve across his chest.

"Yes," she cried. "That's it. Captain Hook!"

David Burton as his alter ego

The shows were an important part of our business, and probably delivered up to half of our sales of The 1805 Collection, either directly or indirectly. It became clear to me, though, that craft shows were on a downward cycle. We tended to see many of the same faces year after year, and sales the second time round in one venue were never as good as the first time. Also, other standholders confirmed that their takings were declining and that average spend per sale was dropping. The market was saturated. Add to that the huge amount of effort needed to set up and run a three or four day show, and many started to query the wisdom of continuing. My view was that we should cover more venues, and not just at shows. I liked the idea of having exhibitions in art galleries. Many of our cities and market towns boast such galleries that always seem to me to be empty of people. However, most galleries are owned either by the artists whose works they contain or else by people who have a particular art genre interest, and neither of these types have a strongly defined commercial sense. Few could be persuaded to clear their gallery for a week or two to host such an exhibition. Furthermore there were problems over pricing. Galleries like to charge 30-50% commission on sales, and would not look at the 15-20% we offered, in spite of the fact that the sales volumes would be almost certainly on a different scale from what they were accustomed to. Finally, it was hard to see how David and Caroline could manage this, given the maximum discount VMP Ltd could make available to them and the gallery, not to mention the cost of staying away for one to two weeks. David was not keen. It never happened.

PART TWO

FLAGSHIP PROJECT

The 1805 COLLECTION

15

THE 1805 COLLECTION: TALES AND TALLIES

THE attraction of the whole project for me was the idea of assembling the nation's most talented artists and craftspeople and turning them loose with this unique supply of heritage material in order to create a fitting tribute to the bicentenary of Britain's greatest naval triumph. Like most collections, it contains the sublime and the strange, the whimsical and the 'wannabe', the collectable and the simply memorable. It is certainly the case that every single maker was inspired by the historic opportunity, and his or her work reflects this.

What follow is both a digest of The 1805 Collection as well as a thumbnail of the makers, together with some of the anecdotes that accompany many of the pieces. There is no hierarchy here, and they appear in alphabetical order of the maker's name. Please note that the quantities shown for each item were correct at the time of writing, but some editions have continued to sell through Nauticalia Ltd.

GEOFF BARNETT

HUMIDOR	
EDITION SIZE:	100
NUMBER SOLD	9
MAKER	Geoff Barnett
LATEST PRICE	£550

Geoff Barnett, a member of the Guild of Master Craftsmen, approached me through our website appeal for makers, and we discussed various products, settling on a humidor as something that would be welcome in The Collection. This finely finished box was available in Victory oak or teak, banded on all edges with wenge and a contrasting feathered or chevron inlay. The handles, lock and quadrant hinges were brass, and a disc of Victory copper was inlaid into the top. The box was lined with cedar and fitted with a humidifier and hygrometer to maintain cigars in top condition.

PHILIP BAUGHAN

PLAYING CARDS BOX	
EDITION SIZE:	200
NUMBER SOLD	3
MAKER	Philip Baughan
LATEST PRICE	£215

This was a nicely made box but just too expensive. Also, we were unable to source any further packs of Nelson playing cards as the producers discontinued the line.

PAUL BIGNELL

QUOIN	
EDITION SIZE:	10
NUMBER SOLD	7
MAKER	Paul Bignell
LATEST PRICE	£199

Paul Bignell became a wood carver and sculptor in wood later in life after service in the merchant navy. When he contacted me to ask if he might make a quoin for The Collection I was reluctant to show my ignorance, but my acceptance not only boosted my knowledge of Nelson's navy it also added a unique piece to our offering. Quoins were used to range the cannons on board ship from a minimum of 400 yards to the maximum range of 1,800 yards. They were wedged under the guns, each with a different angle of elevation depending on the distance required. The gun captain would call the range and the 'powder monkeys' would run to each cannon with the appropriate quoin. Paul's was a half size scale replica of one of *HMS Victory's* quoins, made from solid Victory oak and hand carved with the royal cipher of King George III. This excellent item was kindly sponsored by Tripstamp Ltd of Chichester.

ELAINE BLAKEY

HORATIA'S ROCKING HORSE	
EDITION SIZE:	5
NUMBER SOLD	1
MAKER	Elaine Blakey
LATEST PRICE	£265

The rocking horse emerged as a result of a good idea that did not quite work. **Elaine Blakey** is an amateur woodworker who contacted me to see if I would accept her design of a sort of nautical bookshelf. This was essentially a leather hammock arrangement slung at an angle between two oak ends into which three or four books could be held that would swing with the motion of the ship. It seemed a novel concept so I sent her some oak and in due course the item arrived. Sadly, it was not really robust enough or sufficiently suitable for purpose, so after exhibiting it for a while we withdrew it. Elaine was philosophical about this and asked if she might use the remaining oak to make a miniature rocking horse, and so she did. She produced a scaled down version of a full size rocking horse designed by Judy Fergusson, made of 4mm birch plywood standing on rockers of Victory oak. The accessories are of leather, brass and horsehair. We were both delighted to sell the original.

SILVER NELSON STATUETTE	
EDITION SIZE:	100
NUMBER SOLD	6
MAKER	James Boddy
LATEST PRICE	£236

NELSON'S COLUMN	
EDITION SIZE:	3
NUMBER SOLD	1
MAKER	James Boddy
LATEST PRICE	£15,000

As I mentioned in Part One, **James Boddy** decided to have a quantity of Victory copper made into Britannia standard silver by the Royal Mint. Both James and I had met Anthony Vanderpump whose family had been silversmiths in London for generations, and James discussed the product opportunities for this Victory silver with Anthony. He knew of a mould made from original 1929 drawings of a scale model of Nelson's column standing 3ft high, complete with the four lions and the four plaques commemorating Trafalgar, the Nile, Copenhagen and Cape St Vincent. James had three of them cast, with a base of Victory oak, and they were truly magnificent – with a price to match. It was a great joy to sell Number one to *HMS Excellent* for their Officers' Mess.

The statuette of Nelson on top of the column was cast separately in Victory silver and mounted on oak by David Burton, and six of these were sold.

AMELIA BOWMAN

OAK PENDANT	
EDITION SIZE:	500
NUMBER SOLD	5
MAKER	Amelia Bowman
LATEST PRICE	£22.50

My daughter **Amy Bowman** was making and selling jewellery at the time of The 1805 Collection and was anxious to have something of hers in it. The simple square of polished oak on a silver wire achieved this for her.

JANET BOWMAN

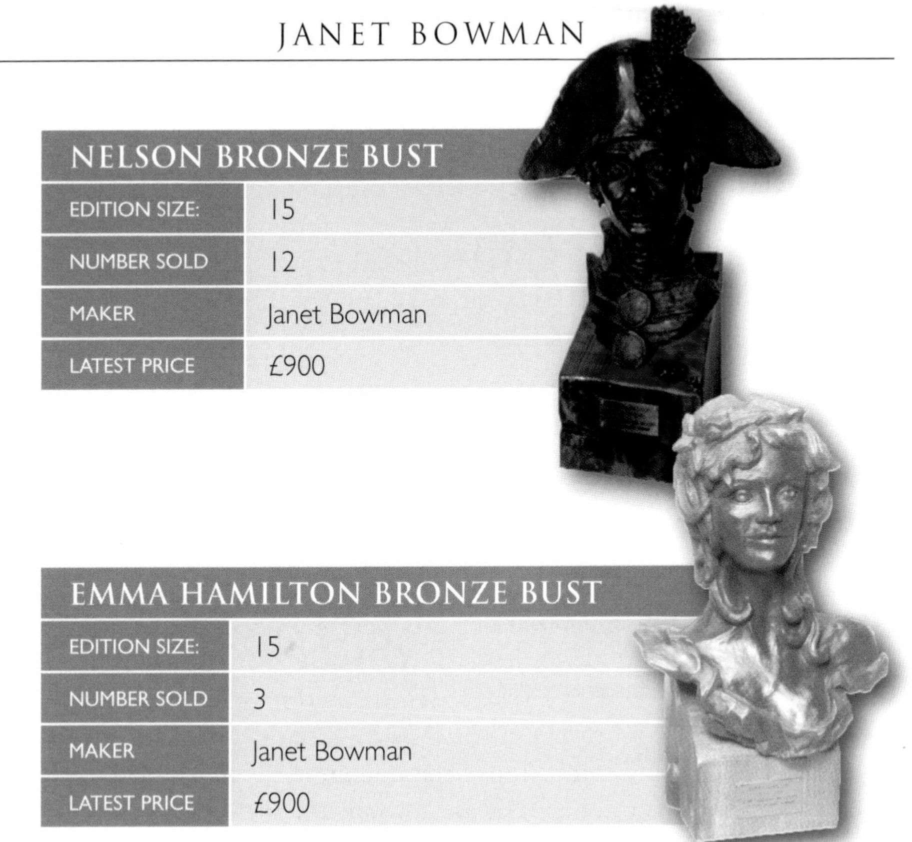

NELSON BRONZE BUST	
EDITION SIZE:	15
NUMBER SOLD	12
MAKER	Janet Bowman
LATEST PRICE	£900

EMMA HAMILTON BRONZE BUST	
EDITION SIZE:	15
NUMBER SOLD	3
MAKER	Janet Bowman
LATEST PRICE	£900

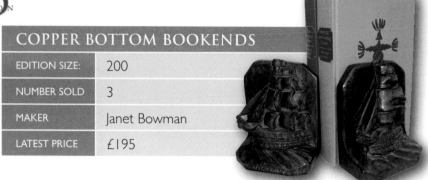

COPPER BOTTOM BOOKENDS	
EDITION SIZE:	200
NUMBER SOLD	3
MAKER	Janet Bowman
LATEST PRICE	£195

My wife **Janet Bowman** decided to start her involvement with The 1805 Collection by producing a cold cast bronze bust of Nelson, and mounting it on a section of Victory oak beam. The likeness, which is life size, is based upon the detail provided by Nelson's life mask, a copy of which was lent to her for the purpose. Happy with the result, she went on to do the pair by sculpting Emma Hamilton, using the various contemporary portraits of her for guidance. Nelson sold well, but Emma less so, and all the Emmas went as part of a pair. It seems Emma Hamilton still has not found great favour with the public, much as was the case when she was alive. My partner in this venture, James Boddy, purchased one pair.

The copper bottom bookends were also of cold cast bronze, and contain a piece of the copper sheathing set into the base of each one. We tried hard to find a company that would turn some of the copper into powder so that it could be mixed with resin and cast, but we were unable to find anywhere in the UK that would do this except at enormous cost. The copper bottom for this piece was the only solution, but it sadly did not sell well. The casting process is not cheap, nor is it price-volume sensitive. A set of bookends required two castings, and there was no way of getting the price down to a commercial level.

ALICK BURT

WRITING BOX	
EDITION SIZE:	20
NUMBER SOLD	4
MAKER	Alick Burt
LATEST PRICE	£2,250

Nelson's writing box is to be seen in the National Maritime Museum at Greenwich. It was never **Alick Burt**'s intention to create a replica of the original, but to use it as inspiration for a similar piece. The external casing is of Napoleon oak (Napoleon had oak forests planted for ship building just as Nelson encouraged them in England). The interior is Victory oak, including a hidden compartment, and the writing surfaces, which depict the crest of *HMS Victory* and also Nelson's last letter to Emma Hamilton the night before the battle, are hand painted (by David Burton) on English hide. Inlaid into the top exterior is a brass plate describing this piece, and there are two brass handles set into the sides.

DAVID BURTON

HERO PANEL

EDITION SIZE:	100
NUMBER SOLD	34
MAKER	David Burton
LATEST PRICE	£85

BATTLES CHESS TABLE (24 INCH)

EDITION SIZE:	100
NUMBER SOLD	3
MAKER	David Burton
LATEST PRICE	£695

TILT TOP FO'C'S'LE TABLE (24 INCH)

EDITION SIZE:	100
NUMBER SOLD	1
MAKER	David Burton
LATEST PRICE	£595

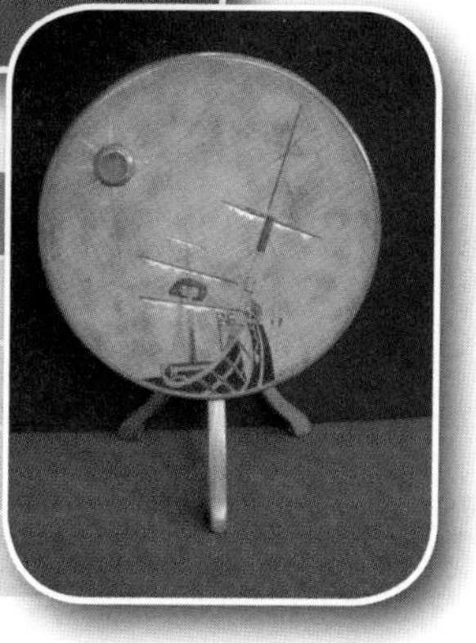

LEATHER TILT TOP TABLE (30 INCH)

EDITION SIZE:	100
NUMBER SOLD	4
MAKER	David Burton
LATEST PRICE	£1,050

BATTLES BAROMETER

EDITION SIZE:	100
NUMBER SOLD	16
MAKER	David Burton
LATEST PRICE	£195

SLOPING BLOCK BAROMETER

EDITION SIZE:	100
NUMBER SOLD	12
MAKER	David Burton
LATEST PRICE	£295

BATTLES CLOCK

EDITION SIZE:	100
NUMBER SOLD	6
MAKER	David Burton
LATEST PRICE	£195

COLLINGWOOD BOWL

EDITION SIZE:	100
NUMBER SOLD	34
MAKER	David Burton
LATEST PRICE	£105

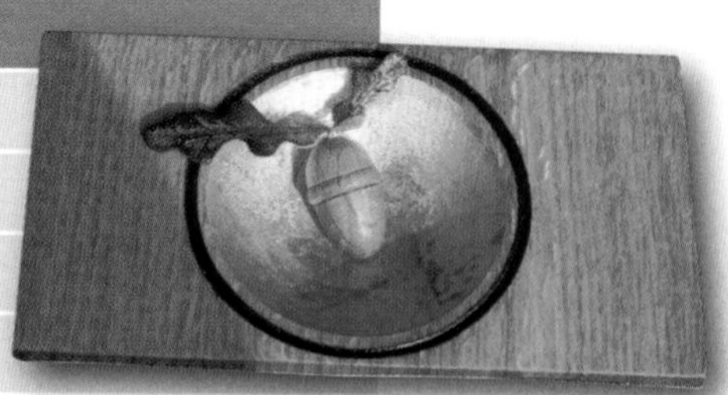

'ENGLAND EXPECTS' PANEL

EDITION SIZE:	100
NUMBER SOLD	33
MAKER	David Burton
LATEST PRICE	£85

VICTORY FO'C'S'LE PANEL

EDITION SIZE:	100
NUMBER SOLD	2
MAKER	David Burton
LATEST PRICE	£395

FULL COPPER SHEET PANEL

EDITION SIZE:	100
NUMBER SOLD	6
MAKER	David Burton
LATEST PRICE	£1,135

HEARTS OF OAK BOWL

EDITION SIZE:	100
NUMBER SOLD	1
MAKER	David Burton
LATEST PRICE	£165

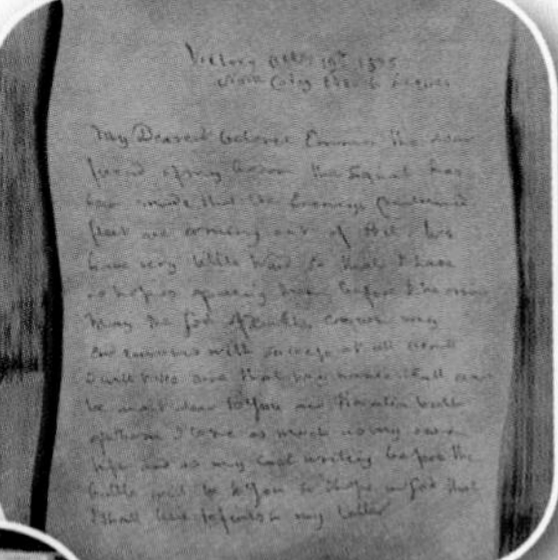

NELSON'S LAST LETTER

EDITION SIZE:	100
NUMBER SOLD	37
MAKER	David Burton
LATEST PRICE	£105

OAK ORLOP PANEL

EDITION SIZE:	5
NUMBER SOLD	1
MAKER	David Burton
LATEST PRICE	£655

RUSTIC BOWL

EDITION SIZE:	100
NUMBER SOLD	2
MAKER	David Burton
LATEST PRICE	£175

WINE TABLE

EDITION SIZE:	100
NUMBER SOLD	15
MAKER	David Burton
LATEST PRICE	£395

WINE TRAY	
EDITION SIZE:	50
NUMBER SOLD	34
MAKER	David Burton
LATEST PRICE	£175

All of our makers came to the project because they wanted to be a part of it. **David Burton** wanted to **be** it. From the start he recognised that this Victory material, which he had been aware of for some years but had been unable to get hold of, could provide new impetus to his struggle to get ahead in the craft business. Furthermore, he had a great interest in Nelson, having been in the Royal Navy. His initial approach to The 1805 Collection resembled a supermarket trolley dash.

His first products were variants on his existing products – namely leather top tables with a Victory theme and small pieces of Victory oak included. Our major craft show host, ICHF Ltd, sponsored one of these. Recognising the need to have products in the lower price range, David used his leatherwork skills, together with his partner Caroline's artistry with the pyrography pen to create three panels. The first, The hero panel, had Nelson's quote: "I will be a hero, and confiding in Providence I will brave every danger." The second was the 'England expects…' flag signal, and the third was Nelson's last letter to Emma written aboard *HMS Victory* on the night before the battle. I tried to get the post office to sponsor Nelson's last letter, but they declined. However, it did evoke the classic comment made by the know-all husband who read the panel to his wife, when she couldn't read Nelson's writing. However, he said it read: " We have no wine, and no way of opening the bottle," rather than "We have no wind and no way of opening the battle".

Keen to find the best mix of price and product attractiveness, David then started using his woodturning and general woodworking skills, producing bowls, clocks, barometers and further wall panels. Perhaps the most successful of these was the Collingwood bowl, which was a turned bowl incorporating an acorn in recognition of Nelson's great friend and second in command, Admiral Collingwood who was known to go about the countryside scattering acorns to encourage oak trees for future generations of ships. We were at the NEC in Birmingham when a lady with a young son and daughter came onto the stand and started examining the items. The girl, who was about nine years old, came over to David and said:

"My name is Collingwood. My great, great-grandfather or something knew Nelson. Do you know anything about him?"

"Yes," said David, "he was Nelson's best mate, and an admiral like Nelson. The French wanted to invade England and were sending their ships to fight against us, so Nelson and your Collingwood went out and gave them a really good slapping!"

"Wow, cool," breathed the girl, and rushed off to tell her mum. They bought a Collingwood Bowl.

As the project progressed, David realised that he could purchase oak and copper from us and make an unlimited amount of items and not have them as part of The 1805 Collection. This way he would not have to pay commission to VMP Ltd, but would have the opportunity to sell them on the stand at our shows since he was managing them. I agreed to this somewhat reluctantly, though we did demand a commission on all those items for which orders were taken at our shows. Inevitably, the stand became dominated by David's own items, and I always felt that this was not beneficial to The Collection overall. It was, though, a pragmatic move, generating ongoing income and further sale of the material. I will deal with David's non-collection products in Part Three.

GILLIE HOYTE BYROM RMS HS BSOE

MINIATURES OF NELSON AND LADY HAMILTON	
EDITION SIZE:	1
NUMBER SOLD	0
MAKER	Gillie Hoyte Byrom RMS HS BSOE
LATEST PRICE	£985

It is ironic that one of the few specific products I wanted in The Collection did not sell. Miniatures of Nelson and Emma framed together in Victory oak seemed a natural 'must have'. I sought out one of this country's leading miniaturists, **Gillie Hoyte Byrom**, whose commissioned works include Margaret Thatcher and The Sultan of Brunei, and she painted, with permission of the National Maritime Museum, two portraits based upon the most celebrated depictions of the famous couple. The oak frame, with its engraved copper plate on the reverse, was made by Howard Reynolds whose other works appear later in The Collection. The fact that they did not sell was not a reflection on the artistry of the works, but rather a failure of VMP Ltd to target the fine art market adequately. It became apparent with this and a handful of other works offered within The Collection, that we needed a very different level of exhibition than that being used for our core craftwork. Regrettably we failed to find an appropriate and cost-effective way to do this.

The technique involved in miniature making is more complex than simply fine painting on a very small scale. The portraits are of vitreous enamel, fired in a kiln at 750 degrees. Each one is made by fusing glass enamel to copper to create a base, and then applying by hand an enamel print from an original painting done by the artist. Gillie has just won one of the highest awards in her field – the Jacques Cartier Memorial Award, offered in the Craftsmanship and Design Awards 2007, Goldsmiths Hall, London – for an enamel miniature of Henry VIII on 18ct. gold.

The Nelson and Emma miniatures are still available from the artist at her own price, but not as part of The 1805 Collection.

TWO COASTER RACK	
EDITION SIZE:	500
NUMBER SOLD	12
MAKER	Gillie Hoyte Byrom RMS HS BSOE
LATEST PRICE	£70

FOUR COASTER RACK	
EDITION SIZE:	100
NUMBER SOLD	37
MAKER	Gillie Hoyte Byrom RMS HS BSOE
LATEST PRICE	£95

TRAFALGAR MEDAL EN GRISAILLE

TRAFALGAR MEDAL EN GRISAILLE	
EDITION SIZE:	1
NUMBER SOLD	1
MAKER	Gillie Hoyte Byrom RMS HS BSOE
LATEST PRICE	£850

Happily, Gillie realised that the Trafalgar bicentenary market still offered some opportunities for her talents, and once again with the woodworking input from Howard Reynolds, produced some items bearing a grisaille painting on china of the Trafalgar Medal that was issued to survivors of the battle of Trafalgar on their return. The coaster sets, in twos and fours, proved popular. The one-off framed Trafalgar Medal en Grisaille is hand painted vitreous enamel on copper with an inner frame of lignum vitae and the outer frame of Victory oak.

ROBERT CADE

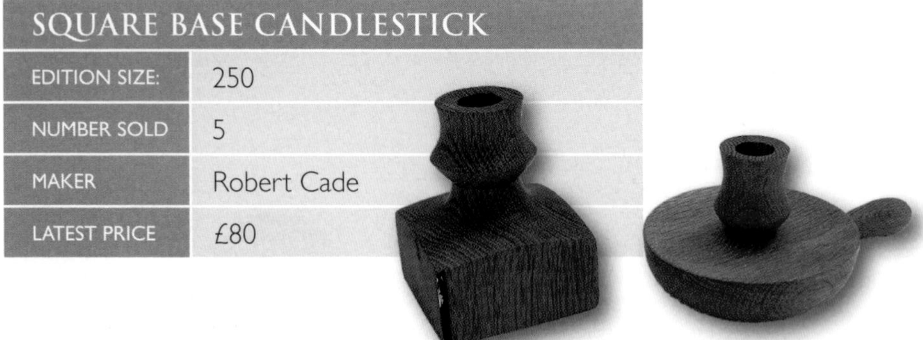

SQUARE BASE CANDLESTICK	
EDITION SIZE:	250
NUMBER SOLD	5
MAKER	Robert Cade
LATEST PRICE	£80

Candlesticks were to have been among my early choices for The Collection, but somehow no one else seemed to share my enthusiasm. I tried without success to have them sponsored by the country's leading candle makers, but they were not interested. **Robert Cade**, who offered the two designs shown, needed some persuading to participate, and in the event the numbers sold vindicated his reservations. The portable candleholder shown, which was a truly contemporary design for *HMS Victory*, did not sell at all.

BILL CARE

GAVEL AND BLOCK	
EDITION SIZE:	200
NUMBER SOLD	17
MAKER	Bill Care
LATEST PRICE	£110

Bill Care's gavel and block was well made and well priced, but my enduring memory is that I had to chase up every single order after the promised 28 day delivery period had expired. Bill was always good humoured and apologetic about it, and I suppose it is a tribute to the demands made on his time by other customers for his work.

DENIS CHAPLIN

COPPER CHESS TABLE AND CHESS SET	
EDITION SIZE:	50
NUMBER SOLD	2
MAKER	Denis Chaplin
LATEST PRICE	£1,050

Denis Chaplin is a traditional blacksmith using both open fire hot forging techniques, as well as more modern methods. I had been looking for blacksmiths who could do something with the copper rivets, and Denis heard about us through the industry grapevine. He asked if he could make a copper chess table, and when I agreed, he came round to pick up some rivets and copper sheathing from his forge in Diss in Norfolk. He spoke in a quiet, measured Norfolk accent, and I sometimes had a little difficulty following him. In essence, he said he felt slightly awe-inspired by the material, and was not entirely sure of his design, but would come back to me with something in due course. Some months went by, but he pitched up one afternoon and produced his table as work-in-progress. I'm not sure what I expected, but it surely was not this. The structure looked to me like a metal barstool with casters on the bottom. He had removed the rollers of the castors and replaced them with turned down section of 35mm copper rivet. The top of the table and the canopy above the castors were nicely turned from English oak, and on the top was a square of hammered out and cleaned up copper sheathing, into which he had etched the black and white squares. He was a little diffident about it, but once I had got over my surprise at what I was looking at I had to confess that it was different. Very different. And why not?

After some discussion I suggested that the etching needed to be a little deeper, and that it would be a good idea if the product included a chess set. He set off home promising to take care of those two points. A few weeks later he arrived again. His first words were:

"I'm sorry if you have difficulty understanding me, but I just knocked my front teeth out with a hammer!"

As he leant into the boot of his car, I could not wait for what was coming next. He had improved the etching as requested, and sure enough he produced a chess set to go with it. He had been to the shops and bought a conventional wooden chess set. He then took plaster moulds of the pieces, melted down some Victory copper and cast the pieces, blackening one set and leaving the other copper coloured. The result was quaint and slightly bizarre, and the price suggested to me that we would be carting this around the shows for months to come. When I phoned him a few months later to tell him we had sold it, his response was characteristic.

"Aren't folk strange?" he said in his soft, Norfolk way.

DAVID CHIVERS

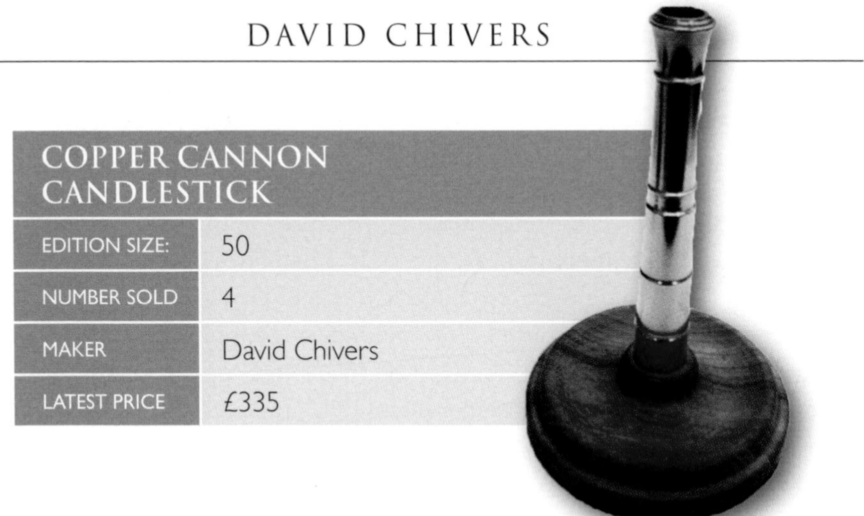

COPPER CANNON CANDLESTICK	
EDITION SIZE:	50
NUMBER SOLD	4
MAKER	David Chivers
LATEST PRICE	£335

PAPERKNIFE AND PEN TRAY

EDITION SIZE:	200
NUMBER SOLD	66
MAKER	David Chivers
LATEST PRICE	£59.50

SAIL CLOCK

EDITION SIZE:	150
NUMBER SOLD	16
MAKER	David Chivers
LATEST PRICE	£295

As well as being a cabinetmaker, **David Chivers** is a keen and experienced sailor from Essex, and counts Keith Musto, of iconic sailing apparel maker Musto Ltd among his friends. He approached me to say that he had various product ideas, including an unusual design for a clock for The Collection, and that Musto would sponsor it. The clock base was chosen from oak that had some distinctive wear in it, and copper sheathing was cut to form a square rig sail pattern resembling *HMS Victory*'s rig. The artistic sentiment expressed through the design embraces the timelessness of the materials coupled with the passing of time in the clock.

"The sail faces away from the clock hands as the desire to sail away from the restrictions of time is strong in so many people," he explained.

David was also keen to try and turn something from the copper rivets. He researched the cannons on *HMS Victory* and produced a faithful replica measuring 23 cms and mounted it on turned Victory oak. It was a good example of the thoughtfulness and care seen in all David's work.

In response to numerous enquiries, David agreed to produce the paperknife and pen tray. Chris Wedlake, maker of the successful Victory oak wine coaster, supplied the turned handle of the knife for David who did not have small enough turning equipment to do this part himself.

JOHN CROXON

PEN STAND	
EDITION SIZE:	25
NUMBER SOLD	25
MAKER	John Croxon
LATEST PRICE	£70

THE HERITAGE VICTORY OAK PEN STAND	
EDITION SIZE:	50
NUMBER SOLD	7
MAKER	John Croxon
LATEST PRICE	£86

THE HERITAGE VICTORY OAK PEN STAND	
EDITION SIZE:	50
NUMBER SOLD	7
MAKER	John Croxon
LATEST PRICE	£86

John Croxon first came to us to select oak for products to be made for a local company that wanted to take part in the Trafalgar celebrations. He had the advantages of being near at hand, as well as having a shrewd sense of what would sell and at what price. His workmanship and reliability were of the highest order. His first product for The 1805 Collection was the pen tray, which quickly sold out the realistic edition size of 25. Shortly after the last of these were sold I was approached by *Heritage* magazine, which wanted to commission a desk accessory item exclusively for their readers to be offered in their Trafalgar bicentenary issue. Having recently secured the casting in Victory copper of a replica of the Trafalgar Medal (of which more in Part Three), I proposed that we offer one of John's pen trays, but with a Trafalgar Medal inset into the stand in place of the inscription on copper sheathing that featured in The 1805 Collection product. It was a fine product, but the response from the magazine's promotion was disappointing, selling only seven pieces. The price point was probably a little high for an off-the-page offer of this type, but it still represented very good value in the overall mix of Victory products that were available, either through The Collection or from our trade customers.

The blotter, which was based upon a design used in Nelson's day, was inspired by a one-off piece of the same design that emerged through an auction house as having been made of Victory oak for the centenary celebrations in 1906. Desk accessories were popular gifts for men, and I had high hopes for it. Although it sold relatively few, it inspired fountain pen maker Conway Stewart to commission a miniature version from John to put into a commemorative presentation set, and this sold very well.

John's visits to select oak were memorable. Besides being a talented woodworker, John was a successful exponent of the sport of fencing, competing successfully at international level and also teaching it. He amazed me by recounting how he was engaged in teaching a blind man to fence – something that had never been done before. Over the period of this Victory project, John made considerable progress in developing a system for this unique tuition, and having fenced myself in younger days I enjoyed hearing all about it.

KATHERINE FERNIE

OAK CABINET	
EDITION SIZE:	7
NUMBER SOLD	1
MAKER	Katherine Fernie
LATEST PRICE	£2,650

Another splendid example of contemporary cabinet making and design came with this cabinet made by **Katherine Fernie**. With the exception of the back panel and interior shelves, this item is made entirely of solid Victory oak, with front inlay and handle of Victory copper. The sides are curved with the oak bent in a similar fashion to the cladding on the hull of a ship. The high-ticket price reflects the quality of workmanship and style of this designer piece.

DANA GOODBURN BROWN

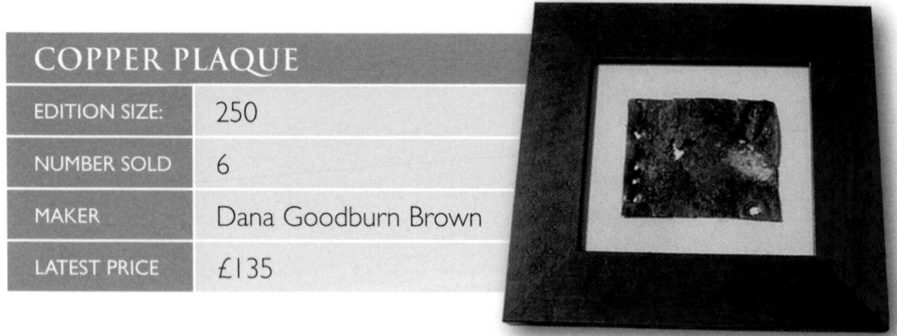

COPPER PLAQUE	
EDITION SIZE:	250
NUMBER SOLD	6
MAKER	Dana Goodburn Brown
LATEST PRICE	£135

Dana Goodburn Brown is an artist specialising in the investigation, care, reproduction and presentation of artefacts and past technologies, and was based in the foundry in the Historic Dockyard at Chatham where *HMS Victory* was built. Her interest in the project stemmed from that specialist background, and she chose to adopt the simple and classical museum-like approach of mounting a piece of Victory copper sheathing and presenting it in a plain oak frame. It was well executed, but some people who admired it simply purchased their own piece of copper and mounted it in a frame of their own choosing for a fraction of the price, albeit without The 1805 Collection certification.

NICOLA HAMPSON

BLOCK AND TACKLE	
EDITION SIZE:	5
NUMBER SOLD	0
MAKER	Nicola Hampson
LATEST PRICE	£3,000

This truly stunning solid bronze casting of a block and tackle similar to those found on *HMS Victory* is mounted on a rugged Victory oak beam measuring 57cms long by 30cms wide, and is extremely heavy. **Nicola Hampson** is a successful and highly talented sculptor, and the fact that this piece did not sell (it is available at the time of writing) is a reflection of our failure to target the fine art market successfully. Part of the problem lies with the high commission charges levied by suitable galleries which would have put the price beyond the reach of most people.

DAVID HARBER SUNDIALS

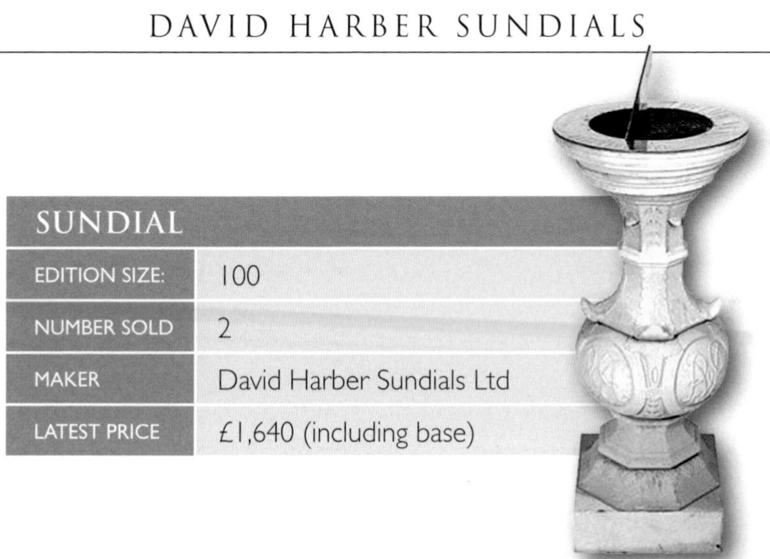

SUNDIAL	
EDITION SIZE:	100
NUMBER SOLD	2
MAKER	David Harber Sundials Ltd
LATEST PRICE	£1,640 (including base)

David Harber is unquestionably the leading designer and maker of sundials in Britain, regularly featuring his work at the Chelsea Flower Show and other major events. His products are both traditional and modern, but all with strong design at their core. He was fascinated by the opportunity to do something with the Victory copper and came up with two products. The first, being the traditional dial shown above, had copper sheathing at the centre of the dial, and the whole mounted on a classical stone carved base. The other design, which sadly did not sell (probably due to cost) was splendidly conceived. It was a rectangular plinth with a full sheet of copper sheathing as its centre, and the dial was calibrated around the edge with the complete chronology of the Battle of Trafalgar. Thus, as the sun made passage through the day, the dial would show the actual state of the battle at that time.

JIM HARRIS

MINIATURE COFFER	
EDITION SIZE:	25
NUMBER SOLD	1
MAKER	Jim Harris
LATEST PRICE	£900

This miniature coffer is a fine example of the cabinetmaker's art. It is based on a traditional coffer design current in Nelson's time, and superbly made. The workmanship and materials used pushed the price to a level that prevented multiple sales, however.

SUE HARVEY

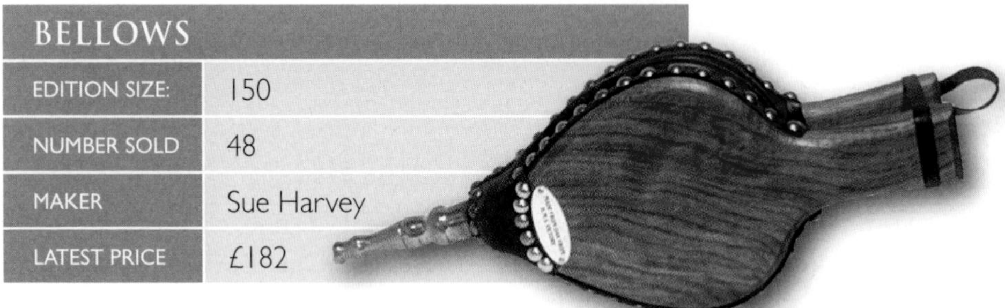

BELLOWS	
EDITION SIZE:	150
NUMBER SOLD	48
MAKER	Sue Harvey
LATEST PRICE	£182

Sue Harvey has the distinction of being the country's only lady bellows maker. With her skills in leatherwork and stitching that come from her main occupation of saddlemaker, making bellows had become a useful sideline and found a market among her regular customers. Wood craftsman and designer Peter Hageman who selected the Victory oak and cut the oak blanks for the bellows that Sue then produced helped her in this particular endeavour. They were a successful product, but eventually it became difficult for Peter to find pieces of Victory oak that were large enough and sufficiently clean of holes, cracks and imperfections to meet the operational requirement of working bellows, and this finally limited their sale to 48 pairs. Peter confided that cutting the large beams was always a nervous time because of hidden copper and iron nails, but in the event he lost no tools to Victory oak

Bellows were in use aboard *HMS Victory*, though not in this small, domestic format. Cooking on board was done on a large timber burning range, and large bellows were on hand to encourage the blaze.

DR MIKE HAYWOOD

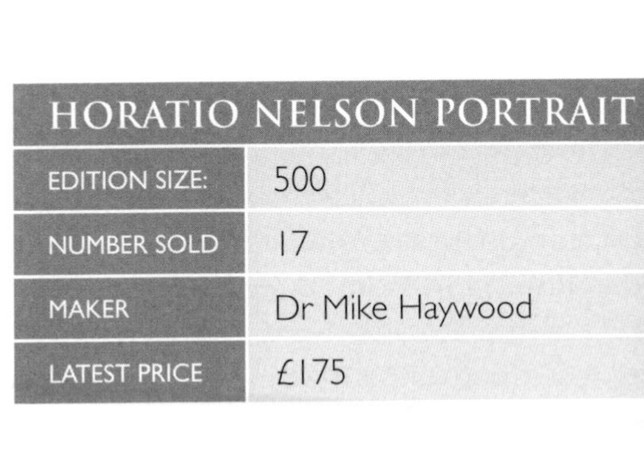

HORATIO NELSON PORTRAIT	
EDITION SIZE:	500
NUMBER SOLD	17
MAKER	Dr Mike Haywood
LATEST PRICE	£175

"HMS VICTORY IN THE STORM AFTER TRAFALGAR"	
EDITION SIZE:	250
NUMBER SOLD	64
MAKER	Dr Mike Haywood
LATEST PRICE	£300

"RELENTLESS PURSUIT"	
EDITION SIZE:	500
NUMBER SOLD	26
MAKER	Dr Mike Haywood
LATEST PRICE	£300

Dr. Mike Haywood came into The Collection as a result of hearing my interview on the Radio Four's *Today* programme. He was in the process of painting *HMS Victory in the Storm after the Battle of Trafalgar* and thought it might be a good idea to do a limited edition print, framed with fragments of oak and copper set into the mount. I could tell from the photo he sent me of the work so far that it was an excellent, dramatic work highlighting an important aspect of the famous battle that is often forgotten. Peter Goodwin, curator of *HMS Victory*, advised him on the technical accuracy of the work, and his own background as an oceanographer is evident in the broiling sea. It is worth mentioning that the foretopsail, which is the only surviving sail from *HMS Victory's* battle engagement and which is shown in this painting jury rigged as a mainsail to get her back to Gibraltar, has now been repaired and can be viewed at the Victory Museum in Portsmouth.

The success of this product prompted Mike to paint another scene of *HMS Victory* as she scoured the seas in search of the French fleet prior to Trafalgar. *Relentless Pursuit* similarly framed with oak and copper as a limited edition, was a successful addition to The Collection, and in turn led to Mike taking his first serious shot at portraiture with his portrait *Horatio Nelson*. This, too, was a saleable product, though I secretly felt that I could discern something of the artist in the face of the hero!

RALPH HENTALL

OAK SPOONS	
EDITION SIZE:	Edition size: 150 each of 3 designs
NUMBER SOLD	47
MAKER	Ralph Hentall
LATEST PRICE	£120

Carved wooden spoons have been a traditional gift expressing love and affection for centuries. Welsh love spoons, for example, are now quite collectable. Probably Britain's greatest exponent of this craft is **Ralph Hentall**, who has been making them for over 50 years. His customers include many celebrities, perhaps the best-known being Margaret Thatcher, for whom he made three and presented them to her at 10 Downing Street. There is also an interesting Trafalgar connection. Since the Second World War, Norway has donated to Britain the splendid Christmas tree that stands each year in Trafalgar Square. On the 50th anniversary, Ralph was asked to carve a spoon from the tree after it had been taken down so that it could be given to the Queen of Norway as a token of thanks from the British people. Ralph presented it to the Norwegian Ambassador in London.

HIDEBOUND LTD

THE VICTORY BOOT	
EDITION SIZE:	250
NUMBER SOLD	59
MAKER	Hidebound Ltd
LATEST PRICE	£140

A 'boot' was a leather drinking vessel in use in Nelson's time, and source of the expression 'fill your boots!' The Victory boot had a base of Victory oak and carried a hand-tooled and painted depiction of Nelson's coat of arms. Leading Norfolk brewery Woodforde's Norfolk Ales, maker of *Nelson's Revenge* bitter sponsored it. The boot had the distinction of being the only product I withdrew from The Collection because of the poor relationship with the maker, **Hidebound**. Enough said.

BARRY HORTON

SHAKER BOXES (SMALL, MEDIUM, LARGE)	
EDITION SIZE:	250
NUMBER SOLD	23
MAKER	Barry Horton
LATEST PRICE	£60 - £85

I was intrigued to receive an email from **Barry Horton** who had seen an article in *Furniture and Cabinet Making* magazine about the project. He is a British furniture maker living and working in France, next to the largest and oldest oak forest in Europe (the Foret de Troncais). His proposal was to make a nesting set of three Shaker style boxes. The sides and base are of French oak, and the top is of Victory oak with an insert of Victory copper the size of the musket ball that killed Nelson. As he said in his letter: "This would not only be symbolic, but amusing and perhaps a little ironic." The set proved popular, and was generously sponsored by the 15th century Bell Inn at Horndon on the Hill in Essex. The Inn features five luxurious suites named after famous mistresses, one of which is Lady Hamilton. I understand that Nelson's flag signal features above the bed, exhorting "Every man to do his duty"!

JIM HUNTER

SHIP'S CAT	
EDITION SIZE:	15
NUMBER SOLD	11
MAKER	Jim Hunter
LATEST PRICE	£250

Jim Hunter is one of the most popular craftsmen on the circuit, and has been specialising in carving cats for longer than he probably wants to remember. His carvings of the ship's cat used particularly clean pieces of oak keeping the grain flow through from head to tail. Someone at the Pet Food Division of international food group Nestlé knew his work, and their Purina Brand sponsored his edition. Sadly, his contact at Purina left the company, and in spite of repeated attempts, I was unable to get them to provide the text for their page in the Deed of Provenance, so a special Deed was never produced for this special edition. Jim, however, must be credited with the funds raised for *HMS Victory* as a result of this sponsorship.

JIM JACKSON MVO, RVM

NAVAL DIRK	
EDITION SIZE:	20
NUMBER SOLD	9
MAKER	Jim Jackson MVO, RVM
LATEST PRICE	£3,425

An email in May 2001 from someone registering on our website as a maker of naval dirks, which are short daggers, requesting just a few grams of oak and a diminutive amount of copper sheet was an unlikely genesis of one of the most stunning items in The Collection. I thought **Jim Jackson** was a hobbyist, but one of my principles with the Victory material was that it should be available to anyone who wanted it, so I called him. It was clear from our conversation that Jim was a serious and experienced craftsman and I explained The 1805 Collection concept to him. Would he care to make a limited edition naval dirk for it? He was interested, and since the quantities of Victory materials were so small I had no compunction in sending him what he wanted. I included a small bronze pin used for securing the copper sheathing to the hull, as well as a couple of steel bolts removed from oak sections. I then forgot all about it.

Almost a year later I received an email from Jim saying he had completed his dirk and would like to show it to me. I suggested he bring it to the Penshurst show in Kent where we were exhibiting. He agreed to come on the Saturday. The show was busy, and we had lots of people milling about the stand, but I could not miss the tall figure dressed in black motorcycle leathers being directed to me by David Burton. I thought perhaps he was a courier.

"Jonathan Bowman?" he enquired. "I'm Jim Jackson and I have brought the dirk." Whereupon he unzipped his jacket and rather reverentially withdrew the most amazing weapon I had ever seen. The best way to describe it is to quote his own description that accompanied each piece:

> *"The mounts of the scabbard are made from the copper cladding from the hull of the Victory and are engraved with a V (for Victory) on one side and an anchor on the reverse. The top mount is engraved with HMS VICTORY, TRAFALGAR 1805. The scabbard is finished with A STINGRAY SKIN. The steel mounts, which are fire blued, were made from a large bolt from the ship."*

"The handle is made from oak from the ship's timbers with spacers made from the same copper cladding from the hull."

"The small finial on the pommel cap is made from one of the original nails for securing the copper cladding which were made of bronze."

"The forged blade of the Dirk is what is known as pattern welded, or Damascus Steel, and involves many hours of beating, folding and twisting to achieve the pattern in the blade which, like a stick of rock, goes right through the blade. There are less than a handful of blade smiths in the UK able to do this quality of work."

The last sentence is an understatement. Jim Jackson held the position of Armourer to HM The Queen from January 1st 1958 until his retirement in 2002. He is a talented, companionable and modest man for whom I have a great respect. He always insisted on delivering his dirks for The 1805 Collection in person to the customer – a fine example of customer care.

David did one show in Cardiff that I did not attend. He phoned me from the stand to tell me he had just taken an order for not one, but two, naval dirks. My immediate reaction was that he was winding me up. When he then informed me that the customers were two middle-aged sisters, I was sure he was. I remember saying:

"Well, I just hope they get on well with each other!"

He convinced me that he was serious when he told me the circumstances. The two sisters had become guardians of their teenage nephew after an appalling tragedy. The boy had attended a party during the course of which some of the partygoers, no doubt the worse for wear, had tried to throw the lad into the pool. He was thrown, but hit the side of the pool on the way in, seriously damaging his back. The situation was made worse by the inept manner in which he was pulled out of the water, further aggravating the initial injury. The boy was paralysed and confined to a wheelchair for the rest of his life. The courts awarded damages and compensation for this life-altering trauma, and the sisters decided to invest part of it on his behalf in a pair of dirks. Jim took them down to Cardiff in person.

Another was purchased by an Anglican church in England to present to a pastor in New York who had devoted much of his life to working with underprivileged children. Jim told me it was to be presented as the *Sword of Light*, and that in accepting the order he had to endure a sermon about Saul on the road to Damascus!

Jim is keeping the last two for his two granddaughters – one of whom was born on Trafalgar Day.

MICHAEL JOHNS

DAVENPORT DESK	
EDITION SIZE:	1
NUMBER SOLD	0
MAKER	Michael Johns
LATEST PRICE	£3,950

In March 2002, **Michael Johns** contacted me through the website and offered to make a Davenport desk. The photo he sent of one recently completed for a customer convinced me this would be a great addition to The Collection. He came down from Tyne and Wear and selected some material for the job, and that was practically the last I heard of him. I managed to make phone contact on a couple of occasions and he explained that pressure of other work had prevented him from completing it, and I began to fear we might never see the finished item. I am delighted to report that in early 2008 he arrived at the offices of Nauticalia Ltd, dropped it off and disappeared back up North. It is clearly as magnificent as I had hoped, and at the time of writing is available for sale.

HELEN JOHNSON

THE SPIRIT OF NELSON	
EDITION SIZE:	15
NUMBER SOLD	1
MAKER	Helen Johnson
LATEST PRICE	£485

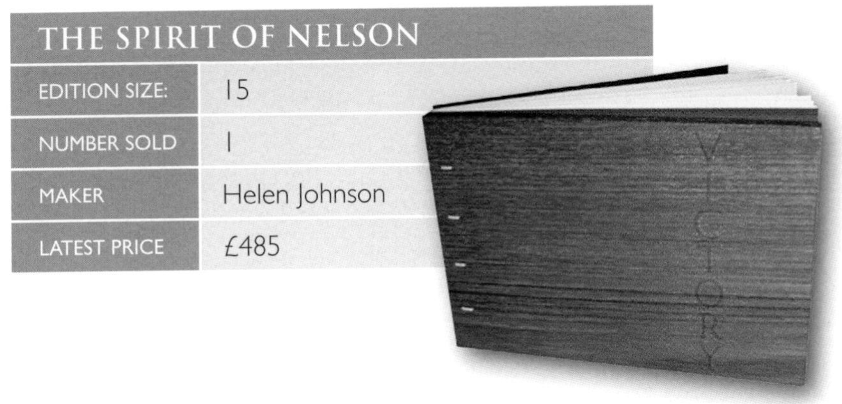

In some ways this book, *The Spirit of Nelson*, was perhaps the most evocative of The Collection offerings, and certainly a unique work of art. It is fitting in my view that there is just one in existence, just as there would be only one original painting. **Helen Johnson** is a respected calligrapher and bookbinder, and this work, which features covers of Victory oak, contains hand written and illustrated works including Nelson's prayer before the Battle of Trafalgar, a poem written by the Duchess of Devonshire shortly after his death and an anonymous poem regarding his famous flag signal. There are also colour illustrations of the flag signal and the crest of *HMS Victory* . The illustrations and lettering are in shell gold and gouache on a mould made Saunders Waterford paper. The blue end papers are Canson Meteints.

JOHN TAYLOR BELL FOUNDERS LTD

BRONZE HAND BELL	
EDITION SIZE:	100
NUMBER SOLD	0
MAKER	John Taylor Bell Founders Ltd
LATEST PRICE	£475

BRONZE SHIP'S BELLS (6 INCH AND 8 INCH)	
EDITION SIZE:	50 of each
NUMBER SOLD	1 (8 inch)
MAKER	John Taylor Bell Founders Ltd
LATEST PRICE	£800 and £950

Nelson is buried in St. Paul's Cathedral, beneath the great bronze bell cast by **John Taylor Bell Founders Ltd**. It seemed appropriate to ask them, of the only two bronze bell founders in Britain, to cast some bells in bronze using *HMS Victory*'s copper. Their bell master was keen on the idea, and even suggested that maybe they could cast a church bell from this material on the bicentenary day in October 2005. I liked the idea, but regretfully the cost would have been great, and require significant sponsorship which was not forthcoming. Nonetheless, they produced three excellent quality bell products using the Victory copper, but sadly only one of the large ship's bells sold. The overall costs of bell founding are high in this country, and put these items out of reach.

STUART KING

APPLE	
EDITION SIZE:	50
NUMBER SOLD	13
MAKER	Stuart King
LATEST PRICE	£120

Stuart King is a well-known artist craftsman, demonstrator, international lecturer and photojournalist who writes regular articles for *Woodturning* magazine. He was pleased to offer an oak apple for The Collection, with the stalk being a brass nail taken from copper sheathing removed from *HMS Victory*'s hull. Hand turned fruit is popular with collectors, and this one proved no exception, with one of them going as far as Saudi Arabia.

TOM KITTLE

SWIVEL MIRROR	
EDITION SIZE:	100
NUMBER SOLD	3
MAKER	Tom Kittle
LATEST PRICE	£215

WALL MIRROR	
EDITION SIZE:	100
NUMBER SOLD	5
MAKER	Tom Kittle
LATEST PRICE	£110

We had one or two enquiries about mirrors so were pleased when **Tom Kittle**, a local craftsman, offered to make two. They fell into the category of 'useful and decorative' and I had high hopes for them. Sadly, by the time they became available, there was already too much competition from other collection products in the same price bracket, and sales were disappointing.

HMS VICTORY FOLDING CHAIRS	
EDITION SIZE:	100
NUMBER SOLD	30+
MAKER	Finewood Furniture
LATEST PRICE	£ 1,095

NORFOLK CHAIRS (LARGE CARVER, CARVER, SIDE)	
EDITION SIZE:	100
NUMBER SOLD	100
MAKER	Finewood Furniture
LATEST PRICE	£795 - £1,095

In many ways **Albert Lain** of **Finewood Furniture** was my ideal maker. A professional businessman with an excellent quality reputation and sound customer base, Albert was alive to the opportunity provided by the bicentenary and was very proactive in selling the products. It was no surprise, then, that his edition of Norfolk chairs sold out. The chairs were made of English oak, with cresting rails of Victory oak. He selected slices of copper rivet with the King's Mark on them, and set these into the cresting rail with a window in the top so that the mark could be seen.

Albert was always on the lookout for PR opportunities. He was able to present one of his chairs (sadly not a Victory one) to HM The Queen for her 80th birthday. He presented a Victory Norfolk chair to Frank Nowosielski, the commanding officer of *HMS Victory*, at the Topcraft exhibition, securing good coverage for the product and The 1805 Collection. His customers for these products included direct descendants of Lord Nelson and Emma Hamilton, as well as TV personality Paul Heiney. Furthermore, through Albert we were able to donate a piece of Victory oak to be used in the restoration of the organ in the Holy Trinity Church at Barsham in Suffolk, which doubtless now plays stirring music.

PETER LANGRAN

COPPER TOP CANE (RIGHT IN PICTURE)	
EDITION SIZE:	150
NUMBER SOLD	16
MAKER	Peter Langran
LATEST PRICE	£185

COPPER TOP CANE (LEFT IN PICTURE)	
EDITION SIZE:	250
NUMBER SOLD	18
MAKER	Peter Langran
LATEST PRICE	£155

Peter Langran retired from the police force and turned his woodcarving skills to the field of walking sticks. He works both with wood and antler, and is to be seen at craft shows around the country, usually attending between 20 and 30 per year. For The 1805 Collection Peter offered two walking canes, based upon designs familiar in 19th century England. The first has a top turned from Victory oak, inset with a disc of Victory copper showing the King's Mark. The second has a solid copper top, turned from one of the rivets. Both canes had lacquered English wood shafts. The canes sold quite well, both for regular use and also for display by collectors.

GRAHAM LAW

LARGE RUM TUB	
EDITION SIZE:	25
NUMBER SOLD	5
MAKER	Graham Law
LATEST PRICE	£850

SMALL RUM TUB	
EDITION SIZE:	150
NUMBER SOLD	20
MAKER	Graham Law
LATEST PRICE	£175

Graham Law was a cooper for more than 40 years, having served a six-year apprenticeship with a Sheffield cooperage, making beer, whisky and sherry barrels for the brewing industry. Each year the Coopers Livery Company would present the new Lord Mayor of London with a traditionally coopered barrel at the Mansion House banquet, and for many years these were made by Graham. He was the natural choice for someone to make the rum tubs for The Collection. When he and his wife Sue came down to meet me and to select some oak he explained how the advent of metal barrels had led to the demise of coopering, and how only a handful of people in Britain still have the skills. He had found it impossible to carry on working as a cooper and now just did it as a hobby.

"So what do you do for a living now?" I enquired.

Graham grinned and said, "I'm a garbologist".

"And what exactly do they do?" I enquired innocently.

"Collect the garbage," he replied.

Sadly, this has been the way of many of our traditional crafts, and was another reason I was keen to represent as many of them as I could in The 1805 Collection.

His first product was a full size 'grog tub' traditionally used by the Royal Navy in old times to serve the daily tot of rum to the crew at the sound of the piped command 'Up Spirits'. It was hard to find good enough lengths of undamaged oak to make the staves for these large tubs with a height and base diameter of 40 cms, but he managed six before it became too difficult, complete with their brass banding and lettering. The small rum tub did not have that constraint, and proved a popular item.

Pussers Rum, the famous Navy rum brand (a corruption of 'the purser's rum') originally offered to sponsor both tubs, but in the end sponsored the launch of The 1805 Collection at the NEC (see Chapter 11).

STEWART LINFORD FURNITURE LTD

THE ADMIRAL'S CHAIR	
EDITION SIZE:	150
NUMBER SOLD	150
MAKER	Stewart Linford Furniture Ltd
LATEST PRICE	£2,995

Stewart Linford Furniture Ltd is a highly successful furniture maker in the historic furniture town of High Wycombe. Its success is due in no small part to its creative and dynamic owner, Stewart Linford. In May 2002 Stewart came to visit me and see the oak, and was enthused by the prospects. He was, however, lukewarm about making items for The 1805 Collection, and preferred the idea of buying material and using his own established production and marketing resources to capitalise on the opportunity. He was, however, less enthused by the prospect of having to fork out large sums of cash to buy the quantity he wanted. In characteristic style, Stewart came up with an innovative proposition. It centred upon his wish to make a limited edition Windsor armchair made largely from English oak and incorporating Victory oak as turned spindles. The product was to be known as The Admiral's Chair. Seeing that I was keen to have it in The Collection, Stewart proposed that he take a quantity of oak, and in exchange provide me with a number of finished chairs. We agreed the retail price for the chairs and a deal was done.

The product was a knockout success, though not through The 1805 Collection. We sold our allocation eventually, but Linford put serious marketing effort behind the item. They worked on their well-established customer list, and threw two parties on board *HMS Victory* to present the finished chairs to the lucky customers. Stewart admitted to me that the exercise was very costly, particularly the second party where 400 guests were entertained on both *HMS Victory* and *HMS Warrior* (moored almost alongside in the Historic Dockyard in Portsmouth). Stewart himself was dressed up as Nelson and his staff appropriately attired as crew, and the champagne flowed. The edition of 150 chairs was sold out within months, and well before they were made, at a ticket price of £2,995 each.

There is more to the Stewart Linford story, with a considerable range of products spawned from the success of The Admiral's Chair, and this will be covered in Part Three.

PETER LLOYD

DESK BOX	
EDITION SIZE:	100
NUMBER SOLD	13
MAKER	Peter Lloyd
LATEST PRICE	£495

In the early days of the project I was keen to find leading makers, and to that end I contacted a number of artists who had made items for the One Tree Project - a project in which 70 artists and craftspeople used every single bit of an old oak tree in a festival of creativity. One of these was **Peter Lloyd**, whose boxes are sought by collectors. He agreed to take part, but since he lived in Cumbria he asked me to select a large beam from which he could make a batch of four or five. I found a suitable piece, just over 1.5 metres long and weighing over 20kg. I phoned Parcel Force to ask about the need for packing, explaining that it was a long and heavy oak beam, and they said it would be enough to just secure an address label and it could be shipped from their depot in Norwich. Jan and I took it across Norwich fully labelled up and waited patiently for someone to deal with us. Eventually our turn came.

"Can't take that – it's not wrapped," I was told.

"But I phoned, and was assured this was all that was needed."

"Can't take that unwrapped – someone might get a splinter handling it." He was not being helpful, and the queue behind us was growing.

"So what should I wrap it in then? Cardboard, newspaper, sacking, what?"

"I don't care. Anything will do so long as it is covered." He made it clear that was the end of the matter.

"Right," I said through gritted teeth, heading for the door with the beam held like a battering ram. A path cleared. Outside, ever practical, Jan said:

"Why don't we use this old duvet cover I put down to protect the inside of the car? They must have some parcel tape inside this place."

The hallowed beam from *HMS Victory* was eventually accepted and made its way unceremoniously to Cumbria inside a yellow candy-striped duvet cover.

Peter's boxes highlighted the distress in the timbers as can be seen from the picture. They were solid Victory oak, and used no metal fasteners. They were just the style and quality I wanted in The Collection, and were accompanied not only by our own Deed of Provenance but also by Peter's own limited edition certification.

BILL MACLENNAN

CAMPAIGN CHEST	
EDITION SIZE:	4
NUMBER SOLD	4
MAKER	Bill MacLennan
LATEST PRICE	£3,999

Bill MacLennan is a former Royal Marines Officer for whom cabinet making is an accomplished hobby. Bill purchased the oak for four traditional campaign chests that he wanted to make for friends and family. By the time of the bicentenary celebrations he had completed the task. The chests are mounted on English oak stands.

INTERKNIFE

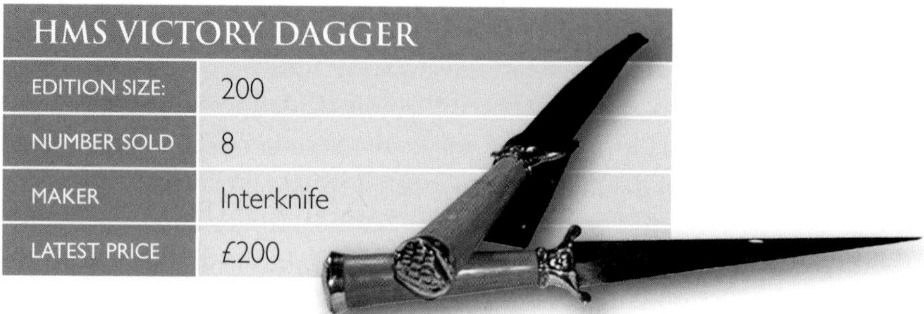

HMS VICTORY DAGGER	
EDITION SIZE:	200
NUMBER SOLD	8
MAKER	Interknife
LATEST PRICE	£200

I came to know **Rod Matless**, who traded as Interknife, through my local pub landlord. The landlord was a great Nelson fan and had purchased some oak for Rod to use in making a dagger for his son (he also purchased one of the Nelson sculptures as a wedding gift). Rod is a blade smith, and his principle market is daggers for pagans (yes, really!). He was certainly one of the most unusual, genuine and helpful of people I met during the project. A true son of Norfolk, he lived with his wife, cat, Doberman bitch and assorted geese and fowl in an old church that he himself had converted to a dwelling. The first time I visited him he showed me around, being careful not to make too much noise as his wife, who had been working a late shift, was asleep where the altar had been with the cat curled up on top of her. The dog showed a friendly interest, then went to its bed in the corner, took hold of its blanket, threw it up into the air and deftly slipped into the bed allowing the blanket to fall neatly on top of it. It was all slightly otherworldly.

For his collection dagger, Rod bought a 1906 Trafalgar centenary medallion on eBay and had copies of it cast from Victory copper. These became the pommel in the oak handle. The blade was engraved according to the purchaser's wishes, and the finished product was contained in a hand made leather sheath.

Rod proved helpful in many ways, particularly with regard to the provision of ceremonial torches for the Drumhead ceremony in Portsmouth in 2005. This story, which still makes me smile whenever I think of it, is recalled in Part Four.

MICHAEL'S FINE CRAFTS

THE 1805 FOUNTAIN PEN	
EDITION SIZE:	250
NUMBER SOLD	250
MAKER	Michael's Fine Crafts
LATEST PRICE	£159.99

THE ADMIRAL FOUNTAIN PEN	
EDITION SIZE:	150
NUMBER SOLD	50
MAKER	Michael's Fine Crafts
LATEST PRICE	£195

Nelson was a prolific letter writer, although his writing quality deteriorated considerably after the loss of his right arm and the need to use his left hand. His last letter to Emma, written aboard *HMS Victory* the night before the battle is the subject of an 1805 Collection edition in its own right (see the section concerning David Burton's products).

Having spent 11 years running a company manufacturing all manner of pens, pencils and other writing products, I knew a good pen would sell well. There was no shortage of good makers on the craft circuit, but Michael Hall of **Michael's Fine Crafts** was undoubtedly one of the best, and what's more, he was very good at marketing his own products. Initially, he was a little sceptical, but soon realised that there was a real opportunity here. He offered his initial product, The 1805 Pen, as a fountain pen, rollerball or ball pen, in single mode or as a set of two or three. The edition sold out, so Michael came up with a new and more expensive design called the Admiral Fountain Pen, of which he sold 50. Both pens were turned from Victory oak, had gold plated nibs and fittings, and were cleverly inlaid with flecks of copper.

His biggest disappointment was the cancellation by Norman Lamont of a special gift pen for Margaret Thatcher. It was to have been presented to her at a Conservative Christmas party, but the event was cancelled and the pen order with it. Nelson would surely approved of part of his flagship being used to write letters by the Iron Lady! I have also been advised, at the time of writing, that a variant of the 1805 Fountain Pen, with the nib and fittings coppered rather than gold plated, is to be presented by the Royal Navy to the Princess Royal on an official visit in March 2009.

ROBERT RACE

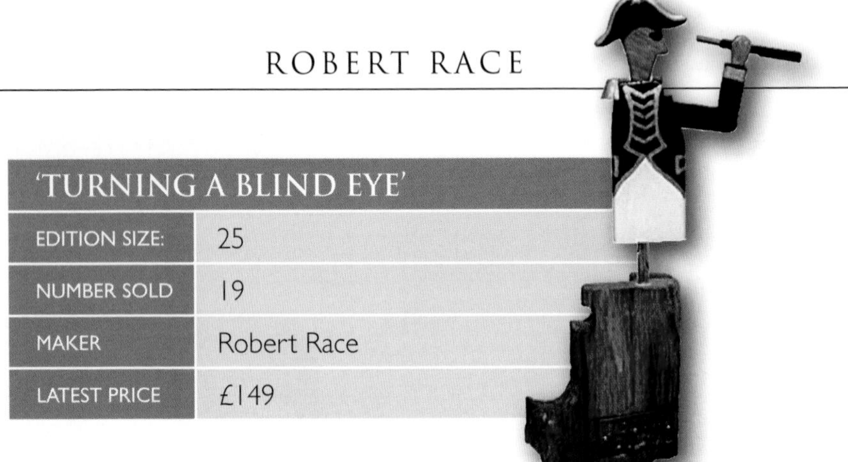

'TURNING A BLIND EYE'	
EDITION SIZE:	25
NUMBER SOLD	19
MAKER	Robert Race
LATEST PRICE	£149

Automata, or moving toys, have been collectable for decades, and I was keen to have one in The 1805 Collection. One of the woodcraft projects of recent years that attracted the country's leading makers was the One Tree Project, and I approached a number of that project's participants to join mine. Among them was **Robert Race**, highly regarded as one of the country's finest exponents of the automaton maker's art.

Robert's toy was a jolly portrayal of Nelson, standing on a rugged piece of Victory oak, his arm by his side clutching a telescope. When the piece is lifted,

Nelson turns his head and brings the telescope up to his blind eye. It was simple, effective, robust and a nice reminder of that story of Nelson that brought the expression 'turning a blind eye' into the English language. I knew the bare bones of this story from childhood, but had forgotten the context. This was remedied for me in what was almost a most embarrassing moment at one of our shows. We had received the artist's proof of the automata just before the show at Stonor Park near Henley, so it was placed in a prime site on the stand. During a quiet period on the first day there was an elderly lady looking at our various exhibits with some interest. To engage her in conversation I asked her if she had seen our latest addition to The Collection, and picked it up so that she could see it do its thing.

"Oh my goodness!" she said. "How fascinating! I'm a Hyde Parker, you know."

I didn't. What's more, I had reached that slightly silly frame of mind that boredom on exhibition stands is inclined to induce. I was about to ask her if that meant she had ancient rights to graze her sheep in Hyde Park, but fortunately stopped myself.

"Yes," she continued, "it was my great, great (great?) grandfather who was in command at the Battle of Copenhagen and gave Nelson the command to withdraw. That is when Nelson did his famous 'blind eye' gesture."

It turned out that not only was this lady the direct descendant of the instigator of this historic moment, but was also the owner and resident of the wonderful stately home of Stonor Park that was hosting our show. She was The Lady Camoys, and was pleased to purchase No. 1 in this edition. It could not have gone to a more fitting home.

It should perhaps be recorded that there is one 'Turning a blind eye' illegally held somewhere but not certificated. No. 12 was sent to the wrong address and was signed for by the recipient. All attempts by the maker to recover it were unsuccessful and a replacement for it was made and delivered to the rightful customer whose name was McNally.

VAL REDDINGTON

COPPER MEDALLIONS	
EDITION SIZE:	5 each of 3
NUMBER SOLD	4
MAKER	Val Reddington
LATEST PRICE	£250

"ENGLAND EXPECT..." ETCHING ON COPPER	
EDITION SIZE:	1
NUMBER SOLD	1
MAKER	Val Reddington
LATEST PRICE	Not known

HMS VICTORY ETCHING ON COPPER	
EDITION SIZE:	1
NUMBER SOLD	1
MAKER	Val Reddington
LATEST PRICE	Not known

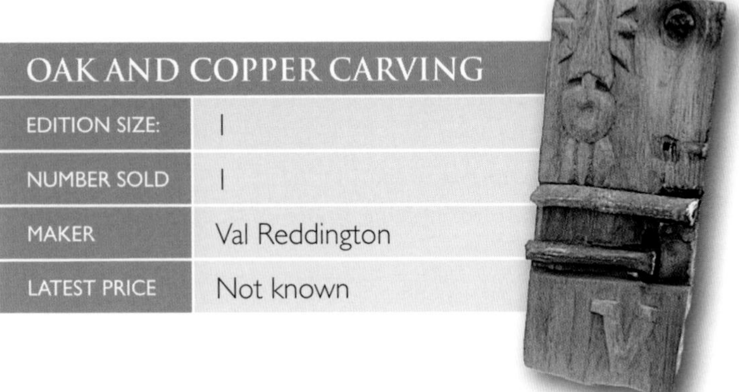

OAK AND COPPER CARVING	
EDITION SIZE:	1
NUMBER SOLD	1
MAKER	Val Reddington
LATEST PRICE	Not known

I met **Val Reddington** at the graduation show at the Norwich School of Art and design where my daughter was also showing her degree work. Val was a mature student doing a masters degree, and I was impressed by the interesting aluminium sculptures she was exhibiting. She was intrigued by the opportunity to do something in Victory materials, and suggested doing some copper medallions. She had experience in this field, having exhibited medallions in the British Museum. She chose to do three designs, with an edition size of five each. The first was the 68 pound cannon, with a Victory monogram on the reverse, the second was the flag signal with a Victory monogram on the reverse, and the third featured

Nike the Goddess of Victory, with Trafalgar 1805 on the reverse. Each weighed 600 grams and measured 8.5 cms in diameter.

In addition to these, Val did three separate one-off sculptures using the oak and copper, all of which sold.

HOWARD REYNOLDS

THE VICTORY CRADLE	
EDITION SIZE:	15
NUMBER SOLD	0
MAKER	Howard Reynolds
LATEST PRICE	£2,500

LETTER RACK	
EDITION SIZE:	150
NUMBER SOLD	20
MAKER	Howard Reynolds
LATEST PRICE	£275

The Victory cradle was a project undertaken by **Howard Reynolds** as part of a cabinetmaking course. It involved research into the style of cradle fashionable in Nelson's time, and this suggested having a hinged lid so that the top could be folded back to enable the baby to be laid down without banging its head. (And they managed this without the benefit of a health and safety executive.) Because of the quantity of oak consumed and the number of hours to make, this item was inevitably too expensive to attract much purchase interest, but I wondered if there was a possible celebrity opportunity. At the time of its completion, Victoria and David Beckham were expecting their first child. I wrote to Victoria and suggested she might like to mark the event by purchasing it or sponsoring it. In due course, I had a polite reply from her office declining. She opted for Romeo rather than Horatio. Perhaps I should have asked her to sponsor the Victory dagger.

Howard's main product, however, was a greater success, and numbered several high-ranking naval officers among his customers. The letter rack once again proved that usefulness was a key factor in purchase decisions for collection items. The Royal Navy chose this as its favourite presentation gift at the time, and recipients included the First Sea Lord and the Director of US Naval Operations in the second Gulf War.

MICHAEL ROSS

TEAR DROP BOX	
EDITION SIZE:	500
NUMBER SOLD	23
MAKER	Michael Ross
LATEST PRICE	£30

SAIL BOX	
EDITION SIZE:	500 total, in three sizes
NUMBER SOLD	27
MAKER	Michael Ross
LATEST PRICE	£28 - £50

Michael Ross, with his expertise in making small, interesting shaped boxes, was able to offer us a couple of products which were both functional and used up some of the smaller pieces of Victory oak. They were also very affordable and we needed items in the sub £50 price range. They were a popular item with ladies.

MIRANDA SALMON

WAVE CABINET	
EDITION SIZE:	5
NUMBER SOLD	1
MAKER	Miranda Salmon
LATEST PRICE	£2,625

I always hoped that we would be able to include a corner cabinet in The Collection, but I had not envisaged such a modern design. **Miranda Salmon** is a designer and cabinetmaker whose work is a real art form. This Wave Cabinet as she called it has a front and sides of Victory oak, with the evocative wave shape set in Victory copper sheathing. It is a practical drinks cabinet designed to take two bottles plus two shelves of glasses.

SAM SAMSON

KALEIDOSCOPE	
EDITION SIZE:	250
NUMBER SOLD	23
MAKER	Sam Samson
LATEST PRICE	£160

WATCH GLASS	
EDITION SIZE:	250
NUMBER SOLD	28
MAKER	Sam Samson
LATEST PRICE	£149.50

BRONZE CANNON BALL	
EDITION SIZE:	21
NUMBER SOLD	2
MAKER	Sam Samson
LATEST PRICE	£258

TWO POUND IRON CANNON BALL	
EDITION SIZE:	200
NUMBER SOLD	2
MAKER	Sam Samson
LATEST PRICE	£160

For some reason, **Sam Samson** always struck me as the craftsperson's craftsperson. Tall, spare and laid back with a rather vague and self-effacing manner, his work was varied, but somehow always different to much of what is seen on the craft circuit. His initial approach to me came as a result of an article in *Crafts* magazine. He wrote: "I am currently developing a kaleidoscope using a variety of old materials – brass, copper, oak etc." He agreed to make one for The Collection. It became a firm favourite for visitors to the stand. Unlike the kaleidoscopes made today which contain coloured fragments that you shake to make patterns, this traditional kaleidoscope contains three front surface mirrors and a fish eye lens, encased in either Victory oak or teak. The patterns you see depend upon what you are looking at, and this will appear as a fascinating kaleidoscopic collage of 12 or more prismatic distortions of the subject. One warm summer afternoon in August we were exhibiting at Stonor Park outside Henley on Thames. The kaleidoscope was one of several items displayed on a central table on the stand, allowing visitors access on all sides. There was an elderly gentleman quietly working his way around the table, examining the items that interested him. I approached him as he neared the kaleidoscope and explained how it worked as a means of getting into conversation. I sensed he might buy something. He picked the piece up and put it to his eye, scanning about for different pictures. Suddenly he stopped still.

"My goodness!" he said. "My word!" he muttered more than once. "Splendid!"

He continued gazing as if in a trance. By this time I thought he was getting just a little carried away with the enthusiasm for Sam's product. And then I saw why. Across the table a well-endowed lady wearing a scoop neck tee shirt was bending over admiring another item in The Collection and revealing substantial cleavage – at least 12 fold through the lens. No wonder his hand was shaking when he put it down.

In spite of initial disinterest in The Collection, Sam agreed to add another product using scientific quality components, and his next offering was the watch glass. A ship's watch lasts for four hours, and its passing is marked by the striking of the ship's bell every half hour. Eight bells signify the end of the watch. In the days of sail, time was kept with a Watch Glass, which is just a large egg timer that runs for half an hour. Sam's product used a high quality scientific standard sand glass, and was housed between oak sections that were chosen for their character and looked like ship's salvage rather than just carefully machined and plain oak. It proved a good talking point at shows, and great for explaining the watch system to children.

The cannon balls, one in iron and one in a gunmetal bronze containing Victory copper, were late editions. They are true replicas of those two-pound balls used on board *HMS Victory*, and are cast from a genuine and original cannon ball. The iron one was a simple sand casting, but the bronze one was an investment or 'lost wax' casting that added considerably to the cost.

Sam also took away a rugged piece of oak beam, almost one metre long, by quarter of a metre wide and forty centimetres thick. He added four legs, making it into a fine one-off coffee table that was sold by the Victory Shop in Portsmouth.

ROD SARSON

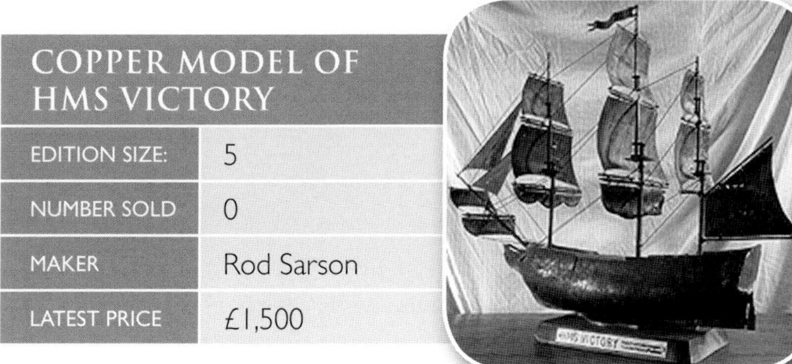

COPPER MODEL OF HMS VICTORY	
EDITION SIZE:	5
NUMBER SOLD	0
MAKER	Rod Sarson
LATEST PRICE	£1,500

Although the copper model of *HMS Victory* never sold, it deserves a mention simply because of its uniqueness. **Rod Sarson** is local to Norfolk, and a very talented artist. This is another of the items that I see more as art than craft pieces, and for which we never managed to find the right route to market. I was proud to have it on the stand, and it certainly drew plenty of interest and comment.

ROBERT SHELTON

ARROW	
EDITION SIZE:	150
NUMBER SOLD	2
MAKER	Robert Shelton
LATEST PRICE	£120

An arrow was possibly the last item I had considered for The 1805 Collection, being 'old technology' for the Battle of Trafalgar. However, when fletcher **Robert Shelton** approached me and explained that archery was a popular sport in Nelson's time, it seemed like a nice idea. The result was a traditionally crafted sporting arrow of the period, containing a splice or 'footing' of Victory oak in the hand-planed ash shaft, and mounted on a display board. I fully expected at shows to have someone ask me whether that was how Nelson lost his eye, and even placed it next to the apple on occasion in the hope that William Tell's exploits at Trafalgar might have been raised, but remarkably no such comments were forthcoming.

SIMPSON'S OF NORFOLK

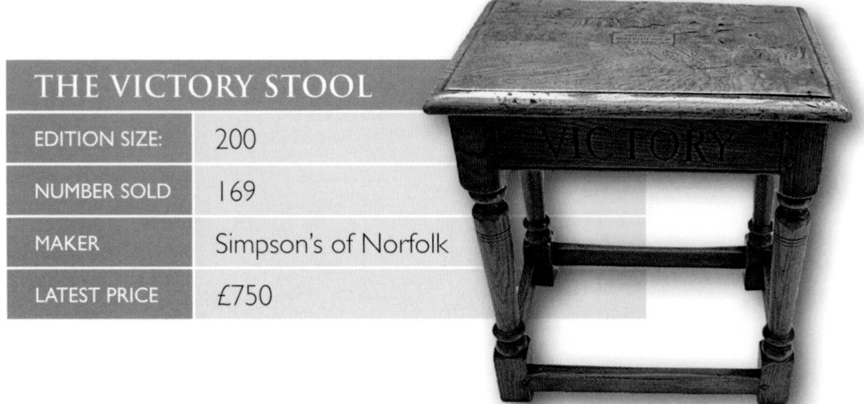

THE VICTORY STOOL	
EDITION SIZE:	200
NUMBER SOLD	169
MAKER	Simpson's of Norfolk
LATEST PRICE	£750

In any collection of art and craft there will always be one piece that becomes iconic – not because it is more beautiful or better made than the others, but because it combines the greatest mix of desirable features that together create the 'lust to own'. The Victory stool had that combination of classical style, exceptional workmanship, practical usefulness and affordability that elevated it to the category of 'antique of the future'. Furthermore, it was hand carved and made entirely of Victory oak while so many other pieces of furniture in The Collection merely contained Victory oak in their construction. By itself it generated in excess of £100,000 of revenue.

The stool was always the centrepiece of our shows. We measured the success of shows by the number of orders for stools that were taken, and as soon as the first one was taken we knew that the show in question was going to be a success. People liked to stroke it. Polished oak makes you instinctively reach out to touch it as though it exudes strength and dependability. In this case, people also felt they were perhaps touching timber that Nelson himself had touched or walked upon. I used to reckon we would have made more money if we had charged people 50 pence to stroke it rather than selling it. Even the Stool, though, was not immune from the cynics. On one memorable occasion at the NEC two bored middle aged men dressed in shell suits and sporting beer bellies were standing, hands in pockets, denigrating the whole display while their wives were more intent on buying something. "Look at this," said one of them in a broad Black Country accent, and reading aloud the inscription on the brass plate in the middle of the stool: "Made of oak taken from *HMS Victory*". He snorted. "If it really was that old that brass plate would be well worn!"

We also had a customer in the West Country who contacted us to say that a top corner had been damaged during delivery. I found this odd as they were extremely well packed. He suggested that the most economic solution might be to send him a replacement top and he, being something of an amateur woodworker, would happily replace it himself. This seemed a good solution until he then contacted me to say that mysteriously the replacement top had arrived split in two. He proposed we try a third time. There is an American military saying that: "Once is happenstance, twice is coincidence and three times is enemy action." It was just possible that our amateur woodworker was turning out copies for his friends. As I was due to go down to Cornwall on holiday I suggested the best solution would be for me to deliver the third myself to ensure it arrived in one piece, and to collect the two damaged ones at the same time. This I duly did. I may well have misjudged him, but I could not afford to take the chance. Apart from the value of the material, the integrity of the limited edition might have been at risk.

The first stool was made in May 2002, making it one of the earliest pieces in The Collection. **Simpson's of Norfolk** was a small, well-established maker of fine furniture, and I contacted Simon Simpson to see if there was anything he would like to do for our project. Initially he voiced the concern heard frequently in later conversations with turners and cabinetmakers that the material would be hard to work and that hidden nails would damage tools. Nonetheless, he produced the stool and liked it so much he bought one for himself. Initially it was priced at £500, but when Simon retired and sold his business the new owners increased the price twice to £750. Eventually they informed me that they were having difficulty finding good enough pieces of timber from which to turn the legs and ceased production before the edition was sold out. I found their decision surprising as there were plenty of sound and sizeable pieces left, but I believe it was more an excuse to stop doing something that required exceptional effort. They started to shed labour, and sadly went into liquidation some short while later.

ROBERT SMITH

CAPSTAN SALT AND PEPPER MILLS	
EDITION SIZE:	500
NUMBER SOLD	97
MAKER	Simpson's of Norfolk
LATEST PRICE	£215

There is just one wood turner who specialises in mills and grinders and dominates the UK market, so we were keen to recruit **Robert Smith** to the project. A former manufacturing jeweller who had taken up woodturning, his capstan design was perfect – chunky and full of character. Unlike some makers, Robert was keen to use distressed oak wherever it was possible so that its origins would be more obvious. He included a top and bottom band of copper sheathing, and incorporated the market leading Peugeot grinding mechanism. The mill was available for either salt or pepper. With a height of 17 cms and a base diameter of 9 cms this item was sure to be a conversation piece at dinner parties, and became one of the iconic products of The 1805 Collection. I purchased a pair for myself.

Robert was also a pleasure to work with. We would meet from time to time in the car park of the Bedford Lodge Hotel in Newmarket, roughly half way between our respective workplaces. This was the venue for unrelated board meetings that I chaired every couple of months, so I would load up my boot with suitable pieces of oak and during the lunch break rendezvous with Robert and transfer timber from my car to his van. It always seemed like one of those drug deals you see in the movies.

MARTIN SMITH

TORTOISE JIGSAW PUZZLE	
EDITION SIZE:	250
NUMBER SOLD	5
MAKER	Martin Smith
LATEST PRICE	£37.50

ACORN JIGSAW PUZZLE	
EDITION SIZE:	250
NUMBER SOLD	16
MAKER	Martin Smith
LATEST PRICE	£45

OAK LEAF JIGSAW PUZZLE	
EDITION SIZE:	250
NUMBER SOLD	2
MAKER	Martin Smith
LATEST PRICE	£70

HMS VICTORY HULL JIGSAW PUZZLE	
EDITION SIZE:	250
NUMBER SOLD	12
MAKER	Martin Smith
LATEST PRICE	£92.50

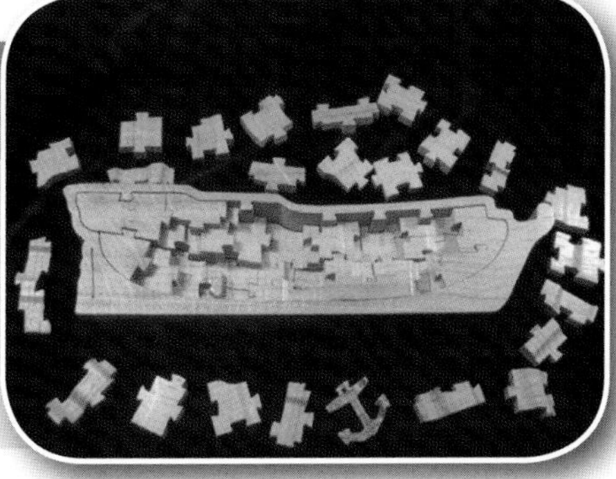

Trigsaw run by **Martin and Shelagh Smith** from Norfolk, could be seen at most of the craft shows with an amazing array of three dimensional jigsaws, and I was anxious to have them on board. They were local, skilful, proactive and offered products at affordable prices. We agreed on three puzzles to give us a range of prices, being the acorn, oak leaf and Victory hull. The first two were three layer puzzles, and the Victory hull had four layers, complete with an anchor shaped piece in one of the middle layers. This was a real family business, with Martin cutting the pieces, his wife Shelagh polishing them and their daughter putting them together. Later in the project they introduced the tortoise as a lower priced puzzle. We struggled to find a Trafalgar related connection for that one.

CRAIG STONE

32 POUND CANNON	
EDITION SIZE:	100
NUMBER SOLD	1
MAKER	Craig Stone
LATEST PRICE	£525

Early in the project I received an email from **Craig Stone** in Australia who was building a 1:16 scale replica of the 32 pound cannon which was the main weapon aboard *HMS Victory*. He wanted to purchase some oak for the base and wooden elements of the model, and cast the barrel from bronze. I was happy to oblige, and he was keen to continue in spite of the punitive postal rates to Australia and that country's tough import regulations for used timber. He sent me photographs of his model as it progressed. Craig is an award winning model shipmaker whose work has sold for thousands of Australian dollars, and the cannon was clearly going to be of the standard and quality I wanted in The Collection. I had not intended having overseas makers involved because of the problems of logistics, carriage costs, duty and the like, but this one seemed too good to miss, and he had already purchased sufficient oak to make several. Craig was enthusiastic about the proposal and so agreed to send his first one to us as artist's proof.

Although we only managed to sell one of this edition, it was always an attraction at shows because of its detail and honesty to the original item. The punishing costs of shipping materials and product back and forth across the world meant that the price was high, and as The Collection developed there was significant competition from other products to tempt Nelson and Trafalgar buffs. I tried to get Rolf Harris to sponsor it, but I never received a reply. It seems that celebrities are inundated with such requests.

RAY SYLVESTER

POMANDER

EDITION SIZE:	100
NUMBER SOLD	3
MAKER	Ray Sylvester
LATEST PRICE	£120

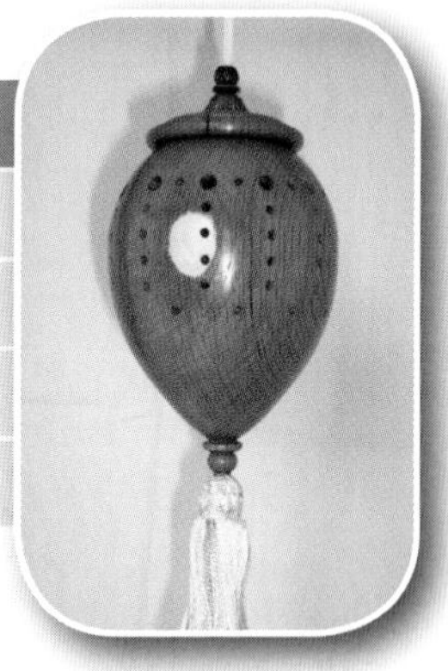

THE BAFFLING BOX

EDITION SIZE:	200
NUMBER SOLD	200
MAKER	Ray Sylvester
LATEST PRICE	£140

GYP BOX

EDITION SIZE:	200
NUMBER SOLD	25
MAKER	Ray Sylvester
LATEST PRICE	£145

David Burton introduced **Ray Sylvester,** who traded as Temima Crafts, to the project. The two had known each other for many years of doing craft shows on the same circuit, and Ray went on to become one of our most successful makers. His debut was a little bizarre – an oak pomander. It was certainly an excellent piece of woodturning, and something of a talking piece, but I could hardly see the public queuing up to buy one. When I raised a quizzical eyebrow at the initial suggestion, Ray assured me that, filled with dried lavender, they were quite the thing in a gentleman's wardrobe in Nelson's day. I doubt Nelson would have tolerated the sniggering from below decks if he had had one to keep his uniform fresh on *HMS Victory*. Still, it was a fine piece of craftsmanship and I was pleased to include it. In the event, only three sold, and Ray was quick to realise that he needed a product with wider appeal.

His answer was almost as bizarre as the pomander in terms of its unusualness. He called it a baffling box. It was cut from a single piece of oak into nine interlocking components including nesting drawers and trays, as well as hidden compartments. In itself it was a jigsaw puzzle. Ray got the pricing on this product just right, and also promoted sales hard himself at his own shows. He recounts:

"I remember one elderly woman saying to her husband, 'Let's buy it dear. It's something the children won't throw away when our time comes!" Many people seemed to be buying them as family heirlooms. We know this because over the past two or three years Ray's wife, Kathy has offered to burn an inscription on the base with her pyrography pen. On many occasions they have asked for the family name to be written there rather than that of an individual. One couple bought three boxes, one for each of their sons. On another occasion, a gentleman took a long time to choose a box, but eventually uttered the words that all craft workers love to hear: 'I'll take that one ...and that one.' A lady in Durham bought a box for her dad who suffered from advanced Alzheimer's disease. She told me that he had served on *HMS Victory* as a young sailor on tourist duty and now talked incessantly about the experience, even though there were times when he didn't know who she was. She hoped that giving him the box would be a way of breaking through to him.

The edition sold out.

When it became clear that demand was outstripping supply because of the limit to the edition, Ray decided to create a new design that was simpler in terms of the number of compartments but slightly more puzzling to undo and put together. He called it his Gyp Box. This one was quite successful, but never reached the popularity of its predecessor.

KATHY SYLVESTER

COPPER EMBROIDERY	
EDITION SIZE:	50
NUMBER SOLD	19
MAKER	Kathy Sylvester
LATEST PRICE	£47.50

Ray Sylvester's wife **Kathy** decided she wanted some of the action, too. An accomplished embroiderer, she selected some of the most worn and holed pieces of copper sheathing and used free-hand machine embroidery and hand stitching to create interesting and artistic designs, mounted on silk and framed with Victory oak. It appealed particularly to ladies who wanted something for themselves rather than as gifts for husbands, fathers and sons.

BRIAN TAYLOR

CRYSTAL VICTORY	
EDITION SIZE:	500
NUMBER SOLD	50
MAKER	Brian Taylor
LATEST PRICE	£55

Brian Taylor became interested in the project as a result of having been an *HMS Ganges* boy and submariner in the Royal Navy. We had been friends for many years, and he ran his own business gifts' company. He took on responsibility for selling the Victory Ltd in-house products to retail outlets (see Part Three), but wanted to have a product in The Collection. He sourced from within the UK a laser etched, 3D depiction of *HMS Victory* in crystal and had a Victory oak base made for it. He had one returned by a customer who complained that the oak was "too distressed". Brian pointed out that Trafalgar was a pretty distressing place for a ship to be, but replaced it with a clean base. This sort of comment arose from a number of customers of The Collection who did not seem to appreciate the character and atmosphere generated from demonstrably old and weathered timbers.

DINING TABLE	
EDITION SIZE:	1
NUMBER SOLD	1
MAKER	Andy Thornton Ltd & David Burton
LATEST PRICE	Full set, with 8 chairs, £20,000

The dining table, complete with two carvers and six side chairs made in the style of Rennie Mackintosh and bearing on the leather backs of the carvers the hand painted portraits of Lord Nelson and Emma Hamilton, became the visual centrepiece of most of the large shows. They were certainly stunning talking points, and for that reason justified the amount of space they occupied both on the stand and in the van, not to mention the physical effort involved in moving them about. Many a time I heard someone (usually a lady) say to David:

"I'd love to buy this but I just don't think I could get it in my dining room," to which David would reply:

"Well, I'll tell you what. You buy it and I'll keep it at my house and then you can come over and have dinner with me whenever you want!"

Or the sotto voce aside while watching it being stroked by a particularly yummy mummy:

"I never thought I'd like to be a table"

"Worth it just to be stroked, though?"

"No, to be laid!"

This item was a collaboration between furniture makers **Andy Thornton Ltd** who made them, and **David Burton** who supplied the hand painted leather centrepiece depicting the crest of *HMS Victory* as well as the chair back portraits. The tabletop was 5ft in diameter, with eight 'book-matched'[1] sections of laminated Victory oak representing Nelson's 'band of brothers'. The hand-painted centrepiece was gilded with 23carat gold leaf.

The downfall of this remarkable set of furniture was its price. It attracted considerable serious interest and the table was finally sold, without the chairs, to novelist and disgraced peer Lord Archer. It is pleasing to think of the interesting people who must now dine at it, and what a talking point it must be at those dinner parties.

[1] A piece of timber, sliced through the centre along the grain will become two identical shaped pieces with matching grain patterns. This is known as 'book-matched'.

PATRICK TITE

VICTORY CAPSTAN TABLE	
EDITION SIZE:	50
NUMBER SOLD	0
MAKER	Patrick Tite
LATEST PRICE	£1,100

LORD NELSON CAPSTAN TABLE	
EDITION SIZE:	25
NUMBER SOLD	3
MAKER	Patrick Tite
LATEST PRICE	£2,125

These two extremely high quality tables made by **Patrick Tite** perhaps illustrated the point that modern design did not sit comfortably with historic material in a commemorative collection of this type. The Lord Nelson Table is solid Victory oak, with black bog oak squares inlaid to represent gun ports, while the Victory table has a Victory oak top with a base made of bleached English sycamore. Both are hand-carved around the tops. They drew much favourable comment at shows, but people were put off by the prices, and serious customers often chose the Victory stool instead.

TIM TUCKER

TRAFALGAR BATTLE PLAN	
EDITION SIZE:	500
NUMBER SOLD	3
MAKER	Tim Tucker
LATEST PRICE	£104

The son of a friend living at the other end of our village had recently set up in business screen printing on canvas and stretching the canvases onto frames. **Tim Tucker's** knowledge and equipment were of a high order, and we thought it might be worth trying a product based upon the famous battle plan of Trafalgar. John Croxon made the Victory oak frame with copper sheathing corners. This product was another late arrival to The Collection, and had too much to compete with.

IVAN UPRIGHT

MINI CLOCKS (LARGE AND SMALL)	
EDITION SIZE:	150 of each
NUMBER SOLD	46 large, 38 small
MAKER	Ivan Upright
LATEST PRICE	£45 (large), £40 (small)

POCKET WATCH	
EDITION SIZE:	150
NUMBER SOLD	8
MAKER	Ivan Upright
LATEST PRICE	£37.50

WATCH PENDANT	
EDITION SIZE:	150
NUMBER SOLD	4
MAKER	Ivan Upright
LATEST PRICE	£32.50

Ivan Upright had the ideal range of gift items at the lower end of the price range, which used up small, otherwise unusable pieces of Victory oak. We saw him at many of the shows, with an impressive array of clocks in turned woods of every description, and it was easy to keep him supplied with our oak. The mini clocks proved popular, particularly with women customers.

GRAHAM WAUDBY

HMS VICTORY HALF HULL	
EDITION SIZE:	50
NUMBER SOLD	0
MAKER	Graham Waudby
LATEST PRICE	£1,500

HEART OF OAK	
EDITION SIZE:	150
NUMBER SOLD	7
MAKER	Graham Waudby
LATEST PRICE	£82.50

OAK TANKARD	
EDITION SIZE:	150
NUMBER SOLD	14
MAKER	Graham Waudby
LATEST PRICE	£215

Half hulls are a specialist collector's item, with few good artists making them. **Graham Waudby** is one such, and was keen to offer a commemorative one of *HMS Victory*. It was a large piece, being a 1:100 scale replica with a hull size of 70cms x 17cms x 9cms, presented on a Victory oak plaque and housed in a handmade carrying case. The below-the-waterline section of the hull is Victory oak. The quality and workmanship demanded a price of £1,500, but this proved too rich for our main market. It joins some of the other high quality, high price items in The Collection that would benefit from specialist art marketing.

The Heart of Oak product was a whimsical notion of Graham's. He took a piece of off-cut material from the half hull, carved it into a heart, and stuck it to a piece of sheet music of the song about Nelson's navy, and added a picture of the great man. He sent it to me in a frame, and we decided to offer it as part of The Collection. We were a little surprised, though pleased, to sell seven of them.

The oak tankard is made in the traditional manner, as it would have been by ship's carpenters of the day, using staves bound with willow applied damp to shrink and tighten on drying, and sealed inside with beeswax. It is a genuine drinking vessel and is made to be used as such, with a capacity of 32 fluid ounces or just over a pint and a half.

CHRIS WEDLAKE

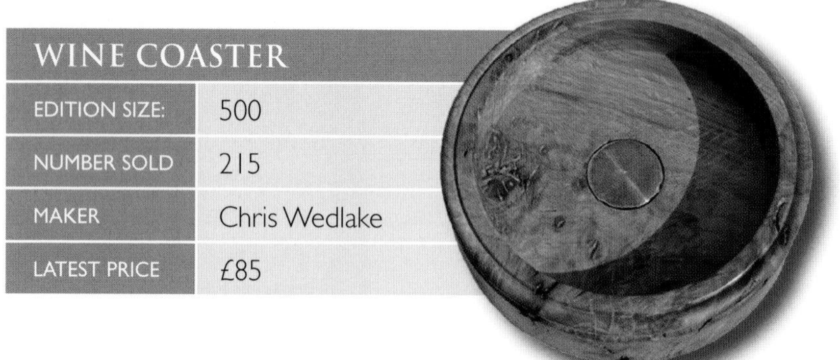

WINE COASTER	
EDITION SIZE:	500
NUMBER SOLD	215
MAKER	Chris Wedlake
LATEST PRICE	£85

The wine coaster, made by former police officer **Chris Wedlake** was another product that proved how success in this context came from products that had a use as well as being decorative and well priced. This item is designed as a stand for a wine bottle, and the numerous customer comments received back praising it as a great dinner party conversation piece show that customers all over the world are using it. It continued to sell through Nauticalia Ltd after I ceased to handle the business, and the sales count has reached 215. The coaster is turned from solid Victory oak and has a slice of copper rivet set into the centre. Victory oak is notoriously tricky to turn because of the many shakes, holes and other distress marks found in it. For most, this was an attractive bonus, but Chris had his share of complainers who seemingly would have preferred something made from MDF. He took the step of including a slip of paper with each product explaining the features of old, reclaimed oak and the provenance of this particularly historic timber.

WILLIAMS AND ROBINSON

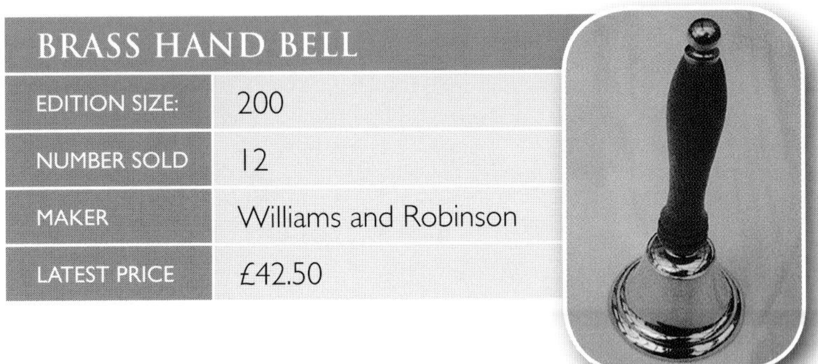

BRASS HAND BELL	
EDITION SIZE:	200
NUMBER SOLD	12
MAKER	Williams and Robinson
LATEST PRICE	£42.50

MAGNIFYING GLASS	
EDITION SIZE:	200
NUMBER SOLD	21
MAKER	Williams and Robinson
LATEST PRICE	£42.50

TELESCOPE	
EDITION SIZE:	200
NUMBER SOLD	3
MAKER	Williams and Robinson
LATEST PRICE	£99

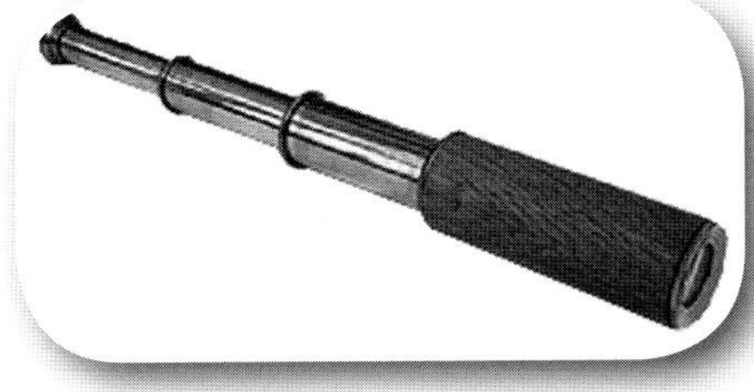

FARMHOUSE STOOL	
EDITION SIZE:	100
NUMBER SOLD	2
MAKER	Williams and Robinson
LATEST PRICE	£340

MILKING STOOL	
EDITION SIZE:	100
NUMBER SOLD	1
MAKER	Williams and Robinson
LATEST PRICE	£250

I knew **Kevin Williams** and **Simon Robinson** as good local furniture makers partly because they had made some items from Victory oak for James Boddy's *Remember Nelson* collection. I had seen their work at the Royal Norfolk Show, so when I visited Simon at their workshop in Taverham they were keen to be involved with The 1805 Collection. The question was, with what product? The Victory stool made by Simpson's of Norfolk was proving a winner, in part because it combined fine workmanship with practicality. It was, however, quite expensive. It seemed reasonable to explore the possibility of offering a lower priced but very traditional stool to complement it. Three and four-legged farmhouse and milking stools were commonplace in Nelson's time, and there was plenty of opportunity to select characterful oak for the tops. The legs are of hand-turned yew. Unfortunately, however, they sold poorly. Perhaps the contrast with the Victory stool was too great.

Not wishing to miss out, they decided to offer some simple, lower priced objects and brought out the brass hand bell, the magnifying glass and the telescope. These items were late editions, and faced mounting competition from the explosion of other lower priced items available in Victory oak in 2005.

DAVID WILLIAMS

NELSON'S COAT OF ARMS	
EDITION SIZE:	1
NUMBER SOLD	1
MAKER	David Williams
LATEST PRICE	Not known

David Williams is an authority on Lord Nelson and provided me with much help and many contacts throughout the project, and indeed acted as consultant on a number of projects relating to the bicentenary. He researched Nelson's coat of arms and produced a hand painted version, signed by the current Lord Nelson and framed it with some Victory oak. We were pleased to sell it to a known collector.

TOBY WINTERINGHAM

STICK BAROMETER	
EDITION SIZE:	50
NUMBER SOLD	0
MAKER	Toby Winteringham
LATEST PRICE	£1,450

This Nelson contemporary stick barometer, which uses mercury in a glass tube to indicate barometric pressure, is perhaps another example of an art product for which The 1805 Collection did not deliver the right audience. **Toby Winteringham** is a highly skilled furniture maker based in Norfolk, and he chose to use the Victory materials to create a unique design. The piece is made of four beautifully marked, book-matched pieces of oak, with a fragment of copper sheathing in the top left quartile.

SHULIAN ZHANG

GLOBE PAINTING	
EDITION SIZE:	10
NUMBER SOLD	3
MAKER	Shulian Zhang
LATEST PRICE	£750

Shulian Zhang was demonstrating her extraordinary skills at painting in minute detail inside bottles and globes at one of our last ICHF shows. I invited her to visit our stand. She knew nothing of Nelson or Trafalgar, but readily appreciated the idea and offered to do a product for us. The resulting globe is exquisite, and will undoubtedly become a collector's item. The painting shows Nelson on one side and *HMS Victory* on the other.

The following products were offered through The 1805 Collection as unlimited editions:

40 YEAR CALENDAR	
EDITION SIZE:	unlimited
NUMBER SOLD	1
MAKER	Michael's Fine Crafts
LATEST PRICE	£159.99

This excellent quality brass calendar, which starts in 2005, is framed in onyx and mounted on turned Victory oak, inlaid with copper. It bears a brass plate on the side with the words: "The 1805 Companion".

BRASS MAGNIFIER WITH COPPER INLAY

EDITION SIZE:	unlimited
NUMBER SOLD	19
MAKER	Michael's Fine Crafts
LATEST PRICE	£168.99

This superb 4x magnifying glass has a handle of Victory oak, inlaid with copper, and comes in a lined presentation box.

ANCHOR ON OAK BLOCK

EDITION SIZE:	unlimited
NUMBER SOLD	16
MAKER	Peter McNamara
LATEST PRICE	£27.50

Timber off cuts, with copper sheathing disc insert, have a replica of the Victory's anchor and rope coil mounted. A plate bears the words 'Timber from HMS Victory' and the base is felted.

COPPER INGOT

EDITION SIZE:	unlimited
NUMBER SOLD	36
MAKER	Janet Bowman
LATEST PRICE	£35

Solid Victory copper ingots with a replica of the King's Mark.

CRYSTAL SHIP'S DECANTER

EDITION SIZE:	unlimited
NUMBER SOLD	3
MAKER	VMP
LATEST PRICE	£395

TRADITIONAL MENDLESHAM CHAIR

EDITION SIZE:	unlimited
NUMBER SOLD	5
MAKER	Finewood Furniture
LATEST PRICE	£1,095

This traditional Suffolk chair has a Victory oak cresting rail with a section of bronze rivet in the centre, mounted to show the King's Mark.

BEAM BOWL

EDITION SIZE:	1
NUMBER SOLD	1
MAKER	Julienne Dolphin Wilding
LATEST PRICE	£650

Rugged oak beam sections were hand carved. Two bowls were made, and one featured on the TV programme The Antiques Roadshow.

THE VICTORY CHAIR

EDITION SIZE:	One offs (two made)
NUMBER SOLD	0
MAKER	Julienne Dolphin Wilding
LATEST PRICE	£4,000

These sculptural chairs were designed to show the origins of selected atmospheric Victory oak beams.

I will always remember this larger than life character with dreadlocks and huge enthusiasm picking up oak beams and saying to them, "Do you want to be a chair? Right, stand there then!"

OAK BEAM LAMPS

EDITION SIZE:	One offs
NUMBER SOLD	12+
MAKER	Alan Sheppard
LATEST PRICE	£150-250

*Many of the lumps of oak were ideal as lamps, and **Alan Sheppard** had a talent for selecting pieces with interesting shapes and features, and highlighting the colours of the wood. He continued to make lamps for Nauticalia Ltd after 2005.*

PAPERCLIP HOLDER

EDITION SIZE:	unlimited
NUMBER SOLD	20
MAKER	Ray Sylvester
LATEST PRICE	£35

These Victory oak domes contain a concealed magnet. They come with paper clips and printed presentation bag.

SCALE REPLICA OF HMS VICTORY

EDITION SIZE:	10
NUMBER SOLD	1
MAKER	Brian Williams
LATEST PRICE	£1,250

This highly detailed 1:525 scale replica was created by the much sought after marine miniature specialist Brian Williams in his "shipyard" in Cornwall. Using a magnifying glass, one can even see the watch on deck!

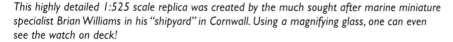

The following artists made proofs for The 1805 Collection but never sold:

Philip Capper, a senior Fishery Officer in Wales, as well as a skilful wood turner has an interest in anything to do with maritime history. He produced a fid, which is similar to a marline spike, used by sailors of Nelson's time. Essentially it is a round length of hard wood that is tapered to a blunt point and is used to open the lay of a rope in order to facilitate splicing. Wooden fids are still used today, and have the advantage over metal marline spikes that they are less likely to cut the fibres of the rope. It proved a source of conversation with visitors to the exhibitions, and would have more than covered its cost if we had £1 for every time someone asked where you put the batteries!

Tony Collins, who is a traditional shipwright, antique restorer and boat repairer, made a splendid set of half-hull models of *HMS Victory's* five ship's boats: an 18 foot cutter, a 25 foot cutter, a pinnace, an admiral's barge and launch. Considerable research and planning went into the creation of these faithful replica hulls, which must some day be an important addition to some collection.

Jo Crutchfield makes a fascinating range of stringed instruments from wood, and is an accomplished musician. Excited by the opportunity to work with this heritage oak, Jo made a large and a small lyre, both of which made artistic use of the natural shapes of the salvaged timber and played perfectly – in the right hands!

Richard Mullard created a traditionally handcrafted stained glass hanging lampshade. It comprised of alternate unaltered Victory copper sheathing segments and six hand-painted images fired into period blown glass panels that depicted scenes from the battle of Trafalgar. It was exciting to have a stained glass artist as part of The Collection, but sadly the cost of such workmanship put the item beyond reach.

Anthony Roberts created a magazine table using oak with copper sheathing set into the top. The novel design included a V shaped compartment that hinged out from beneath to store magazines.

Toby Vint includes furniture design and making in a wide spectrum of interests, and designed a fine pair of modern bedside lights from the oak. I suspect that there was a clash in some people's minds between the historic nature of the oak and the clean 21st century lines of these well-crafted items.

... and finally, the most discussed product that never happened must be the *HMS Victory* shoeshine box. I was approached by **The Traditional Victorian Shoeshine Company Ltd.**, which operates a traditional shoeshine service in London and other locations for special occasions such as the Henley Regatta and Royal Ascot. It was reported that it used to clean the Duchess of York's impressive collection of shoes for £250 per day. Keith Stevens, the dynamic and enthusiastic director of this venture, wrote to me and suggested the creation of a unique shoeshine box using the oak and copper. It was to be: "of an authentic old English style with copper lid and oak foot plate, and the foot plate would be supported by two pieces of oak in the shape of a ship's capstan. The shoe box artwork would tell the story of this famous battle..." We met to discuss the concept and for Keith to see the material he would have to work with. His creativity was boundless. There could be shoe brushes made from the oak, and the polish tins could be made from the copper, with a picture of Nelson on the black polish and *HMS Victory* on the brown. He would research the method used in Nelson's day for shining the boots of naval officers, and he could take his shoeshine team down to Portsmouth, dressed in period naval seaman's attire, and polish the shoes of the guests as they boarded the ship for the bicentenary celebration on October 21st 2005. In the end, the idea sank without a trace. Maybe the material was too difficult to achieve the desired result. Maybe it hit the rocks when I reacted negatively to the idea that some of the oak could have musket balls introduced into it.

PART THREE

IN LINE ASTERN

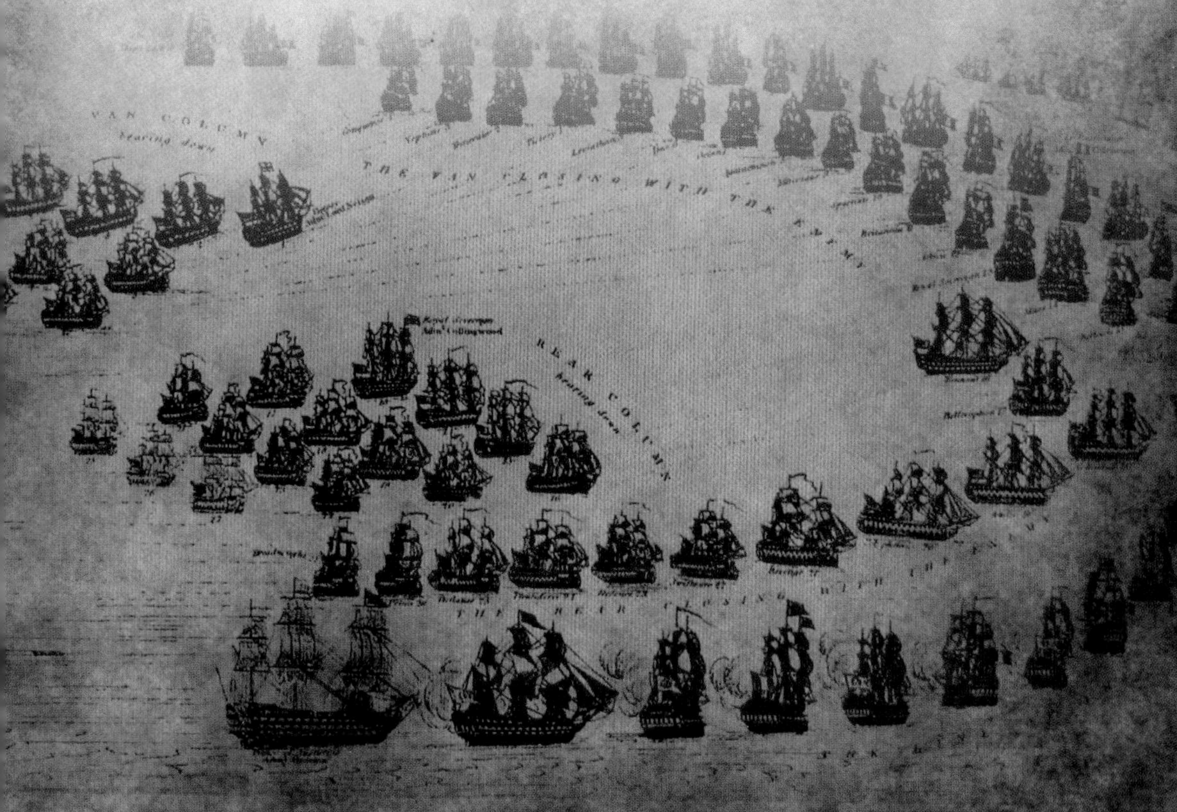

It is usually the case that, when you are out ahead of the fleet, you are not fully aware of just how much is going on behind you in support. So it was with me concentrating on The 1805 Collection. Attracting trade and corporate custom to use the material was a key part of the strategy, and sales for this purpose were always welcome. It was not until after the event, though, that I was able to fully appreciate the depth and breadth of the work done in this sector. I shall deal with it in three sections.

16

Corporate Customers

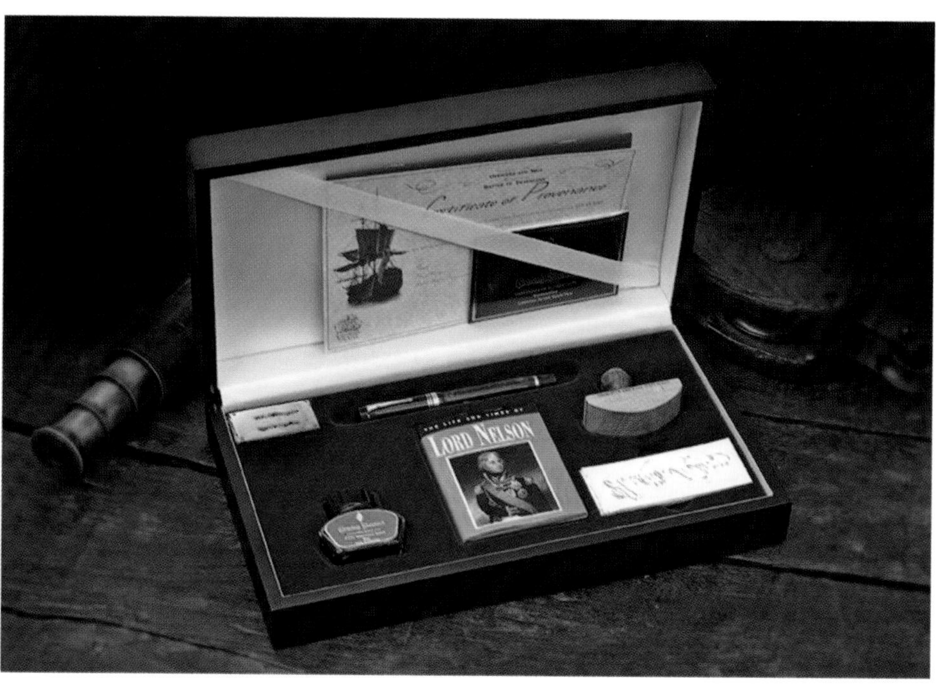

CONWAY STEWART

The name Conway Stewart is almost certainly lodged in the memory of 1950s school children as their first fountain pen – a marvel of marbled plastic, gold nibs and ink sacks, filled by a lever in the side of the barrel and representing a giant developmental leap forward from dip pens and inkwells. It was a nostalgia trip, therefore, to be contacted by the company that had resurrected the brand and asked how best to use the Victory oak for a commemorative pen set. After discussing various options, the company elected to include in their presentation a mini version of the oak blotter made by John Croxon that appears in The 1805 Collection. Their boxed set included a booklet on the life of Nelson with bottle of ink and blotter, plus Certificate of Provenance. We supplied 150 mini blotters for this promotion.

The appeal of this brand to schoolboys of the 1950s and '60s was best illustrated by a group of four friends who attended the Royal Naval College in Dartmouth together and had successful naval careers. In 2005, they bought each other one of these sets for their 60th birthdays as an appropriate link between them, their era and their mutual connection with the hero of Trafalgar.

CROWN AGENTS

The Trafalgar stamp was the most unexpected and arguably most bizarre product to use the Victory oak, but no less successful for that – and highly collectable to boot.

"French printers stick it to Nelson..." proclaimed The Times. "The French printer Cator has achieved what the French and Spanish fleets failed to do 200 years ago – take part of Nelson's flagship," proclaimed a philatelic expert. So what was that all about?

Nigel Fordham was Head of the Crown Agents Stamp Bureau for almost 14 years. He co-ordinated the design and marketing for countries represented by the crown agents of commemorative stamp issues for the Trafalgar bicentenary around the world. Artist John Batchelor had worked with Nigel several times in the past creating stamp artwork, and the two men carried out extensive research at the National Maritime Museum and at the Royal Naval Museum in Portsmouth before coming up with some proposals. During the course of this work Nigel became aware of the existence of the Victory oak owned by Victory Ltd, and thought how unique it would be if this material could somehow be incorporated into the stamp. Further research threw up the existence of a French printing company that had the technology to incorporate wood dust into the printing ink. Nigel came to see me and purchased 50 kg of our scrap oak off-cuts, and after six months of development the French company perfected their ability to print the wood onto stamps.

Her Majesty the Queen granted Royal approval for the stamps, and no less than twelve countries, seven of which are United Kingdom Overseas Territories, issued a set of stamps. The stamp bearing the Victory oak was a painting by Francis Smitherman, with the rest of the artwork completed by John Batchelor. If you run your finger over the hull, masts and spars of *HMS Victory* in the picture on the stamp you can feel the wood dust and touch Nelson's flagship!

The countries that issued the stamp are: Ascension Island, Bahamas, British Indian Ocean Territory, Gibraltar, Nauru, Kiribati, St. Helena, Tristan da Cunha, St Lucia, Cayman Islands, Bermuda and Jamaica. [1]

David Burton

David must be considered the 'default maker' of items using Victory materials. If the companies or individuals mentioned elsewhere in this book did not make it, it was almost certainly one of David's pieces. He was also the most prolific maker in The 1805 Collection. Unlike other makers, David has devoted himself exclusively to working with this material, making not just for his own business but also for Nauticalia to sell in their shops and catalogues. His energy was seemingly endless – not just in making large quantities of art and craftworks, but also setting up and running consumer sales operations. In addition to organising, setting up and running the shows for The 1805 Collection, he also attended many other exhibitions on his own account, usually to a total of some 30 shows per year. Not content with that, David and Caroline rented a shop in Uppingham for a couple of months while it was between tenants, and sold well from it. The result of this success prompted them the following year to buy the shop opposite and to try and maintain the momentum. Unfortunately the Uppingham market for this rarefied type of product range was exhausted after about 18 months, and the shop was closed. At that point they decided to move to Norfolk nearer to the material and to Nelson's home, and rented a gallery in Holt, which they ran successfully from Easter 2005 until the bicentenary in October 2005.

Such is the variety and volume of David's work that it is not possible to

[1] Detail of the connections found by Nigel Fordham between the countries concerned and Trafalgar can be found in the Bicentennial Edition of The Nelson Dispatch, December 2005, produced by the Nelson Society.

provide pictures of it all. Here are samples from all the key product categories. It should be noted that all his products come with some form of Certification that he generated (examples of which are shown below), and these are backed by our recorded sales of oak to him.

TABLES: David developed a technique for using resin, sometimes coloured to suit a product or application, so that smaller and interesting pieces of oak could be brought together in one larger piece. He would use this approach to produce blocks or boards that could then be turned, cut or machined. This resin oak was particularly useful for tabletops, but will be seen in other product categories. His most popular table style was the tilt-top wine table made in different sizes, but he also produced coffee tables. The last one shown is his Artefacts Table, which houses a display of copper rivets, sheathing, and oak that are of particular interest, beneath a glass top.

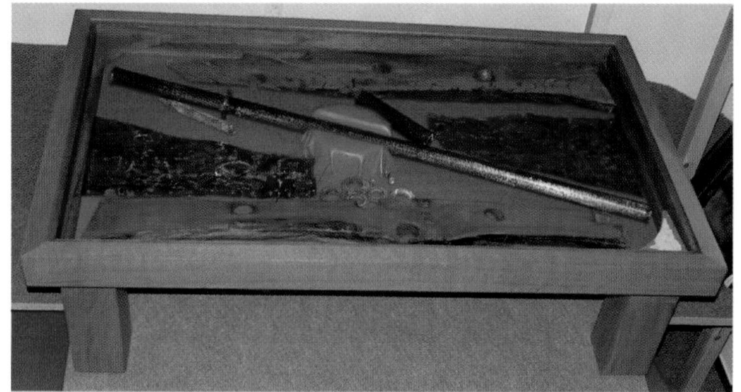

PICTURES: David Burton produced a range of unique pictures featuring fragments of the material.

BOWLS were also produced in a startling variety of shapes and sizes.

COASTERS were made for wine glasses, bottles and the like.

BOOKENDS lent themselves to various designs that maximised the character of the oak pieces.

VICTORY NATURAL SCULPTURES were David's answer to the success my wife had enjoyed at shows with her Victory oak Sculptures which involved selecting unusual shaped pieces of the oak, cleaning and polishing them and presenting them in sculptural form.

THE STOOL in The 1805 Collection had been one of the most successful of all products. When the edition closed, David thought it worthwhile to offer a lower priced alternative but using the resin oak technique.

BAROMETERS AND CLOCKS

BOXES: This particular item appealed to David because of the oak piece from which it was made. Boxes were not one of his staples.

BOTTLE STOPPERS were almost David's Holy Grail, but not quite. The search was always on to find that product which would attract mass gift appeal, priced right and each one sufficiently unique to add interest. It should use up scrap oak and be simple to make. The product sold extremely well in the year of its launch, but slowed inexplicably in 2005. David found a good source of high quality metal stoppers in the Far East and bought a useful quantity at an economic price. At shows customers would pick over the display for ages to find the one that most appealed to them. I think we decided the record was 45 minutes to select one. Quite often it would spark the debate about the wisdom and effectiveness of sealing up an opened bottle of wine, but generally the issue of what to buy dad for Christmas or birthday that was a bit different proved the overriding consideration. The corkscrew was an obvious range extension.

The **PAPERKNIFE** was made from off-cuts of oak and beaten copper sheathing.

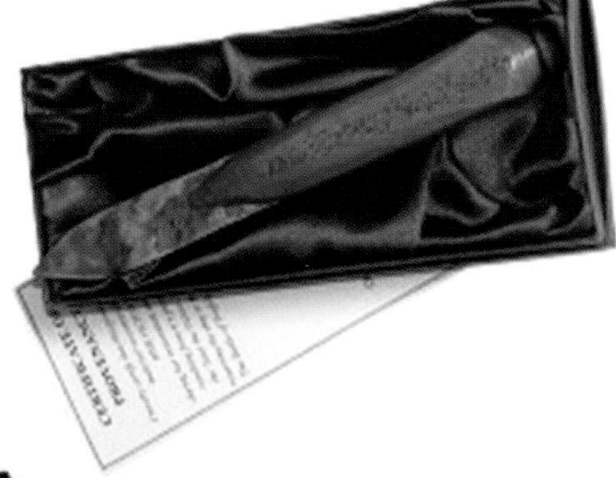

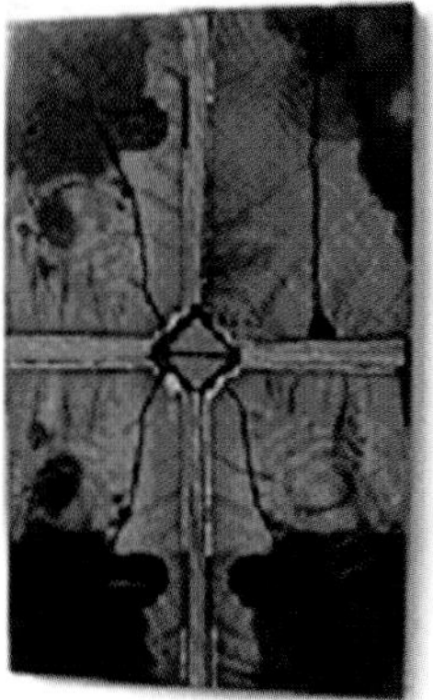

OAK PANELS were another chance to use resin oak and David's artistic creativity.

COAT HOOKS had worked for my wife Jan who had used three or four hand-forged iron hooks on interesting pieces of oak for sale at shows. David tried it with brass fittings.

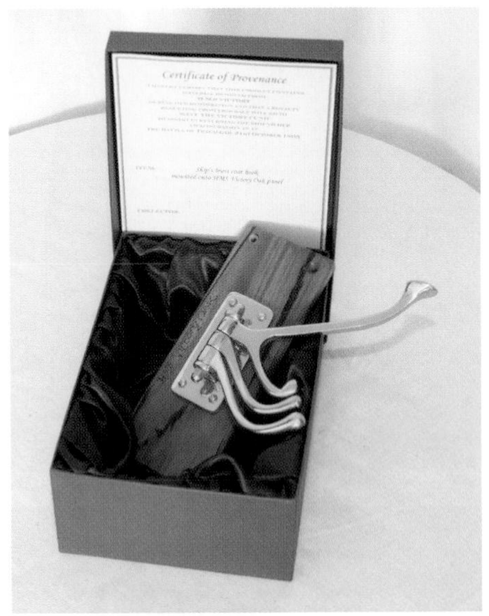

The pewter **HIP FLASK** was another attempt to appeal to the 'man who has everything' gift market.

NUT CRACKERS were produced for the Christmas shows.

An **HOUR GLASS** was inspired perhaps by the watch glass that had done well in The 1805 Collection.

DISPLAY PIECES were made to show off particular artefacts.

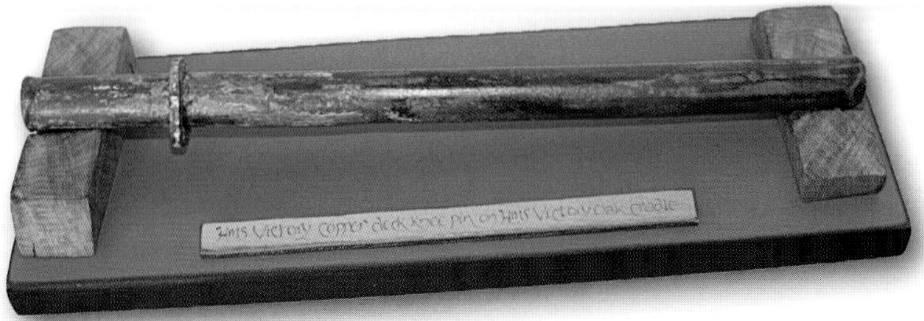

Even **BOOKMARKS** were offered at the low end of the price spectrum.

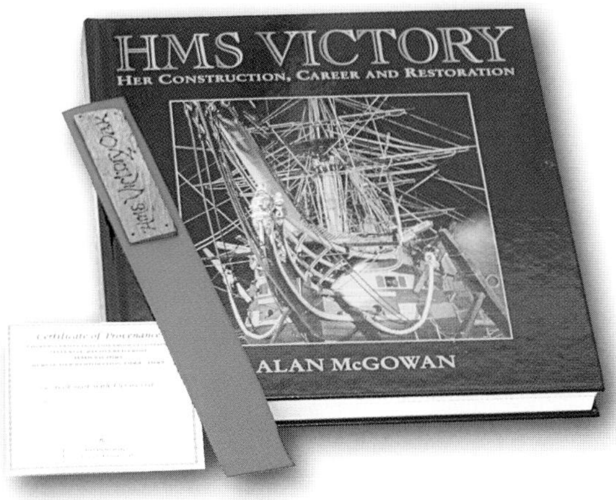

As an artist, David always wrestled with the volume production aspect of his work. Most of what he produced had the individuality in it born of both his creativity as well as the unique nature of each piece of material. Occasionally, however, he would go off on one of his artistic binges and shoot for the stars. The apogee of this was his mega Victory sculpture. In his mind, he saw the complete fleet of Nelson's ships with *HMS Victory* at its head laid out as a massive sculpture at some appropriate and important location for the bicentenary celebrations. It would have been a vast undertaking, unthinkable without serious sponsorship. Efforts to find this proved fruitless, but David was determined to realise his dream in part at least, and created a large sculpture in his gallery in Holt, as seen above.

He also produced its smaller brother.

Certificate of Provenance

'I HEREBY CERTIFY THAT THIS PRODUCT CONTAINS MATERIAL REMOVED FROM H.M.S VICTORY DURING HER 1922 1927 RESTORATION'

COLLECTOR:

DATE:

David Burton
MAKER,
THE FAMOUS TREE COMPANY LIMITED
www.victoryoak.co.uk

Certificate of Provenance

I hereby certify that this hand crafted item contains material salvaged from HMS Victory during her restoration and a royalty resulting from it's sale will go to 'Save the Victory Fund' to assist her long term preservation

Signed

Maker: David Burton www.victoryoak.co.uk

Here are two samples of certificates used for David's work

DEAN'S BEARS

Just to prove that the opportunity afforded by the Trafalgar bicentenary was not limited to those on a testosterone-fuelled nostalgia trip, and that any business could put its tri-cornered hat on and come up with a winner, Dean's Bears brought out a limited edition Nelson Teddy Bear. Dean's are the UK's oldest teddy bear company, founded in 1903 and commenced production in 1915. Their bears are highly collected and are generally regarded as 'must haves' by seriously posh babies.

The Nelson bear was an edition of 500 that sold out, and came in a box with a piece of Victory oak and a certificate. Dean's also made a donation to the Save the Victory Fund.

LUCY ASKEW

Architectural Model Maker and Miniaturist Lucy Askew saw an opportunity to celebrate the bicentenary of Nelson's amazing state funeral in January 2006 by producing a limited edition of his highly ornate coffin, using Victory oak. I saw pictures of some of her work and was keen to have this unusual item in The 1805 Collection but Lucy preferred to handle it herself. Its success proves that was a sensible decision for her.

Nelson's funeral was an extraordinary affair, as was his coffin. The body of the Hero lay in state in the Painted Hall in Greenwich Hospital for three days from January 5th and 7th 1806, when it was estimated that some 15,000 members of the public were able to view it. In Adam Collinwood's words: "…a multitude that almost extended from Greenwich to London returned with disappointment." On January 8th, the body was placed upon the state barge, and, with a procession of barges of the Lord Mayor and principal livery companies of the City of London, proceeded upriver to Whitehall to gun salutes from Greenwich, the Tower of London and on landing. The body lay overnight in the Captain's Room at The Admiralty prior to the public funeral procession on Thursday 9th January from The Admiralty to St Paul's Cathedral. The funeral carriage was hugely ornate, the rear being modelled on the stern of *HMS Victory*. It was drawn by six black horses with all the panoply of a state funeral.

Nelson's inner coffin, in which his body was carried from *HMS Victory*, was made out of the main mast of *L'Orient* and was a gift from his friend Captain Hallowell. The outer coffin, as depicted in Lucy's scale model, was six foot eight inches long, 26 inches wide at the widest point, and 19 inches deep and made from mahogany. It is covered with a rich black Genoa velvet, divided into a number of compartments and panels, and containing no less than 10,000 double gilt nails.

The Lucy Askew scale replica, which is made of Victory oak, is decorated with fine gold plated emblems and ornaments on suitably rich black velvet. It is presented in a black and gold leather case, lined with cream satin with a gold inscription inside the lid. The limited edition of 500 is issued with a certificate of provenance and comes with a commemorative booklet containing a collection of contemporary newspaper reports, eyewitness accounts and images of the funeral.

At the time of writing there are 178 pieces of this special edition in circulation. Interestingly, some of the sales came through Messrs. France, the funeral directors who undertook Nelson's funeral and who are still at their original address in London. A quantity were also sold through Selfridges who had it as part of their launch of their new Wonder Room which opened in October 2007 to serve a growing demand for super-luxury gifts for that special someone who has everything.

John Barnard is certainly Norfolk's, and probably Britain's most visionary contemporary furniture designer and creator. Introduced to the availability of the Victory materials and the impending Trafalgar bicentenary by James Boddy, and no doubt spurred on by James's own passion for the subject, John felt inspired to create a suitably atmospheric dining suite. To this end, John, James and I drove down to Portsmouth together to introduce John to *HMS Victory*. The result was the stunning Victory Suite, consisting of a dining table, chairs, sideboard and coffee table. To create the Victory Table, John spent hours in the barn selecting the most distressed and atmospheric pieces of oak, which, in his own words, he then "embalmed in resin to create a beautiful wood collage capped in bronze. Around the table are Admiralty Chairs, sea thrones of awesome grace and power, their huge arching spines instrument and lyre to ropes and rigging, masthead and spar: all making for the majestic stature, the gravitas."

The design is based on Victory's ribbed frame. The chairs, which incorporate a piece of Victory oak on the arms at the point where the hand naturally falls, are backed with hemp 'rigging'. The Nelson chair at the head is inspired by Victory's stern post, while the Hamilton chair at the foot of the table takes its inspiration from Victory's more curvaceous bow and recalls Nelson's mistress Lady Hamilton. The oak tabletop is capped in place, trimmed with bronze and further secured by black Fenland bog oak wedges.

Complementing the table and chairs are the superb sideboard and coffee table.

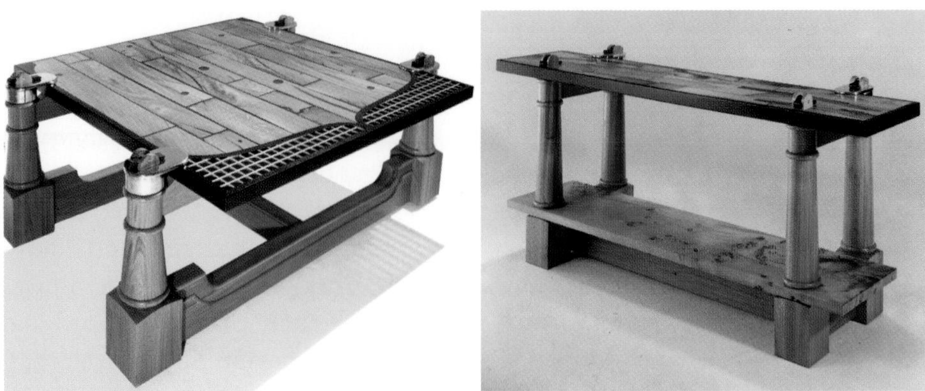

To date, John has made 14 chairs, four dining tables, three coffee tables and one sideboard. The first full set was sold to an Italian lover of design for his London home. Another table is in London, with one on the Isle of Man and one on the Isle of Skye. Three of the tables are 10ft by 4ft and the fourth is 8ft by 4ft. A full set of the Victory Suite would cost a significant five-figure sum.

NAUTICALIA

If The 1805 Collection is the flagship project, then Nauticalia Ltd must be the flagship corporate customer. Founded in 1974 as a floating marine antiques shop, Nauticalia has now secured a virtually unchallenged position in UK and world markets as the leading retailer, wholesaler and direct marketer of reproduction boating and shipping memorabilia. With nine retail shops in key locations such as Covent Garden, London and the Historic Dockyard, Portsmouth, as well as an active wholesale operation supplying consumer product outlets from museums to seaside shops, Nauticalia certainly covers the waterfront. In addition, it is a major direct marketing company distributing as many as three million catalogues per year around the world.

Nauticalia was always the obvious choice of company to take the Victory arisings to market, and indeed they were one of the bidders when the Ministry of Defence put them up for tender. They later admitted to me that they really wanted the copper that they knew could be cast into all manner of products but did not know what to do with a mountain of traumatised timber. In consequence their bid consisted of a very low price for the timber combined with a more realistic price for the copper. Together, this was insufficient to outbid Nick Varley. During the early days of the project I half expected Nauticalia to approach me and suggest some sort of deal, but I was determined not to approach them until I could demonstrate that we had a viable proposition. I needed an adequate negotiating platform. In the event, it was I who made the first approach in 2004, though Nauticalia admitted they had been on the point of contacting me instead.

They started purchasing items for sale in their shops and catalogues. The success of this led both parties to realise that the long-term future of the project would be better served if Nauticalia took it on. I had made it clear to the Sons of Zebedee that I wanted to retire from the business once the Trafalgar bicentenary was over, and so it made sound sense for us to negotiate a hand-over deal with Nauticalia. Rather than selling the businesses Victory Ltd and Victory Marketing Partners Ltd as going concerns it made more commercial sense to both parties for us to wind those businesses up and to sell the balance of outstanding arisings to them. This was accomplished in November 2005.

Since that time, Nauticalia has expanded the product range, using their existing contacts in India and the Far East to cast items from the copper, while David Burton was contracted to make stock items for them from the timber and supplied them with several of his own products. Nauticalia continued to offer much of The 1805 Collection through their shops, and developed an on-going relationship with the new Commanding Officer of *HMS Victory*, Lt. Cmdr John Scivier. The product portfolio not covered elsewhere in this book, and current at October 2008 is shown below.

Cast copper products included three items created by my wife Janet Bowman - the Anchor Chart Weight, the ingot and the Pyramid of Cannon Balls, all of which sold in significant quantity. The latter was based on the 'balls on a brass monkey' idea which is that canon balls were stacked in this manner on a brass ring or 'monkey', and when the temperature fell so low that the brass contracted the balls would fall off, leading to the expression: "It is cold enough to freeze the balls off a brass monkey". Whether this is true is a matter of debate, but it would certainly not have been a practical manner of cannon ball storage on the heaving decks of a ship! My daughter Amy designed the Victory key ring.

Other products introduced by Victory Ltd and continued or improved by Nauticalia are the framed sheets of copper sheathing, the pyrographed etching on Victory oak of Nelson's prayer before the battle, the oak in acrylic key ring and the Boulton Trafalgar medal set in oak with copper corners.

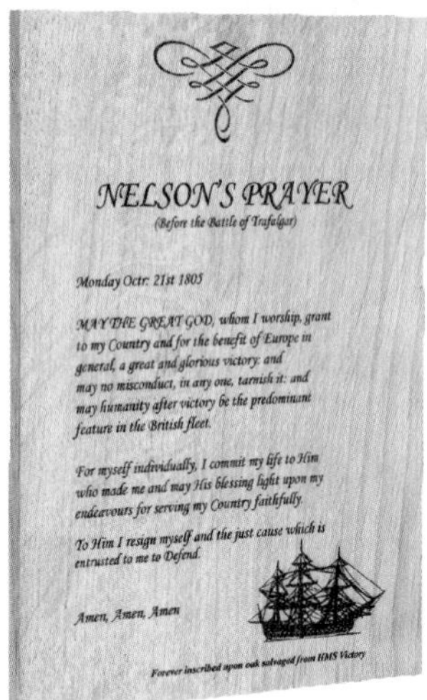

Nauticalia's models of *HMS Victory* mounted on Victory oak plinths have proved popular and appear in two edition formats – the Trafalgar edition of 1805 pieces and the more elaborate Vice-Admiral edition of 821 representing the number of crew.

Then there are the items made by David Burton or on plinths made by him. The change bowl uses the acrylic resin technique while the jack knife is hand pyrographed. The library table is a limited edition of 250 to mark in 2008 Nelson's 250th birthday. The top is made of oak using the acrylic resin technique, and there is a copper disc set into the cross-member. The Nelson bust, Hogget decanter and Nelson figurine are set on Victory oak plinths or bases, as is the nutcracker. The wine coaster is turned from solid oak.

Pen products made by Michael's Fine Crafts proved successful in The 1805 Collection so Nauticalia commissioned their own designs – the Admiral fountain pen and the Nelson 250 limited edition fountain pen commissioned for Nelson's 250th birthday.

One particularly unusual product is The Priest – a limited edition of 250 turned from Victory oak with the end hollowed out and filled with lead to give it weight and balance and then capped with copper. The unusual name for this derives from its use to deliver the 'last rites' to fish. Next to it is the framed picture of *HMS Victory* incorporating some of its oak.

Finally, Nauticalia have continued to sell interesting pieces of oak in their natural state to those who wish to make their own commemorative piece.

NELSON'S NORFOLK VOYAGES

Three years before the national bicentenary celebrations, two local people **Lloyd Addison**[2] and **Ian Weetman** launched Nelson's Norfolk Voyages, a company which developed, manufactured and marketed a collection of unique products made from genuine wood from the *HMS Victory*. It was the first company to purchase Victory materials from Victory Ltd for commercial purposes, and it went about its task with an enthusiasm to honour a local hero.

This collection was essentially aimed at the desktop market with a website www.nelsons-victory.com developed to assist in selling its range of products, with

2 Lloyd, who was a well-known local restauranteur and entrepreneur, died sadly in 2008 after suffering for some time with Parkinson's disease.

the raw material procured from Victory Ltd and made by Norfolk craftsmen, to both British and worldwide markets. The product range included letter openers, gavels and blocks, wine stoppers, rum barrel and dice, paperweights, pens, magnifying glass, calendars, time zone and key fobs.

Each product in the collection was a limited edition and came with full provenance.

The company was successful in selling to markets in the UK, North America, Canada, Australia and the Caribbean, with in excess of 2,000 individual products sold. Examples of their products are shown below.

The following certificate accompanied all editions issued by this company:

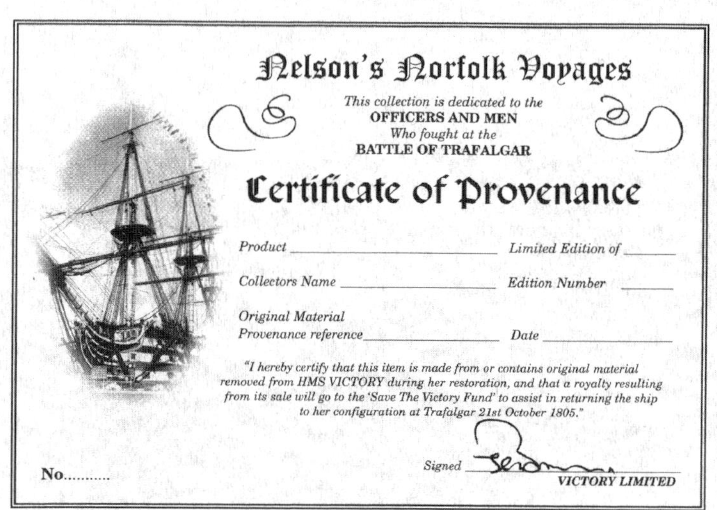

Nelson's Norfolk Voyages

This collection is dedicated to the
OFFICERS AND MEN
Who fought at the
BATTLE OF TRAFALGAR

Certificate of Provenance

Product ______ *Limited Edition of* ______

Collectors Name ______ *Edition Number* ______

Original Material
Provenance reference ______ *Date* ______

"I hereby certify that this item is made from or contains original material removed from HMS VICTORY during her restoration, and that a royalty resulting from its sale will go to the 'Save The Victory Fund' to assist in returning the ship to her configuration at Trafalgar 21st October 1805."

No..........

Signed ______
VICTORY LIMITED

When Pobjoy Mint, Europe's largest private mint, became aware that the copper from *HMS Victory* was available, it applied to the Governments of the British Virgin Islands and the Isle of Man for the rights to produce two unique coins incorporating some of this historic material. The National Maritime Museum in London granted Pobjoy Mint access and permission to use the signature that Nelson adopted when he became the Duke of Bronte.

The design on the magnificent gold coin from the British Virgin Islands features a full portrait of Nelson, Nelson's column, highlighted in copper and the fountain in Trafalgar Square with three ships in the background referring to his life on the seas. Nelson's signature is shown beneath with the value of $125 at the base. The wording 'Admiral Horatio Nelson 1758-1805' is in the surround.

The exceptional silver coin from the Isle of Man depicts The Battle of Trafalgar, showing *HMS Victory* cutting through the French Line. Nelson's signature is shown beneath the image, highlighted with the copper, with the date of the battle underneath. The wording in the surround reads: 'The Bi-Centenary of the Battle of Trafalgar' with the value of one Crown at the base.

The gold coin was only available as part of a set with the silver coin. They are both presented in a handmade box with a detailed booklet explaining and showing the whole process that the copper followed and the certificate of authenticity. This set also includes a piece of copper from *HMS Victory* as it was when it was removed from the ship. This was a limited edition of 999 sets.

Approved by Buckingham Palace the obverse of each coin carries a fine effigy of Her Majesty Queen Elizabeth II by Ian Rank-Broadley FRBS FSNAD.

A framed set was auctioned in Cannes by the Pobjoy Mint and raised £1,000 for the Leukaemia Research Fund.

In February 2004 I was contacted by a businessman whom I had never met. He invited me to meet him and a colleague in London to discuss the possibility of selling some of our products on one of the TV shopping channels. Not one for daytime television, and certainly not one for shopping channels, I had no knowledge of the matter whatsoever but was intrigued by the opportunity. I met **Steve Booth of ViaTel Ltd.**, a company specialising in putting together specialist or themed buying programme propositions for this medium, particularly with the international market leader QVC. In essence he would put together a programme proposal with a range of products to be sold by QVC on air. Steve would negotiate deals with suppliers of selected merchandise and then negotiate a package deal with QVC. Once agreed, QVC would purchase the items at a volume they felt they would shift on the programme, and Steve would make his commission. He had recently put together a successful programme with QVC based on Concorde memorabilia, following the final, nostalgic commercial flight of that supersonic aircraft. His plan was to persuade QVC to run a mega two-hour Nelson and Trafalgar bicentenary show on the actual day – 21st October 2005. He was sensibly planning well ahead.

Initially I was presented with a wish list of products from Steve and asked to make my own suggestions. His list included some items from The 1805 Collection. This is where we ran into problems. First, he wanted samples which would be difficult midstream in a limited edition series. The makers were not keen to release samples, whatever guarantees of them being returned were made. Also, there was no room for manoeuvre on prices for these to enable him to make the margin both he and QVC would want to make. Finally, all these items were made to order and were not available "off the shelf". In the end, the only real solution that gave Steve flexibility to price and to use his own buying power was for Victory Ltd to supply him with quantities of oak and copper cut to agreed sizes and for him to have made into products for the programme. We agreed a format for certification of these QVC products that carried the ViaTel logo and my signature. The products included copper suspended in a resin block, a framed pewter coin with the story of the King's Shilling, and oak and copper, framed and mounted oak and copper and a photo of *HMS Victory* with oak and copper.

He also persuaded me (for a fee!) to act as co-presenter and resident expert on the show. The prospect of doing live television – and it was very much a live show rather than recorded – was a little daunting, particularly for a show of two hours duration. I had to go up to the studios in London for an audition and screen test that consisted of a ten minute run with the show's presenter, on video. This was then considered by the QVC programme director to assess my suitability. They felt I was up to it and I was scheduled in with presenter Dale Franklin from midday to 2pm on Trafalgar day. Although quite nervous before going on air, I have to congratulate the production team and the presenter on their ability to make me feel at ease and to guide me past any banana skins. My role on the programme was to add contextual comment about each of the products as they were offered for sale, and to give background commentary about Nelson, the battle and the ship herself. For this I was on familiar territory and felt at ease. The thing I found most difficult was being asked to comment about products that had been sourced elsewhere and contained no Victory materials, particularly when some of them were not to my taste. I knew I had to be enthusiastic and positive. It is quite hard for someone who is not a professional salesman to say things like: "This is a quite exquisite example of a fine china replica of a snuff box that Nelson would almost certainly have used had he taken snuff, and the masterful execution of the portrait of his beloved Emma on the lid is probably the most sensitive I have seen" when in fact you would have been tempted to lob it into the canal.

The point, as I had learned when putting The 1805 Collection together, is that different things appeal to different people and one should not let one's personal preferences override that. During the programme from time to time people would phone in and talk to us on air. I was particularly gratified when a gentleman phoned in and said that he had met me at one of our shows and had purchased an item from The 1805 Collection. He was most complimentary about our project, and it gave me a real boost, helping me to relax.

I left the studios at around 3pm to assurances from the production team that it had gone well and that they were pleased with my performance. I suspect they were just being kind. Nevertheless, they told me later that they had sold some 80% of the stock on air, and I understand that to be a satisfactory outcome. For myself, I was only too pleased to get on the train to Norwich and get home in time to host a Trafalgar Night dinner for about 40 people at our local pub.

REMEMBER NELSON

My business partner **James Boddy** was driven in this venture largely by emotion. He was a huge fan of Nelson and was caught up with the romance of the conquering local hero and his colourful love life with Emma Hamilton. When he appreciated that Victory Ltd, by virtue of the quantity of oak and copper it needed to sell, was not best placed to create the sumptuous and lavish product collection he wanted to see in tribute to them both, he set up Remember Nelson Ltd to fulfil this ambition. It was, in James's own words, "...a hobby company - rather a passion than a business". In particular, James wanted to honour Nelson's dying wish: *"I leave Emma, Lady Hamilton, therefore, a legacy to my King and Country, that they will give her ample provision to maintain her rank in life."* The nation failed in this, as Emma died penniless a few years later in Calais. James wished to put the record straight.

The products that were created in the two years or so leading up to the bicentenary paid scant attention to their commercial viability but all were stunning. The official launch of this extravagant gesture took place in the crypt of St Paul's Cathedral, the place of Nelson's entombment, in May 2005. In 1802 Nelson had ordered from Chamberlain's (now Royal Worcester and Spode Ltd) an ornate set of china tableware bearing his coat of arms for his home with Emma at Merton. Nelson died in battle before the account for this tableware was settled with Royal Worcester, and the debt remained unpaid by Emma. At the launch event, James presented a cheque to Royal Worcester Ltd for £120/10/6, being the full amount of the original debt, indexed up to today's value of £3,750. Royal Worcester donated the amount to the Royal Navy Association.

Many of the items in the Remember Nelson Bicentenary Collection (which can now be accessed through Nauticalia Ltd) did not contain Victory oak or copper. These were predominantly Royal Worcester porcelain and Dartington crystal. However, many of the choicest objects were mounted on Victory oak plinths, or otherwise contained Victory copper. Chief among these were:

- The Trafalgar bowl, made in fine bone china in an issue of 822 to honour the courage and skill of the 822 crewmembers of HMS Victory at Trafalgar, priced at £295

- The Nelson and Emma bicentenary vases - a hand painted pair of George III style vases from Royal Worcester, one bearing a facsimile image of Nelson's famous portrait by Lemuel Abbot and the other Emma's image taken from one of George Romney's Attitudes painting. This was an edition of 47 pairs – one for each year of Nelson's life, and priced at £5,850 per pair.

- The bicentenary bowl. Standing nearly 13 inches tall, this crystal bowl was hand-engraved by Dartington Crystal's Master Engraver, Nick Davey, and shows the famous flag signal about the rim, together with a profile of Nelson on one side and detailed etching of the battle on the reverse. The Victory oak stand incorporates a piece of Victory copper. The bowl is in an edition of 47, priced at £1,950

- The Trafalgar medal (not a replica of the Mathew Boulton medal) is a hallmarked, piedfort-quality medal containing 2 troy ounces of Britannia silver that in turn contains copper from *HMS Victory*. It features a profile of Nelson on the obverse and the fouled anchor logo of the Royal Naval Association on the reverse. The edition was limited to 1805 at a price of £79 each.

- Victory cufflinks, made from Victory silver, featuring a fouled anchor on a blue background overlaid with vitreous enamel, and priced at £178.50 per pair.

- Horatio and Emma figurines sculpted by Bob Russell and then cast and hand-painted by David Fryer. Standing more than 14 inches tall on their Victory oak base, these figurines were limited to 200 each with a price for the pair of £7,995.

- Horatio Nelson and Emma Hamilton fountain pens in Victory silver and enamel, designed and made in England by The Onoto Pen Company, and offered in editions of 100 at a unit price of £1,495

- The Burnham chair is a traditional East Anglian design in burr oak and yew, incorporating a fouled anchor panel in the chair back made from Victory oak along with a Victory silver medal bearing a cameo portrait of Nelson and commemorative inscription. The words 'Remember Nelson' carved into the chair back recall the flag signal given by Captain Sir William Hoste at the Battle of Lissa in 1811 that inspired his seamen to an overwhelming victory against the French.

- The Trafalgar suite – sofas, armchair and footstool, upholstered in a unique Nelson fabric designed in-house and manufactured in Belgium especially for this tribute, are made in Norfolk with beech wood frames and acorn finials of Victory oak. Prices range from £795 for the footstool to £2,795 for the three seat sofa.

- The Nelson's Column candelabra in Victory silver with a Victory oak base is a candelabra version of the Nelson's Column mentioned in Part 2. They were offered singly or as a pair (one with Nelson atop the column, and the other with Emma) with a price for the pair of £37,500.

Nelson and Emma Vases

Bicentenary bowl

The Trafalgar suite

The Trafalgar bowl

Richard Lucraft is a specialist distributor of limited edition artworks, both through his own extensive customer list and also through galleries When he approached me to suggest a product offering containing Victory oak and copper, I had to advise him that we could not do this through The 1805 Collection as we already had an agreement with Dr Mike Haywood to market a similar product. Therefore his preferred route, was to purchase oak and copper from us and to market it himself. He shared market research data for a proposed range of three products featuring well-known works of marine artist Geoff Hunt RS MA, and these data promised favourable sales.

The three prints offered in this Special Commemorative Edition were: *Victory on the Atlantic Chase, 1805; Victory Breaks the Enemy Line, Trafalgar 21st October 1805;* and *Victory Races Temeraire for the Enemy Line, Trafalgar 21st October 1805.* Each one was signed by the artist, hand numbered and limited to 850 copies. A Certificate of Authentication that also describes the historical background to the subject was offered with each one. They were offered framed at £280 and unframed at £220. In spite of the research and the superb quality marketing material used for this promotion, the outcome was disappointing and failed to sell out. When I advised Richard that I was writing the book of the Victory project his somewhat terse reply was: "Well, it's hardly going to be a best seller, is it?"

Oops!

After his success with the Admiral's chair (see Part II), **Stewart Linford** was keen to extend the range of Victory oak furniture products. Equally, I was not keen to trade products for oak as per the arrangement with the Admiral's chair, so we negotiated a phased payment programme for a further significant quantity of oak and copper rivets.

"This was the best product range we have ever had. It was worth more than £2 million ," Stewart told me.

The Admiral's Collection comprised of the following products incorporating Victory oak and copper:

TRAFALGAR BICENTENARY WINDOR STOOL

LATEST PRICE	£1,995

SQUARE MEAL COASTER

LATEST PRICE	£259

Made from oak from HMS Victory and packed in a presentation box

CAPTAIN HARDY BOOKENDS

LATEST PRICE	£1,477

A pair of bookends, made using oak and oak and copper from HMS Victory

LORD NELSON CHART TABLE

LATEST PRICE	£2,690

Lord Nelson chart table, made in oak and oak and copper from HMS Victory. Carved painted flags adorn the rails spelling out the famous signal "England Expects that every man shall do his duty"

THE TRAFALGAR HANGING SHELVES

LATEST PRICE	£2,690

Made using oak and oak and copper from HMS Victory

HMS VICTORY PEN AND CASE

LATEST PRICE	£477

Made using Victory oak packed in a presentation box.

ADMIRAL NELSON'S SIDE CHAIR

LATEST PRICE	£3,125

Made using burr oak, oak and oak and copper from HMS Victory

NELSON'S COLUMN CANDLESTICK

LATEST PRICE	£765

Made using oak and oak and copper from HMS Victory

HMS VICTORY LAMP TABLE

LATEST PRICE	£3,515

Made from oak and Victory oak and copper.

HMS VICTORY TELESCOPE

LATEST PRICE	£875

Made using Victory oak and copper and packed in a presentation box.

HMS VICTORY PAPER KNIFE

LATEST PRICE	£756

Paper knife with box made using Victory oak and packed in a presentation box.

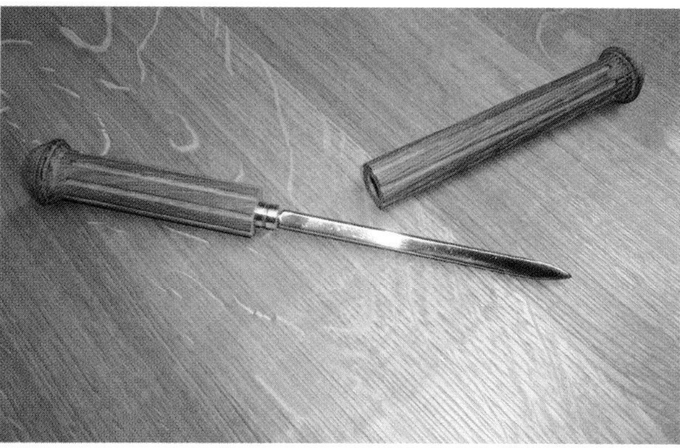

BATTLE OF TRAFALGAR LIMITED EDITION PRINT

LATEST PRICE	£3,850

Limited edition print set in a frame made from oak, and Victory oak and copper.

HMS VICTORY PAPERWEIGHT

LATEST PRICE	£220

Made using oak and copper from HMS Victory and packed in a presentation box

The Westminster Collection is a major British supplier of collectables of all sorts, particularly coins, stamps and other limited edition products. They act as distributors of such items for the British Royal Mint, the Royal Australian Mint, the Royal Canadian Mint and the United States Mint in the UK. In 2004, two of their marketing team came to view the Victory material and discuss opportunities with me. They chose to purchase some quantities of oak and copper sheathing fragments which they incorporated into two products – a commemorative Trafalgar Pack, and a limited edition print. The latter was a depiction of *HMS Victory* breaking the French and Spanish line at Trafalgar, based on the original by Stephen Arch in an edition of 1805 individually hand signed and numbered. According to their marketing department, both products sold well and the promotion was one of their best in recent years.

The Society for Nautical Research, which ran the Save the Victory Fund and was helpful to Victory Ltd in many ways during the project, teemed up with the Woodland Trust for a joint project to commemorate the battle of Trafalgar. Mindful of the concerns Nelson and Collingwood had about replenishing the oak stocks that were so depleted in building and maintaining the fleet, this project aimed to create massive new planting of oak woods and trees in Britain and to educate and inspire young people about trees and conservation.

Voluntary work, sponsorship and fund raising activities led to an impressive result. Significant amongst the fund raising tools was the making and sale of 10,000 key rings made from Victory oak. This was, in the words of the Woodland Trust's marketing department, "one of the best selling items we have ever had in our catalogue range". We were particularly pleased to be able to supply a ton of small off-cuts and less attractive pieces to a company called Wooden Wonders Ltd who were contracted to make the product. That company's general manager told me later: "We won't forget that job. I'll take it to my grave with me! We broke so many blades, but just about broke even."

The centrepiece of the Trafalgar Woods project was called Victory Wood, and consisted of a 328-acre site in Kent, not far from Chatham where *HMS Victory* was built. In addition to this, there were no less than 26 other Trafalgar Woods named after Nelson's ships of the line as well as a further six woods named after his support vessels. In total, 858 acres of new woodland was created to celebrate this bicentenary. The tree planting count, both in the woods and among private supporters, was an impressive 446,000 trees. 15,000 of these trees were planted in the new woods by 6,000 schoolchildren, and a further 75,000 trees were planted by the same number of children in their school grounds. It was a privilege to be involved with this project, and we planted two oak trees on our own property to mark it.

1805 — 2005

This is to certify that this keyring is made from wood taken from HMS Victory – Nelsons flagship

MD Victory Ltd in co-operation with the DSA, MoD

From the early days of the project I had hoped to find ways of using the Victory material in some form of appropriate regalia. As a royal warrant holder for 11 years, I had met Bryan Toye who held Her Majesty The Queen's warrant for insignia, and whose company produces medals such as the OBEs that are awarded in the honours' list. Their business is widely based, and comprises the manufacturing and sale of civil and military regalia, including the weaving of ribbons and narrow fabrics, ties and neckwear, flags, leisure wear, trophies, awards, medals, badges, cufflinks, buttons, jewellery, gold and silverware, cutlery, glassware, watches and clocks, commemorative issues and limited editions. I went to see Brian at their shop in London to discuss opportunities.

We decided on two products – one being a commemorative medal to be offered for the 2005 Fleet Review (covered in the next section), and a pair of cufflinks for sale to the public. These featured a disc of Victory copper sheathing set in Sterling silver, and were accompanied by a Certificate of Authenticity bearing Bryan's signature. They were an unlimited edition and sold for £35.

Toye, Kenning & Spencer Ltd also carried a display of 1805 Collection products in one of their shop windows in the West End of London in the months leading up to the Trafalgar bicentenary, generating useful sales for both parties.

TRAFALGAR 200

Trafalgar 200 (T200) was the agency appointed by the Royal Navy to market and promote the bicentenary celebrations, particularly the International Fleet Review and other events. It was, in fact, a marketing agency in Horsham, Sussex that won the contract to carry out this work for the duration of the events. They had an active and effective website which gave details of all events, as well as an online shop for suitable memorabilia. They listed about 20 of our products, mostly from The 1805 Collection, and generated good business. Under the terms of the contract we had to include paperwork with all despatches that carried the two logos shown above, for which we paid a fee. The total commission taken by T200, including the fee mentioned was slightly higher than we gave to others who took orders on behalf of our Collection partners but was overall very worthwhile. The relationship was proactive, professional and very cordial.

'VERYBIGMABEL'

"**Chris Blenkiron** from Costessy", as he always refers to himself when leaving phone messages, would be amused to see himself described as a corporate customer. A retired National Health Service professional, Chris is a keen amateur wood turner who lives locally and first came across our Victory material when we were showing The 1805 Collection at the Forum in Norwich in the early days of the project. With his slight stature, drooping moustache and amiable disposition I always felt he should have arrived on a burro and wearing a sombrero rather than astride a motor scooter and wearing a crash helmet. The scooter had a storage box behind the seat with the characteristics of Dr. Who's police box – it swallowed up startling quantities of assorted lumps of oak, teak, pitch pine, copper sheet and rivets. His arrival was always welcome, not just for the inevitable chat or 'mardle' as the say in Norfolk, or for the occasional bottle of wine from his English vineyard smallholding, but because he took away loads of off-cuts of material returned by other makers which would most likely have otherwise gone to waste.

Initially, Chris made odds and ends for friends and family, and even sold some to Victory Ltd for sale on our website and at exhibitions. In 2004, however, he discovered eBay and rapidly became our principal eBay vendor, trading as 'verybigmabel'. To date he has sold upward of 400 items on this website, ranging in price from £6 to £100. His main products are small turned vases, pens, light pulls, bottle stoppers and assorted paperweights which he sells all over the world, particularly to America. They carry the Victory Certificate of Provenance except for the very small items that have 'Arisings from *HMS Victory*' stickers. His main products are shown below.

WILLIAM BRITAIN

Toy soldier and military model maker William Britain had two porcelain scenes made commemorating Nelson and his death at Trafalgar. A limited edition of 200 of each was made with Victory oak bases, although they were also available unlimited without oak. The first was the Nelson Deck Scene depicting a number of officers on the deck of *HMS Victory*. This quickly sold out. The later Nelson Death Scene limited edition did not sell quite so well, largely because collectors who wanted both scenes felt that having one on the oak was sufficient. The editions were sold through the normal collectors' distribution outlets, particularly MKL Models who still have a few of the Death Scene available at the time of writing.

Boulton's Trafalgar Medal was designed, engraved and sunk by Conrad Heinrich Küchler and struck at Matthew Boulton's steam coin press at the Soho Mint. It was an unofficial medal created by Mathew Boulton and offered to all those who had participated in the battle. The seaman's version was in pewter and the officer's version was in copper, although some were also struck in silver. Although this gesture by Boulton was intended to honour those involved, it is reported that many of the seamen saw it as an insult and threw them into the sea!

Worcestershire Medal Services restruck the medal in their Birmingham factory, offering a silver edition of 1805 pieces and a bronze edition of 3,610 pieces. These medals were presented in a handmade case and included a piece of Victory oak and a Victory copper ingot. The pictures below are of original medals.

17

IN-HOUSE PRODUCTS

The original strategy called for a small number of in-house products that we could offer at low prices and high volume to retail outlets, particularly featuring small scraps of the material that would otherwise be wasted. We started with just two, the Certificate with an oak fragment, and the acrylic blocks with a piece of either oak or copper sheathing. These were stocked in the early days by the museum shops at the Royal Navy Museum in Portsmouth, the Nelson Museum in Monmouth and St Paul's Cathedral, and latterly by Nauticalia Ltd in its shops. We struggled to break into high street gift and souvenir shops, though a small number of London venues took them in 2005.

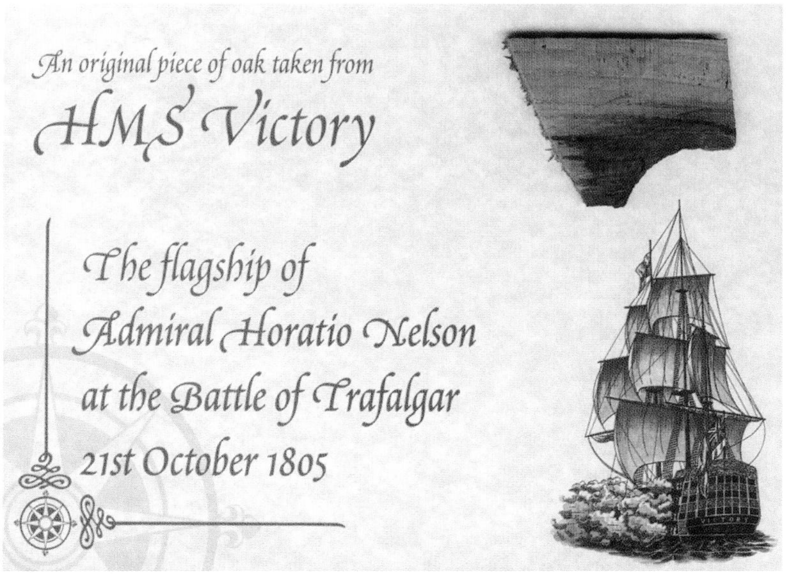

An original piece of oak taken from
HMS Victory
The flagship of
Admiral Horatio Nelson
at the Battle of Trafalgar
21st October 1805

From 2004 we gradually increased the number of products available to retail outlets, on our website and at shows. The impetus for these products was usually either a response to customer suggestion or else a particular scheme of my own.

DAPHNE PAIN PAPERWEIGHTS

At one of the business gift exhibitions, I came across Daphne Pain Paperweights. This company produces a range of paperweight modules that can incorporate your own design. We established that they could just accommodate a thin sliver of oak and also a piece of copper sheathing, that could be presented in gift boxes. I had my daughter design a suitable background and we launched two new retail products that used up small fragments of material. They proved popular with our retail outlets.

Over the years we collected dustbins full of sawdust, and I always hoped we might find a use for this. Julienne Dolphin Wilding, the energetic and imaginative sculptor in wood who had made the Victory chairs and the beam bowl that was featured on the BBC's *Antiques Roadshow* programme, was the first to try. She took away a bag full to play with and returned some time later and presented me with… a 'beef jelly'! She had purchased from an antique shop a traditional copper jelly mould of around Nelson's time, mixed the sawdust with some resin and baked it in the oven. It turned out slightly over-cooked. It was, she advised me, a representation of a delicacy that might have been eaten aboard ship, and how many did I want? I feared my marketing skills fell way short of being able to turn this into a commercial shooting star so I reluctantly declined the offer. I often pick up the original with a quiet chuckle and remember this rather special lady.

In the end my daughter **Amy Bowman** came up with a more possible product. She sourced some small, stylish glass bottles with corks, filled them with sawdust and attached with a rubber band a label she designed herself. The finished item had the sort of quirky appearance of the bottle in Alice in Wonderland with the words 'Drink me' on it. She called it Cannon Blast. We succeeded in selling it through Nauticalia and some of the museum shops and shifted around 200 bottles. The cost of the bottles and the hand-filling filling meant that by the time the retail outlets had added on their customary 100% mark-up the item was quite expensive, so the sawdust mountain was not significantly diminished.

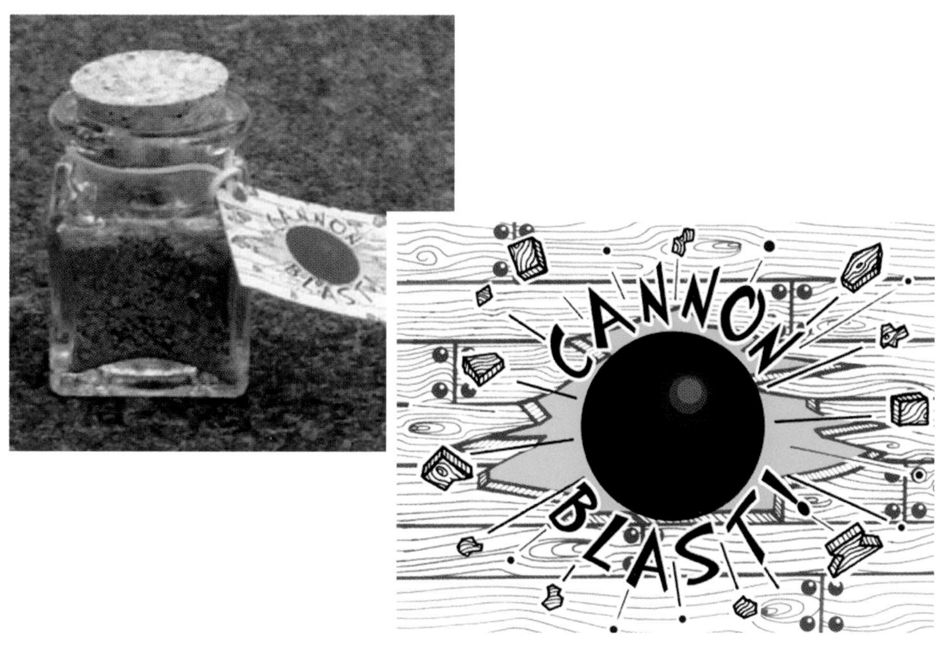

USING THE COPPER

By 2004 I knew we needed to move up a gear with product development, and also to find a way of using the copper. There was an inevitable limit on the amount of copper rivets and pieces of sheathing that could be sold on their own, or even incorporated into sculptures, and we had over six tons of sheathing plus nearly four of rivets. The best chance seemed to be to have items cast in copper or bronze (which would be at least 95% Victory copper). We had worked with one or two art foundries in The 1805 Collection for items such as Val Reddington's medallions, but they were telling me that the toxic fumes from the uncleaned copper were too dangerous to work with. The only hope, I was advised, was to find a large commercial smelter of scrap alloys and to have them melt down large quantities of the sheathing and turn them into ingots. This process would remove the dirt and the worst of the fumes and make it acceptable material for art foundry usage. I contacted a company in Willenhall called **Brookside Metal Company Ltd** and went up to meet their General Manager Steve Moore. My dealings with this company proved to be a complete delight, and not the hassle I had imagined.

Large scrap foundries are not elegant places of work. This I knew from my early career working with one of the world's largest forging and casting groups, also based in this industrial Black Country location. The offices are plain and functional and the work areas resemble something from Dante's inferno. Large, hanger-like buildings with cavernous, dark and soot encrusted interiors, bereft of any softening features, house huge furnaces and crucibles. The dirt floors are churned up by the constant criss-crossing of heavily laden fork trucks carrying stillages of scrap metal. Huge sliding doors remain open to allow passage of these trucks from the scrap piles outside, so any kind of heating is pointless; the furnaces provide ample warmth in the winter, and in summer the accumulated heat can be unpleasant. Light comes mostly from the daylight through the doors and from the orange glow of the furnaces. Overhead safety lights supplement this as needed. There is a constant cacophony of the clatter of metal and the roar of the furnaces, and the overall atmosphere is topped off by the smells and fumes from molten metal. In this environment, work men dress in steel capped boots, donkey jackets and hard hats, often donning goggles and ear protectors. It is a tough environment.

I shipped six tons of copper sheathing to Brookside and we agreed that the process of melting it down and casting it into ingots would take place in my presence, using fully cleaned crucibles from which all extraneous material had been scoured, so that I could verify that what went in was pure Victory material and that what was cast from it was the same copper. They understood the need to verify provenance and were happy to accommodate me on this. When I arrived on the agreed morning I was introduced to the foreman who was overseeing this job and handed a copy of the melting procedure prepared for those involved in it. The single sheet of instructions had been laminated so that it would survive the day. As can be seen from the copy of this document shown below, it had been overprinted onto a colour watermark picture of *HMS Victory*. I was pleased with this touch as it showed that they were taking the project to heart. As I read it I laughed aloud at the first line of the third paragraph: *"Having inspected the copper for shot – that is the Brookside shot blaster shot and not the French or Spanish cannonball sized shot…"* I was also puzzled by the reference in the following sentence to the addition of "2kg brass taps".

"What are brass taps?" I asked.

"Taps made of brass, of course," was the answer. "Like you have on an outside pipe."

I had forgotten momentarily that I was in a scrap metal facility. They had stacks of old brass taps, and the successful casting of copper required a small addition of brass. Simple really.

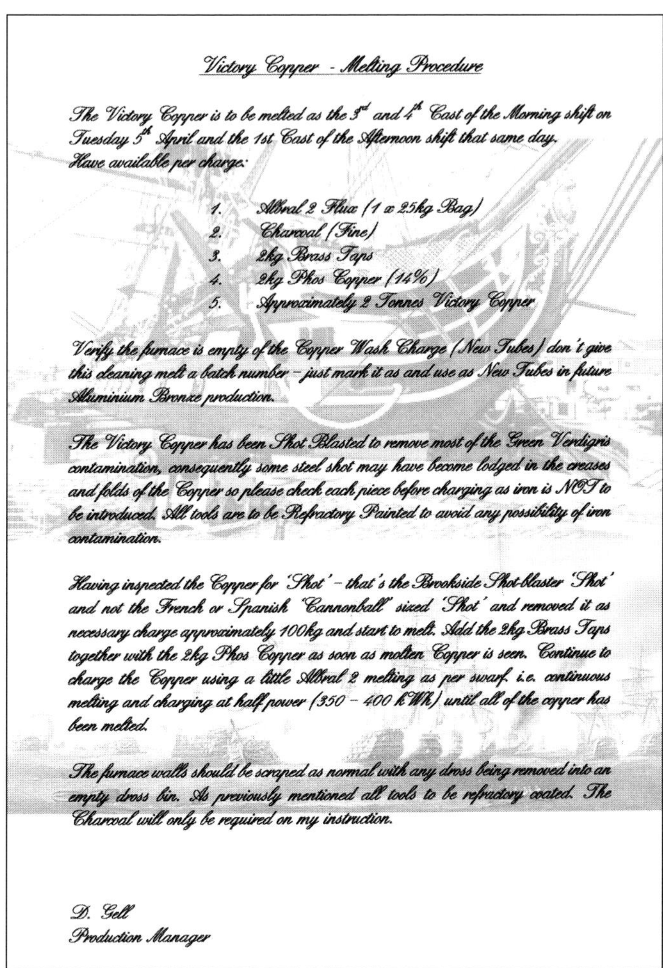

Victory Copper - Melting Procedure

The Victory Copper is to be melted as the 3rd and 4th Cast of the Morning shift on Tuesday 5th April and the 1st Cast of the Afternoon shift that same day.
Have available per charge:

1. *Albral 2 Flux (1 x 25kg Bag)*
2. *Charcoal (Fine)*
3. *2kg Brass Taps*
4. *2kg Phos Copper (14%)*
5. *Approximately 2 Tonnes Victory Copper*

Verify the furnace is empty of the Copper Wash Charge (New Tubes) don't give this cleaning melt a batch number – just mark it as and use as New Tubes in future Aluminium Bronze production.

The Victory Copper has been Shot Blasted to remove most of the Green Verdigris contamination, consequently some steel shot may have become lodged in the creases and folds of the Copper so please check each piece before charging as iron is NOT to be introduced. All tools are to be Refractory Painted to avoid any possibility of iron contamination.

Having inspected the Copper for 'Shot' – that's the Brookside Shot-blaster 'Shot' and not the French or Spanish 'Cannonball' sized 'Shot' and removed it as necessary charge approximately 100kg and start to melt. Add the 2kg Brass Taps together with the 2kg Phos Copper as soon as molten Copper is seen. Continue to charge the Copper using a little Albral 2 melting as per swarf. i.e. continuous melting and charging at half power (350 – 400 kWh) until all of the copper has been melted.

The furnace walls should be scraped as normal with any dross being removed into an empty dross bin. As previously mentioned all tools to be refractory coated. The Charcoal will only be required on my instruction.

D. Gell
Production Manager

The Production Manager explained that there was great enthusiasm in the plant for this project as it was so different from their every day scrap founding, and they felt honoured to be involved. He asked if he could photograph the process for the record, and I was pleased to know that there would be someone else beside myself keeping a photographic reference of the process. Imagine my surprise when, some two weeks later, I received a computer disc with a sequence of photographs, very professionally shot, of the whole process, and the entire sequence set to romantic music! The commitment, humour and attention to detail that emerged from such a macho and challenging work environment remains one of my most enduring memories from the whole Victory project.

When the truck arrived to deliver the cast ingots to me they, like the carriers of the original oak from Portsmouth, were unable to get their vehicle up my drive. The driver had a tight schedule, so he insisted on off-loading between five and six tons of ingots, each one weighing around 8kg, on the verge at the end of my driveway and a good hundred yards from the barn. Jan and I had no option but to fetch my rather decrepit wheelbarrow and start the tedious and laborious task of carting them up piecemeal. Happily, and before we had made many journeys, our postman arrived with the morning delivery. On seeing our plight he immediately pushed the remainder of his mail to the front of his van and set about loading ingots into the back and transporting them up to the barn. He made seven or eight such trips and we got the job done in no time.

I show below the Brookside Metal Certificate of Analysis carried out on the copper prior to undertaking the smelting.

BROOKSIDE METAL COMPANY LIMITED

UP COMPANY

Bilston Lane, Willenhall, West Midlands, WV13 2QE.
Telephone: (01902) 365544 Fax: (01902) 636671
Registered in England No. 3059787

Date: 07.04.05

CERTIFICATE OF ANALYSIS

Customer's Name — VICTORY LIMITED
Customer's Address — P O BOX 120
WYMONDHAM
NORFOLK
NR9 4JZ

Our contract No: CS — DO No: 25
Customer's Order No:
Material: VICTORY CONVERSION INGOTS
Specification:

Colour: NONE
Batch Numbers/s: G 14122 G 14123

Analysis:

	G 14122	G 14123
Copper	BAL	BAL
Tin	0.01	0.02
Lead	0.07	0.07
Zinc	<0.01	0.01
Iron	<0.01	<0.01
Nickel	0.04	0.04
Phosphorus	<0.01	0.01
Arsenic	0.09	0.09
Silicon	<0.01	<0.01
	100.00%	**100.00%**

CERTIFIED THAT THE SUPPLIES DETAILED HEREON HAVE BEEN INSPECTED AND TESTED IN ACCORDANCE WITH THE CONDITIONS AND REQUIREMENTS OF THE CONTRACT/PURCHASE ORDER AND, UNLESS OTHERWISE NOTED BELOW, CONFORMS IN ALL RESPECTS TO THE SPECIFICATION/S RELEVANT THERETO.

Signed .... L. Beaven Position: Production Controller

Part of "the Mountstar Group"

PART THREE – IN LINE ASTERN

TRAFALGAR MEDAL

As well as Boulton's Trafalgar Medal produced by Worcester Medal Services, it seemed appropriate to reproduce the front or obverse face in Victory copper. It was offered in a box as a stand alone item with a small leaflet enclosed, as well as featuring as an insert in the Heritage Pen Stand of The 1805 Collection. The work was done by **White Rose Castings** in Chesterfield who were introduced to me by Rod Matlass, maker of the Victory dagger in The 1805 Collection. This small art foundry turned out to be very flexible and helpful in producing copper castings for the project

NORFOLK MEDALLION

To recognise the fact that Nelson was a Norfolk hero, and being a local Norfolk business, I decided to offer a special edition of the Trafalgar Medal with an inscription on the reverse side of Nelson's words: *"I myself am a Norfolk man and glory in being so."* Just 100 of these were issued and I gave the last one to our neighbour who is the current Lord Lieutenant of Norfolk.

TRAFALGAR CROSS

It is all too easy to view the Battle of Trafalgar in a macho, triumphalist way but the reality today is that it was a significant milestone in the creation of a modern Europe that is united. The highest profile and most spectacular celebration was undoubtedly the International Fleet Review that took place in Portsmouth in June 2005. Upwards of 40 navies from around the world, including a significant presence from France and Spain, took part in this event. We clearly needed to offer something relevant for the occasion.

I asked my daughter Amy to consider and design something symbolic which would emphasise the sacrifices of all parties in that conflict and point to the unity and comradeship that subsequent years have brought. She came up with the Trafalgar Cross – a simple cross bearing the fouled anchor. She registered the design for our use. I hoped it would find favour with the Royal Navy and possibly be adopted for symbolic use during the celebrations, particularly at the Drumhead Ceremony which took place the day after the Fleet review (of this, more later). To that end I sent a copy of the proposed design to the Chaplain of the Fleet in Portsmouth for comment. In spite of telephone follow-up I received no response of any kind. Disappointed but not discouraged we decided to produce the item in oak and copper.

Mick Lock, who had been responsible for the enormous task of moving all the oak and copper from Portsmouth to Norfolk at the beginning of the project, had frequently sought to be involved in producing something from it. His many talents included cabinet making, and so he undertook to make the oak cross and to fit the copper anchor. **White Rose Castings Ltd**. did the copper casting from the ingots recently completed by Brookside Metal Company. The product, which measured 11cm x 7cms, was presented in a high quality jewellery case, along with an explanatory leaflet also designed by Amy. It retailed for £75. I sent a complimentary one to the Chaplain of the Fleet, but sadly, and in spite of two phone calls to his office to check that it had been received, no acknowledgement was ever received. I am happy to say this was the only time throughout the project that I met with anything but complete propriety, helpfulness and professionalism from the Royal Navy.

THE ENGLAND RUGBY WORLD CHAMPIONS MEDAL

The one element of our material stock that was not being used for anything but itself was the rivets. These came in about four different diameters and of varying lengths, and it seemed to me that the obvious opportunity was to slice them up like salami and stamp or strike them into medals. But medals for what? I kept trying to convince myself that sport must be the key. When England won the Rugby World Cup in 2005 I thought this was it. If you slice the rivet at an angle rather than at 90 degrees you get a rugby ball shaped disc. I spoke to several metalworking companies and it seemed as though the most cost effective way of putting an image or words on a disc of this shape was computer-controlled engraving. I had one of them make me up a sample to my design and went to see Grays Ltd, manufacturers of rugby balls for the RFU, to see whether they might become involved in the project. They expressed interest, and I worked up the following proposal:

Background

Victory Ltd is the sole owner of all oak and copper removed from Nelson's flagship HMS Victory during the 80 years since she was dry-docked and renovated. The material was acquired from the MOD who partner us in our use of the material to raise ongoing funds for support of HMS Victory and to underscore its authenticity. Details of our project can be found on www.nelsonsvictory .com

The Victory Medal

Part of the material removed from the ship consists of copper rivets of various sizes. For this project we propose to use those whose diameter is 35mm. They are in various lengths up to 4 ft. [As an historical aside, the copper for these was mined in the Amlwch mine in Anglesey. This was one of the contenders in the TV programme "Restoration" and has received Heritage lottery money for its restoration]

We propose to slice the rivets at an angle, like salami. This will produce an oval (or elliptical circle) to echo the shape of a rugby ball. The slices will be about 50mm thick and we plan to leave the edges with their original green patination in order to signal their origin. The surfaces will be polished, and both will carry a design, either engraved or stamped.

The copper "medals" will lie in a slice of Victory oak with copper corners made from the sheathing taken from her hull, and the whole placed in a high quality presentation case with a leaflet explaining the item, its origins and certifying the authenticity of the material, along with the edition number.

We plan to produce a limited edition of only 250 of these medals, with no.1 and no.2 to be presented to Sir Clive Woodward and Martin Johnson (if they will accept them). We will produce an "artist's proof" (number 0) which will be donated by ourselves and the RFU (at our expense) to be auctioned on or about Trafalgar night 2005 with the proceeds going to Save the Victory Fund

The balance will be sold at a price of £250 each.

Routes to Market

We propose to reach the market in the following ways:

1. By direct mail, using the RFU database
2. By email shot using the Victory Ltd database
3. By exposure on the Victory Ltd website
4. By advertorial in the Rugby press

NB We welcome alternative suggestions from the RFU, and their assistance in securing the agreement of Sir Clive Woodward and Martin Johnson to accept medals.

Publicity Points

The following sentiments, ideas and facts could be useful in creating a story relevant to the project:

- 2005 is the bicentenary of the battle of Trafalgar (final score: England 18, France 0!)
- Nelson, who died on HMS Victory having won the battle, was arguably our nation's greatest hero, and Trafalgar our most momentous naval victory. The spirit of Nelson embraces outstanding leadership, courage, determination, creativity and patriotism. These qualities have been clearly demonstrated by our victorious squad.
- The legacy of Trafalgar was British control of the seas for 100 years from which grew empire, trade and the society we now know. In this society our popular heroes are more often found on the field of sport than the field of battle. It is fitting that the "arisings" from Nelson's flagship should honour our national sporting triumphs.
- Nelson's battle strategy was to defy the normal set-piece war of attrition expected by the superior French and Spanish fleet and instead to create a melee. There are rugby parallels here.
- The oak and copper are a limited heritage resource. These items will become highly collectable, and thus a vehicle for sustaining the memory of England's rugby success into the long-term future.

- In accordance with our agreement with the MOD, 10.5% of the material value of all the copper and oak in the project will revert to the ongoing support of HMS Victory, together with the funds raised from auction of the "artist's proof". The project is therefore supporting a major national treasure and contributing to the bicentenary celebrations.

Together we approached the RFU in Twickenham. They liked the idea, but by the time we got to them they were fully absorbed in preparing for the British Lions tour of Australia and felt there was not sufficient time to roll out the project. By the time they returned from the tour, the World Cup would be history. With regret I shelved the idea.

NORWICH CITY PREMIERSHIP MEDAL

Generally it is better to be stopped at the outset, however promising an idea looks, than to be led half way up the path and then dumped. This is what happened on the next approach to the sports market. It may be a bit of a stretch to align Nelson with football, but the elements of Nelson being a Norfolk man, Norwich City FC making it into the Premiership for the 2004/5 season and Victory Ltd being a local company seemed worth exploring. I put together a similar proposal to that offered to the RFU, as follows:

The Norwich City Victory Medal

Background.

Victory Ltd is the sole owner of all oak and copper removed from Nelson's flagship HMS Victory during the 80 years since she was dry-docked and renovated. The material was acquired from the MOD who partner us in our use of the material to raise ongoing funds for support of HMS Victory and to underscore its authenticity. Details of our project can be found on www.nelsonsvictory .com

The Norwich City Victory Medal

Part of the material removed from the ship consists of copper rivets of various sizes. For this project we propose to use those whose diameter is 35mm. They are in various lengths up to 3 ft. [As an historical aside, the copper for these was mined in the Amlwch mine in Anglesea. This was one of the contenders in the TV programme "Restoration" and has received Heritage lottery money for its restoration]

We propose to slice the rivets like salami. This will produce a circular medal shape to echo the shape of a football. The slices will be about 50mm thick and we plan to leave the edges with their original green patina in order to signal their origin. The surfaces will be polished, and one or both will carry a design, either engraved or stamped. We propose the club crest to be on the front face.

The copper "medals" will lie in a slice of Victory oak with corners of copper sheathing removed from the hull of HMS Victory, and the whole placed in a high quality presentation case with a leaflet explaining the item, its origins and certifying the authenticity of the material, along with the edition number.

We plan to produce a limited edition of either 250 or 500 of these medals, the first 25 (?) to be presented to the squad. The balance will be sold to Norwich City supporters.

Proposal

We would like to suggest that this become the ***Norwich City FC Victory Medal.*** *Key points of our proposition are:*

- Victory Ltd will supply the copper and oak for the medals presented to the squad, free of charge.
- Norwich City FC will create the design and origination both for the medal and the leaflet which will feature information about the club and its winning squad.
- Norwich City FC will arrange suitable publicity for the project and the presentation to the squad.
- We will produce an "artist's proof" (number 0) which will be donated by ourselves and Norwich City FC to be auctioned on or about Trafalgar night 2005 with the proceeds going to Save the Victory Fund.

Publicity points

- The following sentiments, ideas and facts could be useful in creating a story relevant to the project:
- 2005 is the bicentenary of the battle of Trafalgar (final score: England 18, France 0).
- 2005 will see NCFC back in the Premiership.
- Nelson, who is Norfolk's greatest son died on HMS Victory having won the battle. He is arguably our nation's greatest hero, and Trafalgar our most momentous naval victory.

The spirit of Nelson embraces outstanding leadership, courage, determination, creativity and skill. These qualities have been clearly demonstrated by our victorious squad.

- The battle strategy was to defy the normal set-piece war of attrition expected by the superior French and Spanish fleet and instead to create a melee. There may be soccer parallels here!
- The oak and copper are a limited heritage resource. These items will become highly collectable, and thus a vehicle for sustaining the club's success and profile into the long-term future.
- In accordance with our agreement with the MOD, 10.5% of the material value of all the copper and oak in the project will revert to the ongoing support of HMS Victory, together with the funds raised from auction of the "artist's proof". The project is therefore supporting a major national treasure and contributing to the bicentenary celebrations.

The project was agreed at a volume of 750 pieces at a price of £95, with NCFC to receive 40% of sales generated – enough, I believed, to make it worth their while putting some effort into it. I had the first 50 sets made, with the medals cut from rivets and struck by **Charles Neal & Son (Finchley) Ltd**. Regrettably the experience of working with NCFC was not a happy one. I struggled to get them to communicate with me so deadlines were missed and it became clear that this was very low down on their priorities. Eventually I was invited to present a medal during half-time at one of their home matches to Bryan Gunn, who is a well-known and highly respected former player and Director. At this point in the game fans are busily stocking up with food and drink and taking comfort breaks and so the presentation attracted little notice. This is not the place to engage in recrimination, and doubtless there were failings on both sides, but the lack of publicity and follow-up ensured failure. There are less than a dozen sets in circulation.

Certificate

This medal and plinth are made of original materials removed from HMS Victory in a limited edition of only 750 pieces.

Edition no.

Issued to:

Signed:

Lt. Cdr F. Nowosielski MBE RN
Commanding Officer, HMS Victory

The oak plinth bearing this medal is original material removed from Nelson's flagship, HMS Victory. The medal itself is a section of copper rivet used to fasten the massive timbers of her hull, and the corners are copper sheathing that protected the bottom of the ship. These materials were removed during restoration between 1922 and 1999.

The Spirit of Nelson

The battle of Trafalgar, which freed Britain from the threat of French invasion and secured 100 years of empire, was won by inspired leadership, ground-breaking strategy, great courage and seamless teamwork against a determined and unflinching adversary. This is the legacy of Admiral Lord Nelson.

Sporting excellence demands these same qualities. This medal is a tribute to First Division cup-winners Norwich City and the spirit of Nelson that it will bring to the Premiership in the bicentenary year of his greatest and final triumph.

Norwich City
Football Club

Norwich City Return to the Premiership

and a bicentenary tribute to Horatio Nelson, Norfolk's greatest son
2005

Norwich City Football Club
2004-2005 Squad

1	Robert Green	15	Youssef Safri
3	Adam Drury	16	Simon Charlton
5	Craig Fleming	17	Marc Edworthy
6	Darren Huckerby	18	Paul McVeigh
7	Phil Mulryne	19	Mathias Svensson
8	Gary Holt	20	Damien Francis
9	Mattias Jonson	21	Darren Ward
10	David Bentley	22	Ian Henderson
11	Jim Brennan	23	Ryan Jarvis
12	Paul Gallacher	24	Jason Shackell
13	The Fans	26	Thomas Helveg
14	Leon McKenzie	27	Gary Doherty

Norwich City Football Club
Return to the Premiership

After a nine-year absence the Canaries returned to the Premiership - and did it in style! A momentous season saw Norwich lift the famous First Division championship trophy after finishing eight points clear of their nearest rivals.

Norwich City Football Club is proud to work with Victory Limited to pay tribute to the bicentenary of the Battle of Trafalgar.

"I am a Norfolk man and glory in being so."
Admiral Lord Nelson

The 1805 COLLECTION

Victory Ltd
PO Box 120, Wymondham, Norfolk NR9 4JZ
Tel: 01603 757633 Fax: 10603 758170

www.nelsonsvictory.com
mail@nelsonsvictory.com

FLEET REVIEW MEDAL

Determined to have a successful medal made from the rivets I approached medal makers **Toye, Kenning and Spencer Ltd** who were making the cufflinks described in the previous section. The proposal was to design a ceremonial medal to be offered exclusively to those sailors of all nations who took part in the Fleet Review. They came up with a superb product that was priced at £39.95. The ribbon was white with a red stripe to echo the Cross of St George that Nelson always flew from his flagship, and it was presented in a dark blue medal case. We created a colour leaflet for mailing to participating ships. It proved difficult to obtain direct mailing addresses for the foreign naval ships taking part. However, I contacted the Naval Attaché at the embassies of all participating nations, and almost without exception they agreed to forward the mail shot to their participating vessels. I despatched suitable quantities to all and hoped for the best. In the event it turned out that most of them failed to do this, possibly because the medal was being sold rather than given or awarded. Nonetheless we sold some 200 medals to ships from many nations, notably those we had been able to contact direct.

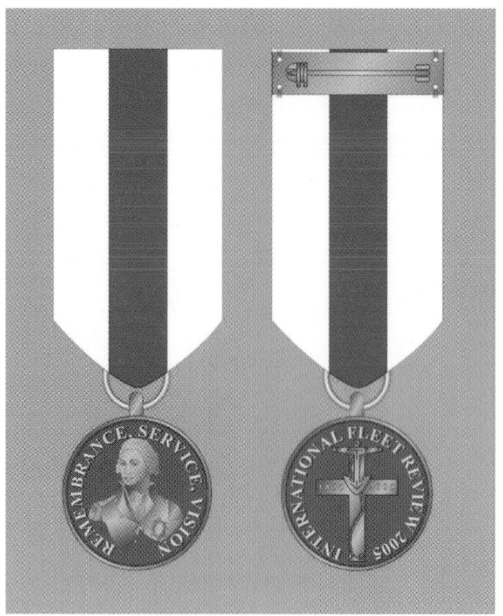

OAK AND COPPER PICTURE FRAMES

From time to time we would be asked at craft shows for picture frames. On the face of it, picture frames seemed an obvious product, but in reality the nature, size and quality of the oak did not lend itself to production of long, thin mouldings. However, at one of the shows we met **Kath and Dave Glenister** of Glencraft originals, and Dave offered to make a few small frames for photos or similar size pictures. He produced ten frames measuring just 5 inches by 5 inches, and we sold these off the stand in subsequent months. Unfortunately there is no picture available, but Victory Ltd Certificates of Provenance accompanied them. My wife Jan also made up framed copper sheathing fragments using off-the-shelf box frames, and we sold dozens of these at the shows.

VICTORY BAILS

This was my swan song project, and born more out of hope than experience. England's cricketers had, in the late summer of 2005, won the ashes for the first time in quite a while. It presented another opportunity to celebrate an English sporting victory with Victory. There was a possibility that the MCC might see the connection and take it forward, but in view of the fact that I was about to pass the whole Victory venture over to Nauticalia it would depend on a number of timing and other pressures. I decided to go ahead anyway, and asked **John Croxon** if he could make them. John had already indicated to me that he wanted to retire from the woodwork scene, but being a sporting type himself he agreed to make a few initial sets to test the water. The finished bails were personalised with the purchaser's name etched onto them using pyrography. Nauticalia set an edition number of 500, and 170 were sold at £49.95 per pair before the pyrographer retired to Spain and England's Ashes victory became a fond memory. I had exchanged several emails with the Chief Petty Officer aboard HMAS Anzac following the fleet review as a number of his colleagues purchased Fleet Review Medals. I could not resist offering the Bails, and this was met unsurprisingly with some straightforward but good-humoured Aussie vernacular!

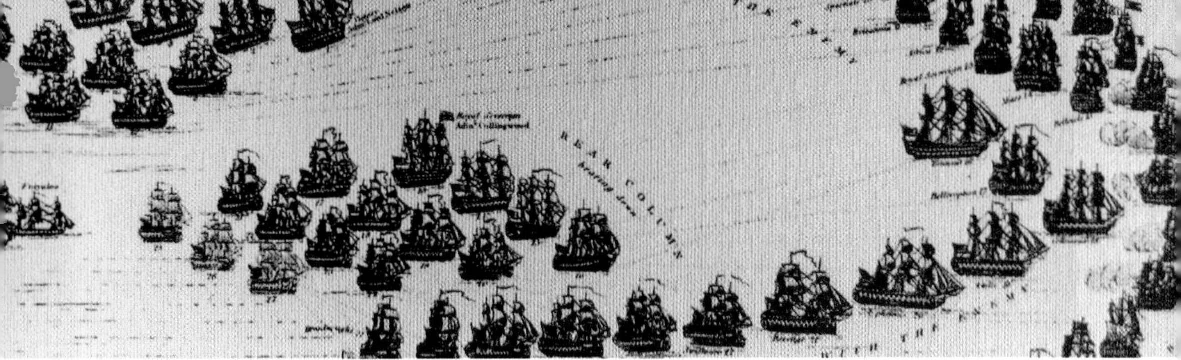

18

SPECIAL PROJECTS

There were some rather unusual projects that involved Victory oak and copper and generated considerable personal interest for me. No doubt the material has been used in other projects not mentioned here, but these are the ones of which I have personal knowledge.

THE STATE COACH BRITANNIA

I stopped for lunch at about 1pm, returning to my office about 40 minutes later. There was a message on the answer phone from someone in Australia called Jim Frecklington. He asked me to call him back as soon as possible and then he would phone me so that I did not have to pay for the call. I was intrigued. It was the middle of the night in Australia, but I figured that if he had phoned me in the last hour he would probably still be awake, so I called his number. It rang a few times before a sleepy and possibly mildly irritated voice answered.

"It's two o'clock in the morning, for Pete's sake!"

"I'm sorry," I replied "but you indicated it was important. My name is Jonathan Bowman and you called me a short while ago."

Jim called me right back just as he promised, full of enthusiasm for his project. "Are you familiar with the Australian State Coach?" he enquired.

Curiously enough I had seen it up close only a short while ago while on a royal warrant holders' visit to the Royal Mews at Buckingham Palace where the Australian coach is housed.

"I built it," Jim explained. "My company is the only one in the world that still has the knowledge and skills to build these, and sadly we are all getting old. I'm in my seventies and many of my craftsmen are approaching the end of their careers

– or even their lives. So, while we still can, we are building the coach for the next monarch who will almost certainly be a king. We are building a King's coach, the Royal Coach Britannia. This coach will be a time capsule, incorporating historic materials from places like Windsor Castle and York Minster. I was wondering whether you might be prepared to donate some oak from *HMS Victory*?"

"Of course, just tell me what you want and where to send it," I replied.

We discussed the detail, and he really only wanted a smallish piece to include in one of the doors. A few hours later he phoned again.

"I was just so excited I could not sleep, and I got to thinking some more about your oak. The pinnacle of the coach will be a King's Crown, gilded and housing cameras for security and broadcasting purposes. We would have to line the inside of the crown with metal to house the cameras, but that won't be a problem. The question is, do you have a piece of oak big enough to do this?"

We discussed rough sizes and I assured him we could find something to do the job.

"How about lining the inside with copper sheathing from the ship?" I suggested.

"Fantastic," he enthused. "Let me work on this idea and I will get back to you."

It was probably a couple of months before I heard from Jim again.

"Listen, can you recommend a wood carver in the UK good enough to take on the crown for me? he said. "It would make more sense to have a local craftsman come and source the materials from you and do the job over there to my specification."

A few months earlier I had met a highly skilled wood carver called **Howard Boyd** who had come to select some oak with a view to making a large and highly ornate chess set for The 1805 Collection. I had seen his work and had no doubt he could do the job. I put the two men in contact with each other. Not long after that, Howard came down for the day and spent careful hours choosing the right pieces of oak and some copper. He explained how the crown would be made in four sections, joined and gilded.[3]

[3] Howard's account of this complex process is to be found in appendix v.

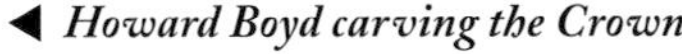

◀ *Howard Boyd carving the Crown*

▼ *Jim Frecklington with the coach*

The crown in situ.

The State Coach Britannia is complete now and is truly stunning. It is currently housed in Australia while decisions are made about its future use, given that it is designed as a King's Coach. A two-page spread on the coach was carried in the *Daily Telegraph* of June 17th, 2006. At no time did I contact the press as there was a fear that the construction of a King's coach might be misinterpreted as a sign that the Queen was considering abdication.

DRUMHEAD CEREMONY TORCHES

Probably the most heart-warming project for me was the one that was at the core of the bicentenary celebrations at the Fleet Review weekend in June 2005. Trafalgar 200, the company responsible for the sales and marketing activities associated with the celebrations, and an important customer for Victory Marketing Partners Ltd, contacted me. They asked whether I would be prepared to donate some oak and copper for three ceremonial torches for the Drumhead ceremony, and whether I could recommend a craftsman skilled in working with both materials to make them. The answer was yes to both.

The Drumhead Ceremony is a military tradition that dates back several centuries to times when a religious service was held on the battlefield after a battle to honour the fallen. Those present would form three sides of a square with the top being an altar built from the regimental drums and covered with their colours. What kind of torches did they have in mind? They did not have a specification, but we decided they would be flame-carrying torches such as used in the Olympic Games.

Rod Matlass, maker of the Victory dagger, had all the skills and lived locally. I phoned and asked him, and we discussed the matter on the phone. Much to my amazement, he arrived not more than three hours later with his first mock-up for my consideration.

"How are you going to make the flame bit?" I asked him. "Can you buy some kind of mini gas bottle to incorporate or what?"

"Oh, that's no problem," he assured me. "I make torches all the time when we go to these pagan shows where I have my stall to sell my daggers. We camp and I make a torch. It's easy. You just need an empty baked bean tin, a toilet roll and some liquid wax. You force the toilet roll into the tin, soak it in wax and then light it. It burns all night!"

I was speechless. I could not see the First Sea Lord being impressed by a canned, flaming toilet roll on a stick being marched across the arena accompanied by the Band of the Royal Marines.

"But won't a bean can be too big and out of proportion?" I ventured, trying to kick the idea into the long grass without causing offence.

"Yeah," he said, "I'll need to get my head round that, but I'm sure it won't be a problem."

Sure enough, I had a call from Rod a couple of days later.

"I've cracked it," he said. "I'm going to use a lady's deodorant can and fill it with citronella oil and a wick. The citronella will burn with a bit of black smoke making it easier to see during the parade."

And so, with the help of Impulse body spray, the technical side of the project was resolved. A real Norfolk solution, I thought.

Just when I thought we were ahead, I had a message from Trafalgar 200 to say that they wanted the design of each torch to be different and symbolic. The three themes were:

- **REMEBRANCE** – "In the rising of the sun and its going down, we will remember them."
- **SERVICE** – "Blown by one wind, tossed by one wave, loyal to one bond."
- **VISION** – "Peace, justice, freedom, security, hope, friendship."

I was quite sure of Rod's ability to make the torches and hoped that the requirement for artistic interpretation of concepts and poetry would not throw him. On the contrary, he enjoyed the interpretation challenge and made three evocative designs with which Trafalgar 200 and the Royal Navy were well pleased. All were turned from oak with the words engraved on polished copper sheathing. For the Remembrance torch, the copper was in the shape of a cross; on the Service torch, the copper was heart shaped; for the Vision torch Rod used the oldest and roughest and most distressed oak he could find, combined with some beaten steel from a bolt to represent the birth of something new and strong from what had been discarded. His next idea showed just how much he had entered into the spirit of the event.

"Why don't we ask the vicar of Burnham Thorpe church to bless the torches before the ceremony since he is the latest successor to Nelson's father who held that post?"

He made the call and the Rev. Jonathan Charles was delighted to oblige. In early June 2005 he structured his Family Service around the three themes, and the Drumhead torches were duly blessed in Nelson's family church. Rod was there with his whole family – the first time they had been together as a family to a service in a church, he later admitted – and my wife Jan accompanied me to join a small congregation. It was a very special touch.

On June 29th 2005, the day after the International Fleet Review, this ceremony was held on Southsea Common, giving an opportunity for all to remember those lost in war. The arena, constructed for the event, hosted some 6,000 veterans of recent wars, including two World War One veterans aged 109 and 104 years, as well as senior military figures and dignitaries from many nations. The service was multi faith, led by the Bishop of Portsmouth. Flags, including those of the 35 nations whose navies were represented at the Fleet Review alongside the colours of all branches of the military, were paraded in a march past with the salute taken by HRH The Duke of York, himself a Falklands veteran, and accompanied by HRH Prince Michael of Kent. At noon there was a fly past and also a "sail past" by *HMS Invincible* that was viewed by all inside the arena. A veteran, a Royal Marine and a cadet paraded the torches, one after the other. It was a very moving event. Rod and his wife and Jan and I had been given VIP tickets in recognition of our contribution, and sitting there in our stand among the gold braid and the medals was almost surreal. As the torches paraded, Rod turned to me and said,

"I can't believe I'm here. Those torches I made are being seen by millions of people on TV!"

It was an emotional moment.

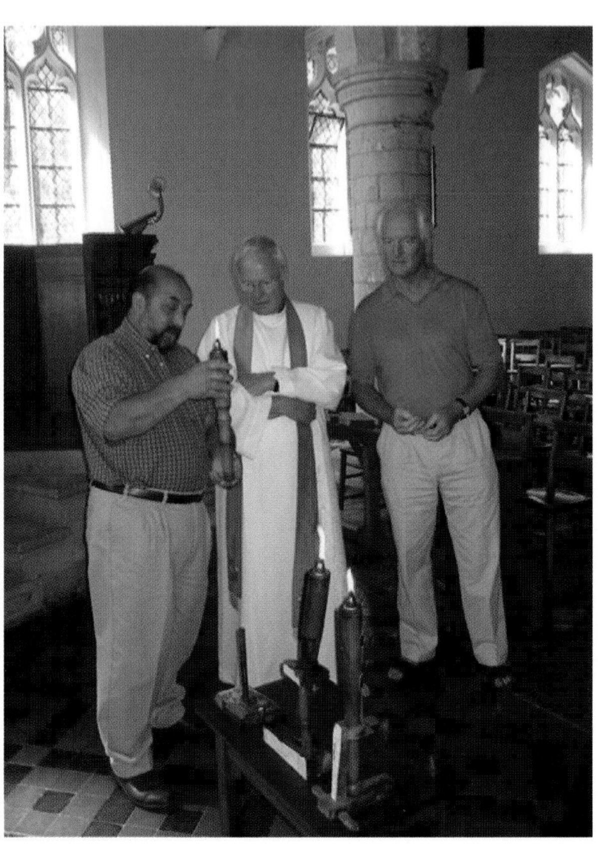

THE SPIRIT OF MYSTERY

On the 18th November 1854, seven Cornishmen, disillusioned with their lives in Cornwall and lured by stories of gold being found in Australia, set sail for the antipodes in an open 37-foot lugger called *Mystery*. Four months and 11,800 nautical miles later they arrived in Melbourne – an astonishing feat of seamanship in those days in so small a craft, particularly for fishermen who were mostly experienced in coastal sailing and could have had no idea what the Southern Ocean could throw at them.

One hundred and fifty years later the idea of honouring this feat took root in fellow Cornishman and adventurer Pete Goss. Apart from being an experienced round the world sailor, made famous during the Vendee Globe race in 1996/7 for his dramatic rescue of fellow competitor Rapael Dinelli in hurricane force winds, Pete is also a skilled craftsman in wood. At a boatyard in Cornwall Pete built a close replica of *Mystery* which he named *Spirit of Mystery* and set sail on 20th October 2008 on the same route without recourse to engines or modern electronic navigation aids. The trip is a tribute to those seven original seafarers.

Hearing about the availability of timber from *HMS Victory*, Pete felt it would be appropriate to incorporate some in *Spirit of Mystery*, and acquired a piece from Nauticalia Ltd which I selected from the remaining stock held in Norfolk. It turned out to be ash rather than oak, but he used it in the construction of the chart table, as seen in the picture below (by kind permission of Mark Lloyd, Lloyd Images).

In 2005, as part of London's celebration of the Trafalgar bicentenary, the annual Great River Race became part of the Sea Britain Festival. It was held on September 17th, the day following the Thames Nelson Flotilla. This symbolic re-enactment of Nelson's state funeral in January 1806, saw an extraordinary number and variety of craft on the stretch of the Thames between Greenwich and Whitehall. The Trafalgar Great River Race itself was in no way outdone by the previous day's spectacle. The race, with competitors from around the world, was run, as ever, over a tough 22-mile course between Richmond in Surrey and Greenwich. There were some 1,600 individuals on the water in more than 260 boats including Chinese dragon boats, skiffs, gigs, Hawaiian war canoes and Viking longboats.

The Masters International Crew in a Chinese Dragon Boat manned by 16 paddlers, a cox and a drummer won the trophy. This achievement was the more spectacular for having come from the back, through the whole field, passing 176 boats to finish in 2 hours 6 minutes and 32 seconds – an average speed in excess of 10mph. This was *HMS Victory*'s cruising speed (maximum 12 knots).

I was approached by Stuart Wolff, director of the race, and asked to donate some oak and copper for a special trophy for this event, which I was pleased to do. The work of creating the trophy was undertaken by Mark Edwards who worked with four others to produce a truly splendid piece. Mark designed the piece and did the sign writing; Sylvia Wicks cut the lettering from the Victory oak, Rosemary Dodd painted the laurel leaves around the edge, Bill Colley turned the copper rivet to produce the cannons and the painting was done by Nancy Petley Jones

PART FOUR

AFTERMATH

19

Small Business Takeaways

LIBRARY shelves are full of literary wisdom about all aspects of setting up and running businesses, and cover every known business function. Many of them are well worth reading if you are embarking on your own business venture. Furthermore, there are government supported small business advice services available at little or no cost to entrepreneurs around the country. These sources are invaluable, and I suppose my first 'takeaway' would be: ***use them.*** What I am offering here are the lessons of my own experience. None of them are new, and most of them are obvious when considered intellectually. The reality in business, however, particularly if you are trying to do everything by yourself, is that you are not interested in theories, wisdom or business models, but rather with getting the orders in, getting them out and keeping the bank off your back. During my business career I have read many of the so-called cutting-edge business books, attended high protein training courses and dealt with all manner of business problems from shop floor to boardroom. That did not stop me from making all manner of elementary mistakes at the coalface while running this small enterprise. The pressure of day-to-day issues often means that you take short-term decisions without properly considering the impact those may have down the line. I suppose what follows is a mixture of "I only wish I had…" and "Wow, that worked well". I hope it may touch a chord or give pause for thought to those tempted to 'go it alone'.

1 **Get your personal expectations crystal clear at the outset.**

This is not the same as the business plan or strategy but has to do with what is in it for you. If you have other shareholders or family members involved in the enterprise, make sure they know exactly what you want in return for your efforts and get their agreement – preferably in writing. Equally, be sure their requirements are also well understood. These are people you need on your side in the future of the business, and crossed wires can cause real difficulty, usually at times when you absolutely do not want any more problems. Keeping your morale high is important for success, and this is all about managing expectations.

2 **Make sure the market is there for you.**

That fundamental piece of business wisdom was absent for Victory Ltd. Because this was a unique situation with monopoly characteristics, the whole project was a risky punt. I knew there would be a market, but where and of what size was unknown and unknowable. Whatever business you plan to start, do the proper amount of research about market size, demographic, growth trends and competition. You cannot create a credible business plan without that.

3 **Have a realistic business plan.**

The bank will want to see something that they can be comfortable with if they are to provide working capital, so it is worthwhile making this exercise meaningful when you undertake it. It is tempting to get carried away with the enthusiasm of starting a business and forecast sales far higher than can be achieved, so take a conservative pill first and then halve the number you first thought of. If you make your base plans such that you can exceed them you will bolster the confidence of yourself, your shareholders and the bank. Learn from your experience. If something does not work, ask yourself why, and if it does work, do more of it.

4 **Get your paperwork/computer systems right from the outset.**

All your transactions need recording, both for your own information as well as for the Inland Revenue and VAT. Today there are some good, simple off-the-shelf computer suites that allow you to record orders, despatches, customer information etc. Make sure you keep a simple cashbook that records daily all cash in and out of the business. I designed my own sales and purchase ledgers on a spreadsheet at the beginning, but as the business grew more complex these started to creak ominously. The temptation, when pressure is on, is to keep sticking patches on in the hope that your system will hold up. The longer you go on with this, the harder it is to go back and recapture your history on a system that will do the job. No one starts a business because they like doing the books, but if you don't get the books right at the outset you will spend your time doing the books and not doing the business.

5 **Add value to the business.**

Mostly when people set out to run their own business their perception of financial value focuses on how much they will be able to draw out of the business as their personal income, and see growth as meaning they can increase their income. All of that is important, but it is easy to overlook the fact that the route to real wealth comes from increasing the underlying value of the business so that the capital value of the business is significantly higher than the investment made. That way, when you come to sell the business you reap a large capital gain – just as you expect to do when you buy a house and sell it a few years later after you have modernised and expanded it. It is important when starting a business to think about where and how you want it to end. You may have visions of setting up something that can be passed to sons and daughters; you are more likely to be thinking of your own medium to long term needs, however, and you should not overlook the 'pension' concept of the value of the business when you want to retire or move on. Some people start businesses mainly to create a valuable asset that can be sold as soon as possible and then go on and start another. In any event, try and make sure that you create real perceived value in your basic business asset. For Victory Ltd the challenge was to take a mountain of scrap material and show that it had value beyond its intrinsic worth. Many businesses will try to achieve the same thing by branding – building the image of the business so that people will see important values in that brand no matter who is actually running the business.

6 **Working from home.**

There are some clear advantages to working from home when you first set up your business – notably the reduced overheads associated with renting office space, as well as the chance to offset some element of domestic cost against the business and gain the tax advantage. Not having to commute to work also saves time, money and environmental damage. However, there are some downsides that need to be recognised before turning the spare bedroom into Mission Control. First, you need the self-discipline to build a mental barrier between the home space and the office. I have a friend who works from home but still puts on a suit and tie to 'go to work' upstairs. Notwithstanding, there is still the temptation to just pop up to the office to sort out the emails when you should be relaxing with your family, and this temptation grows as the pressure builds. The ultimate problem comes when the business is generating high levels of personal stress. In normal work conditions you can escape for a period by leaving the office and seeking the sanctuary of home. When you work at home you cannot separate them and you have nowhere to go to relax. It is not much fun when you start to hate your home because of the pressure it represents. Finally, if you have been working away for years and you suddenly become a fixture at home, your partner is not going thank you when you start appearing at one o'clock and asking "What's for lunch?"

7 **Business relationships.**

Relationships with family and friends tend not to prosper when money is introduced. Business relationships involve people and money and need to be approached with professionalism rather than emotion. In my view, the basis of this is to recognise that the best deal is one in which all the parties benefit. There is little room for machismo in sound business practice. Back in the 1970s, I attended a leadership course and prior to the opening presentation, delegates registered and assembled with cups of coffee. I was standing talking to three other delegates when a man introduced himself into the group and offered us a plate of chocolate biscuits. There were just three biscuits left and the first person took one, leaving just two. As he offered the plate round to the other three of us we all declined, realising that one of us would not have one. It was normal and (perhaps) typically British etiquette. He then introduced himself as one of the speakers on the course and told us that we had just failed our first leadership initiative. "The successful business leader," he told us, "would always grab the last biscuit. There are always winners and losers, and the successful business leader would have taken the last biscuit ahead of his rivals!" I thought it was rubbish then, and am convinced it is rubbish now. Certainly, there are plenty of sharks out there and they need to be handled carefully, but respect and trust build better long-term business relationships. My attitude was always that we could only make money out of this project if we enabled others to do the same. Points that were reinforced to me during the Victory project are:

- New customers are important, but retaining and building business with existing customers is even more important.
- The customer is always right – providing he pays his bill.
- Cock-ups can work to your advantage if handled right. If you give a customer poor service or a defective product, be swift to put it right and err on the generous side. A customer who has been wronged and feels aggrieved can become a real ambassador for you if you exceed his expectations.
- Suppliers should always be paid on time, and as a supplier you should expect no less.
- Walk away from a deteriorating relationship before it becomes explosive. You may or may not win a confrontation, but unless you have clear legal support for a fight, the battle will probably not be worth the aggravation when you have more important things to do.
- Your bankers and accountants make money from you. Make use of their advice and expertise in return for that.
- When you are working with partners their approach may be better than yours. Look at the whole picture rather than just a section of it, and consider the long-term implications as well as the short term ones when weighing up their suggestions. It pays to be pragmatic.
- If you accede to a demand, make sure the other party understands why you did it in case they think you are a pushover who can be exploited.
- Business relationships are still personal relationships. It pays to establish cordial one-to-one relations with individuals you customarily deal with.

8 **Cash is king.**

All businesses need financing. I recall the first lesson of my MBA programme in America in 1967 when the lecturer made the following statement: "The two most important rules in business are: always employ the best people, and always use someone else's money." I have never had reason to doubt the soundness of that rather simplistic statement, but the bit about using other people's money needs handling with caution and both points become more relevant when your business is off the launch pad and gaining altitude (or perhaps, 'off the mooring and sailing well'). It is essential to keep a close weather eye on cash flow to ensure that at the very least you can service your debt. There are plenty of examples of profitable businesses that go bust because they run out of cash. This is particularly the case when the business is going through a growth phase and you are investing in resources to service that growth. Current economic events at the end of 2008 ram home the message that nothing grows forever. Never extend your debt beyond the point where you are comfortable you can cover it with your assets in an emergency without disembowelling the business at the same time. Victory Ltd and VMP Ltd did the vast majority of their business on a cash-with-order basis. It is rare to be able to do that, but any model that allows you to come close to this will help you sleep at night.

9 **Credibility.**

It is almost a cliché that reputation is hard won and easily lost. It was obvious from the 'off' with the Victory project that we needed to give absolute reassurance to everyone that what we were selling was oak from Nelson's flagship and not lumber from my woodshed, so our first priority was to bring on board all those who could verify that, and to ensure that every piece we sold had certification. Our example may seem an extreme one, but every new business needs to build a reputation for integrity and honesty. People being asked to part with hard-earned cash need to know that they are not being hoodwinked, and no more so than in our current sceptical society. Victory Ltd never once made a claim that the timber and copper sold had been at Trafalgar – just that it had been part of *HMS Victory*. No doubt some of it had been, but we could not say with certainty which bits had and which had not.

> Once any business can be shown to be making exaggerated claims about its product or service it will be a wounded business, and rivals will exploit that until it is a dead business.

And finally, to those eager to start their own business I would say this: be absolutely sure that you want to do it, that you have the skills and tenacity to do it and that you will derive satisfaction, if not pleasure, from doing it. Businesses are tough, unforgiving and constantly demanding bedfellows. You will spend far more time on them than you originally envisage, so you must derive some pleasure from them or they will bury you. You must watch them like a hawk because failure to know exactly what is happening with them can mean they steal up behind you and bite you right where it hurts. We may salute our heroes that died in battle, but I have never heard of landmarks raised in honour of failed businesses.

20

A VICTORY LOST

NELSON would have been mortified. Recognition for what he saw as his simple duty to king and country was what drove him. He basked in the limelight of his victories and the honours bestowed upon him. He had earned them all, as was the testimony of London's most prestigious and outstanding landmark, Nelson's Column in Trafalgar Square, donated by the Great British Public in thanks for his life and deliverance from the hated French. Take a straw pole today in London or elsewhere in Britain and the vast majority of people do not know who Nelson was, what he did, why it changed our lives or what Nelson's Column celebrates. This is no better illustrated than by a letter to *The Times* from JA Robinson, of Ightham, Kent: "London's landmarks can be tricky to identify. In 1990 my young daughter confidently asserted that the tall thing in Trafalgar Square was Nelson's Mandela." Sadly, the bicentenary of Trafalgar has not changed that ignorance.

In 2002 I wrote to Tessa Jowell the then Secretary of State for Culture, Media and Sport, appraising her of The 1805 Collection and our aspirations to provide a suitable commemorative tribute for the bicentenary of Trafalgar. In her reply she stated: "Although my Department has no plans to commemorate the 200th anniversary of the battle of Trafalgar, plans for a series of events to mark the bicentenary of Trafalgar in 2005 and to celebrate Britain's unique relationship with the sea are currently being prepared by the Official Nelson Commemoration Committee (Colin White, Director, Trafalgar 200, National Maritime Museum, London SE10 9NF)".

The first point to emerge from this was that the British Government did not wish to be seen to be driving the celebrations. Governments don't take risks. In our new millennium mode of dictatorial political correctness and 'perception is reality', the Blair hologram of Cool Britannia could not support the possibility that we might upset France and Spain and appear as jingoistic warmongers.

The simplest way to dodge the issue was to pass the buck to another hologram – the Official Nelson Commemoration Committee (ONCC).

I mentioned the ONCC in Chapter 11. I have also alluded to an undercurrent of antagonism to the project encountered in some conversations and meetings, most particularly with the National Maritime Museum and the ONCC. It is now widely agreed among those who had any involvement with the 2005 events that the ONCC achieved virtually nothing. Sea Britain was a splendid and successful festival, and Trafalgar 200 with the Royal Navy acquitted itself admirably with their contributions in Portsmouth and elsewhere, but the opportunity to educate and inform was wasted.

One absurdity that illustrates officialdom's cringingly embarrassed view of the bicentenary was the instruction that the naval battle re-enactment so brilliantly mounted as part of the International Fleet Review should refer in its commentary to the two sides as 'red and blue' rather than Britain and the Combined Fleet. The re-enactment was undoubtedly, to all who heard and saw it, a staging of the Trafalgar story. How much better it would have been had this great historical milestone been presented, both nationally and internationally, as the point from which the modern, progressive, influential and essentially united Europe emerged. Each year on November 11th our nation and its allies remember those who gave their lives in two world wars and subsequent conflicts, and reflect upon the lessons of war from which we constantly fail to learn. In an era when politicians have mastered the art of 'spin' to nauseating effect, it is regrettable that this once-in-a-hundred-years chance to teach the lessons of history was so badly missed.

Speaking of the lessons of history, I was asked by two primary schools in Norfolk to come and talk to their pupils in October 2005 about *HMS Victory*, Nelson and Trafalgar. It was a joyful experience for me to talk to these young children. My working life had been spent in a factory and office environment and the classroom was something I had not visited since I was in short trousers myself. Not only was I pleased to have the chance to pass on some of the interesting bits of the Trafalgar story, illustrated with lumps of Nelson's ship, but was quite overcome by the enthusiasm and exemplary behaviour of my young audiences. What took my breath away, however, was what one of the headmistresses told me afterwards.

"Can you believe it, Mr Bowman? I had to get special permission to do this and teach about Nelson and Trafalgar. You see it is not on the curriculum!"

If our current culture of political correctness and the nanny state irritates you, you may enjoy Appendix III.

21

PROJECT STATISTICS

THE size and scope of the Victory 'arisings' project has more to do with the efforts and imagination of all those who participated in it, as detailed in Parts Two and Three. For those who prefer to look at numbers, the following may prove of interest.

1. We purchased 34 tons of timber and 10 tons of copper. When stored on racks, the total volume of space required was just short of 300 cubic metres. This is roughly equivalent to a four bedroom house stacked floor to ceiling.

2. *HMS Victory* weighs in at 3,500 tons. The timber and copper removed during the 1922 to date refit, which Victory Ltd acquired amounted to just 1.25% of that total. So to answer the question posed to me on Radio Four's *Today* programme "is there anything left of the wretched ship?" and to those many people we met during the project who seemed concerned that we were vandalising a national treasure, I would say: "We put back more than we took out" (see 6 below).

3. The 1805 Collection was created by 63 artists and craftspeople from all over Britain, plus one from France and one from Australia. Together they produced 118 product editions, selling a total of 2,775 pieces to a value of £1.15 million. The greatest success stories were furniture, due to the exceptional professional production and marketing skills of Stewart Linford Furniture, Finewood Furniture and Simpsons of Norfolk with the Admiral's chair, the Norfolk and folding chairs and the

Victory stool. After those, the fountain pens from Michael's Fine Crafts, with much lower unit values, did exceptionally well. Other products notable for their high volume sales were Ray Sylvester's baffling box and Chris Wedlake's wine coaster. David Burton takes the prize as the most prolific contributor to the collection overall.

4. Victory Ltd sold the remaining oak and copper to Nauticalia Ltd at the end of 2005. Total revenue to our company from sale of the arisings over the period of the project was just over ten times its purchase price.

5. The estimated retail value of all items sold through The 1805 Collection, Victory Ltd's in-house products and the commercial customers identified in Part Three is between £4-5 million.

6. In total, this project generated funds for the ongoing restoration of *HMS Victory* in excess of £80,000.

APPENDICES

Appendix 1

1805 Collection Deed of Provenance

Certificate of Provenance

"I hereby certify that this contains material removed from

HMS Victory

during her restoration, and that a royalty resulting from its sale will go to the 'Save The Victory Fund' to assist in returning the ship to her configuration as at The Battle of Trafalgar, 21st October 1805."

Item

Edition Number Of

Purchaser

Date

Lt Cmdr Frank Nowosielski
Commanding Officer,
HMS Victory

Sym Taylor
Chief Executive,
The Disposal Services Agency,
Ministry of Defence

Jonathan Bowman
Managing Director,
Victory Limited

PATRON

Vice Admiral Sir Peter Spencer KCB ADC
SECOND SEA LORD AND COMMANDER-IN-CHIEF NAVAL HOME COMMAND

ACKNOWLEDGEMENTS

The 1805 Collection is indebted to the following organisations for their assistance and support:

The Official Nelson Commemorations Committee (ONCC)
to which editions in *The Collection* may be submitted for approval and from which guidance has been sought in its creation.

The Disposal Services Agency, Ministry of Defence,
and its Chief Executive Sym Taylor for supplying and authenticating the material.

International Craft and Hobby Fair Ltd
who have agreed to tour *The Collection* at the 8 major UK Craft Exhibitions each year between 2002 and 2005.

Lieutenant Commander Frank Nowosielski RN
COMMANDING OFFICER, HMS VICTORY
with thanks for his advice and support.

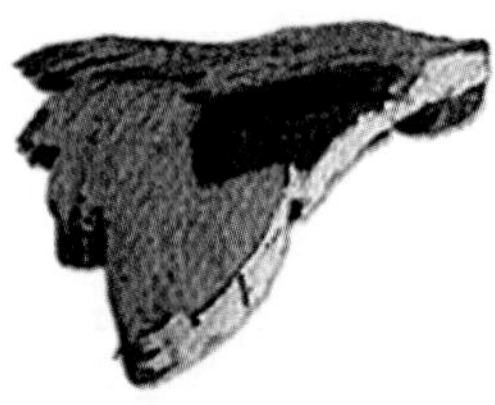

Appendix II

This email circulated during 2005. I lost track of how many times I received it.

HEALTH AND SAFETY VERSUS THE BATTLE OF TRAFALGAR

The Battle of 1805 was a significant naval scrap - Britannia vs. Spain (Pre Beckham, Owen & Real Madrid) and notable for zero US influence, other than Hollywood recreations that portray Nelson as a paid up Republican!

Dramatis personae
Nelson - Admiral of the Fleet
Hardy - his loyal mate

Nelson: Order the signal, Hardy.

Hardy: Aye, aye sir.

Nelson: Hold on, that's not what I dictated to the signal officer. What's the meaning of this?

Hardy: Sorry sir?

Nelson (reading aloud)**:** England expects every person to do his duty, regardless of race, gender sexual orientation, religious persuasion or disability. What gobbledygook is this?

Hardy: Admiralty policy, I'm afraid, sir. We're an equal opportunities employer now. We had the devil's own job getting 'England' past the censors, lest it be considered racist.

Nelson: Gadzooks, Hardy. Hand me my pipe and tobacco.

Hardy: Sorry sir. All naval vessels have been designated smoke-free working environments.

Nelson: In that case, break open the rum ration. Let us splice the main brace to steel the men before battle.

Hardy: The rum ration has been abolished, Admiral. Its part of the Government's policy on binge drinking.

Nelson: Good heavens, Hardy. I suppose we'd better get on with it ...full speed ahead.

Hardy: I think you'll find that there's a four knot speed limit in this stretch of water.

Nelson: Damn it man! We are on the eve of the greatest sea battle in history. We must advance with all dispatch. Report from the crow's nest please.

Hardy: That won't be possible, sir.

Nelson: What?

Hardy: Health and safety have closed the crow's nest, sir. No harness. And they said that rope ladder doesn't meet regulations. They won't let anyone up there until proper scaffolding can be erected.

Nelson: Then get me the ship's carpenter without delay, Hardy.

Hardy: He's busy knocking up a wheelchair access to the fo'c'sle Admiral.

Nelson: Wheelchair access? I've never heard anything so absurd.

Hardy: Health and safety again, sir. We have to provide a barrier-free environment for the differently-abled.

Nelson: Differently-abled? I've only one arm and one eye and I refuse even to hear mention of the word. I didn't rise to the rank of admiral by playing the disability card.

Hardy: Actually, sir, you did. The Royal Navy is under-represented in the areas of visual impairment and limb deficiency.

Nelson: Whatever next? Give me full sail. The salt spray beckons.

Hardy: A couple of problems there too, sir. Health and safety won't let the crew up the rigging without hard hats. And they don't want anyone breathing in too much salt-haven't you seen the adverts?

Nelson: I've never heard such infamy. Break out the cannon and tell the men to stand by to engage the enemy.

Hardy: The men are a bit worried about shooting at anyone, Admiral.

Nelson: What? This is mutiny.

Hardy: It's not that, sir. It's just that they're afraid of being charged with murder if they actually kill anyone. There are a couple of legal-aid lawyers on board, watching everyone like hawks.

Nelson: Then how are we to sink the Frenchies and the Spanish?

Hardy: Actually, sir, we're not.

Nelson: We're not?

Hardy: No, sir. The Frenchies and the Spanish are our European partners now. According to the Common Fisheries Policy, we shouldn't even be in this stretch of water. We could get hit with a claim for compensation.

Nelson: But you must hate a Frenchman as you hate the devil.

Hardy: I wouldn't let the ship's diversity co-ordinator hear you saying that sir. You'll be up on disciplinary.

Nelson: You must consider every man an enemy, who speaks ill of your King.

Hardy: Not any more, sir. We must be inclusive in this multicultural age. Now put on your Kevlar vest; it's the rules. It could save your life.

Nelson: Don't tell me - health and safety. Whatever happened to rum, sodomy and the lash?

Hardy: As I explained, sir, rum is off the menu! And there's a ban on corporal punishment."

Nelson: What about sodomy?

Hardy: I believe that is now legal, sir.

Nelson: In that case ...kiss me, Hardy.

Appendix III

Gunner Jo - A Poem

by Marriott Edgar

I'll tell you a seafaring story,
Of a lad who won honour and fame
Wi' Nelson at Battle 'Trafalgar,
Joe Moggeridge, that were his name.

He were one of the crew of the Victory,
His job when a battle begun
Was to take cannon balls out o' basket
And shove 'em down front end o' gun.

One day him and Nelson were boxing,
The compass, like sailor lads do.
When 'Ardy comes up wi' a spyglass,
And pointing, says "'Ere, take a screw!"

They looked to were 'Ardy were pointing,
And saw lots o' ships in a row.
Joe says abrupt like but respectful,
"'Oratio lad, yon's the foe."

'What say we attack 'em?' says Nelson,
Says Joe 'Nay lad, not today.'
And 'Ardy says, 'Aye, well let's toss up.'
'Oratio answers 'Okay.'

They tossed... it were heads for attacking,
And tails for t'other way 'bout.
Joe lent them his two-headed penny,
So the answer was never in doubt.

When penny came down 'ead side uppards,
They was in for a do it were plain,
And Joe murmered 'Shiver me timbers.'
And Nelson kissed 'Ardy again.

And then, taking flags out o' locker,
'E strung out a message on high.
'T were all about England and duty,
Crew thought they was 'ung out to dry.

They got the guns ready for action,
And that gave 'em trouble enough.
They 'adn't been fired all the summer,
And touch-holes were bunged up wi' fluff.

Joe's cannon, it weren't 'alf a corker,
The cannon balls went three foot round.
They wasn't no toy balloons either,
They weighed close on sixty-five pound.

Joe, selecting two of the largest,
Was going to load double for luck.
When a hot shot came in thro' the porthole,
And a gunpowder barrel got struck.

By gum! there weren't 'alf an explosion,
The gun crew were filled with alarm.
As out of the porthole went Joseph,
Wi' a cannon ball under each arm.

At that moment up came the 'Boat-swine'
He says 'Where's Joe?' Gunner replied...
'E's taken two cannon balls with 'im,
And gone for a breather outside.'

'Do y' think he'll be long?' said the 'Boat-swine'
The gunner replied, 'If as 'ow,
'E comes back as quick as 'e left us,
'E should be 'ere any time now.

And all this time Joe, treading water,
Was trying 'is 'ardest to float.
'E shouted thro' turmoil of battle,
'Tell someone to lower a boat.'

'E'd come to the top for assistance,
Then down to the bottom he'd go;
This up and down kind of existence,
Made everyone laugh... except Joe.

At last 'e could stand it no longer,
And next time 'e came to the top.
'E said 'If you don't come and save me,
I'll let these 'ere cannon balls drop.'

'T were Nelson at finish who saved him,
And 'e said Joe deserved the V.C.
But finding 'e 'adn't one 'andy,
'E gave Joe an egg for 'is tea.

And after the battle was over,
And vessel was safely in dock.
The sailors all saved up their coupons,
And bought Joe a nice marble clock.

APPENDIX IV

THE VICTORY CROWN

THE Victory crown was carved by OH Boyd in his Lincolnshire studio and completed on 17th February 2005.

Named because it is carved from timbers from *HMS Victory*, Nelsons flagship; These timbers were recovered from her during a major re-fit in 1926 and supplied by Jonathan Bowman of Victory Ltd., as was the copper sheath from the hull of the vessel from which the interior liner to hold the surveillance equipment secreted in the recess beneath the crown, was formed.

Significantly carved in this year, 2005, which is the 200th anniversary of the Battle of Trafalgar where Nelson defeated the combined fleets of France and Spain and met his death on the quarterdeck of his flagship Victory, shot through the spine by a ball from a French snipers musket.

Beginning with a telephone call from Australian Jim Frecklington who was charged with building the new Royal Coach Britannia this crown probably has more significance than any other ever carved because it is a piece of the Victory herself. Also contained within the body of the crown is a segment of oak gear teeth made by John (Longitude) Harrison the Barrow upon Humber carpenter in 1726. Harrison invented and made the world's first accurate sea clock which contributed so greatly to Britain's great advances in navigation and superiority at sea. The crown represents all that is finest in our great maritime tradition and celebrates the talents of two great men whose contributions to our nation were invaluable and complemented each other.

All that was specified was that the crown had to be 12 inches in height, be modelled on the male monarch's version of the Imperial State Crown and had to be hollow to take modern surveillance equipment.

A full scale drawing was done from the two photographs of a previous crown that Jim took whilst at the Royal Mews. These photos were vague to say the least but from them I was eventually able to construct a scale, discounting perspective, which gave me dimensions that I believe to be accurate.

The previous crown was done in imperial measurements and when I realised this was able to use this to good effect and fill in gaps by educated guesswork. There were some difficulties with interpretation but by and large logic solved the grey areas. The most difficult were the fleur de leys, the velvet and vaguest of all, the ermine trim which is almost my own version.

Having made a full sized working drawing I had then to decide the construction, bearing in mind that the timber I was using could be up to 300 years old and has to last another 300 or so. Part of this difficulty is the size of the timber and its nature.

The crown represents a large piece of work as one lump, over 10 inches in diameter and up to 12 inches high. Pieces as big as that are not readily available due mostly to the fact that they come from a fighting ship and as such are frequently re-enforced with copper rods to withstand the stresses and strains of cannon and combat, not to count those of long sea voyages. So holes abound.

Also, I was worried about the shrinkage. Wood only shrinks along its width, not along the length and because of that a large block could, in time, become ovaloid in shape. This would put undue stresses on the bridges and other details. I therefore decided to build the main body of the crown from four pieces; these pieces were cut in such a way that they put the tree back together. Roy Smith, the saw man did this with great skill, arranging the growth rings as they would have been when the tree was growing as closely as was possible. This has the effect of making the shrinkage uniform thereby cancelling out the ovaling phenomenon, giving maximum stability.

It does have the disadvantage from a carving point of view of having to carve through pure growth rings making the detail liable to spalling off, so the carving process was more difficult than usual and had to be treated with unusual care.

A trip to Norwich to meet with Jonathan Bowman of Victory Ltd was most interesting and we eventually selected what we thought would be enough sound and clear timber to be able to make the crown together with half a sheath of copper from the Victory's bottom. This is all carefully weighed out and donated by Jonathan on behalf of Victory Ltd.

The timber was converted in the workshops of Roy Smith, a retired journeyman joiner who has had a lifetime of experience with timber, in both the winning and the working.

The timber was found to be reasonably and workably sound but not as clear as we would have hoped. It is difficult to judge the condition of painted timber with holes hidden inside it and it was not until it went through the saw that we were really able to tell fully what we were dealing with.

The block was accurately fitted together gluing each block individually to each other allowing at least 24 hours to cure, the last piece being fitted very accurately indeed. This was because we wanted as perfect a glue line as possible.

When the glues were cured it went back to Roy Smith for turning to the pattern I had decided and made the former for from the master drawing. This was a particularly hazardous time because of the age and brittleness of the timber, also the depth of the recess where the copper liner would fit but Roy's skill and experience come through and we finished with a good solid blank with only two sizeable holes to deal with.

Marking out very accurately the positions and stations of the fleur de leys and crosses I next made a pattern of the fleur de leys and applied it to the block with dry mount glue, carving through it for accuracy and then removing the remaining pattern. This, though accurate was very messy and I would think twice before doing that again because of that. This process was repeated for the crosses. The bridges were to stand on the crosses so they were carefully and accurately levelled in relation to each other.

Before carving could begin one of the holes fell right within one of the fleur de leys and had to be dealt with. A perfectly matching piece of timber was found and after cleaning the hole I made a plug with the grain going exactly the right way and fitting perfectly, this was then glued into place and left to cure for 24 hours. Carving began and the fleur de leys and crosses completed before the bridges were cut.

A pattern was made for the bridges and try as I might, I could not find four matching pieces that were suitable. They were either too short, not the right size, got a shake (crack) or fell right where a hole occurred. This left me in a fix as it meant another trip to Norfolk to pick yet more timber and this was a full days outing as Norfolk is a very difficult journey from here and I was in the middle of moving house with all its attendant difficulties. Using my initiative I rang Jonathan Bowman who gave permission to use timber I already had for another project for these bridges. This suited the work perfectly and I transferred the designs and duly bandsawed them out.

The next big job was getting the bridges to join and fit the crown and each other perfectly whilst keeping the correct angles and inclinations. Carefully marking out I cut the tenons and chopped the mortices on the crosses together with the 45 degree angles at their meeting at the apex, taking care to be as accurate as possible and constantly adjusting for fit until perfect.

The next puzzle was how to shape the bridges with the profile following a completely vertical line through them, including the fillets. To do this I cut a separate bridge that screwed into the bridges proper to lock them in exactly the right position and using great care bandsawed them through by sliding them on their tenons on the table. This had the disadvantage of leaving a screw hole where some of the bridge pearls were to be, these were filled later.

More tweaking and the bridges fitted exactly on the cross platforms and against each other.

When downwards pressure was applied to the top of the structure it was apparent that the whole thing was very strong and a lightweight person could probably have stood on it.

Using the master pattern I made patterns for the lay of the 9 pearls for the individual bridges and pricked through in the time honoured way for exact position, then using pair of compasses scribed the circles in the right places.

Carving them to depth was awkward in that they were a difficult shape to hold so I made a former to fit in the vice which solved this problem. Holding the pieces was generally difficult because of the strength of the timber, the more pressure it takes to carve it, the more it takes to restrain it but with fiddling and tweaking we managed as we usually do.

The pearls were then generally shaped and refined until uniform in size, the undercutting coming later together with the grounds on which they sit.

Having got the bridges properly joined I had to interpret the velvet. From the photograph, which showed only one side, I determined the profile and the lay of the folds. These I drew carefully on to paper and shaded them so that they could be properly understood, once this was fixed in my head I simply did it as best as I could from that position and then worked round each station until a good representation of a velvet liner was formed.

Time was taken to make sure that there were no pockets where water could stand and graceful curves were added to each fillet for the same purpose.

In carving this I managed to get rid of one major dowel hole but opened up other things, including dead and buried worm holes but this solved more problems than it showed. We are dealing with ancient timber after all.

Once the velvet was dealt with we came to the jewelled band; analysis showed that the crosses, which stand on the 90 degree points and are the points for the bridges meeting, contained the main jewels. The 2 large rectangular stones diametrically opposite each other and the 2 triangular jewels at the other diametrical opposite; the other 4 oval stones occur at the 45 degree angles where the fleur de leys happen. These were set into the raised land left for the purpose by the turner, the background being carved away.

To carve the pearls that form the setting that surrounds the jewels took careful setting out and it became apparent just how many there were, the main rectangular stone being surrounded by 26 of them so great care was taken, even so, their small section with the direction of the grain and the age of the timber meant some later forming with abrasive papers would be necessary to tidy up.

The rope twist that happens below the cross and fleur de leys band was next. The number of twists was clearly visible on the photo so that was a simple matter of division and a 'V' groove was set in for the purpose at the right pitch, this was further refined and continued through to give the effect.

Beneath this ring and above the jewel ring is a curved dentil like band which again was carefully laid out and set in, this leaves only the ermine trim and this I had great difficulty with the interpretation because of the lack of clarity of the photographs. I could see however that there was a regular form, probably to represent the black part that happened at each station of a jewel so I set those in and using what I thought to be appropriate carved a representation of the fur.

The copper liner to house the electrical equipment was made from a copper plate from the sheathing of the 'Victory'. The ships hull beneath the waterline was covered in this way to prevent infestation from the Toledo worm, a voracious boring worm found in warm waters that can virtually render a ship useless in a very short time by undermining its timbers, also the copper prevents the growth of marine algae's and molluscs which foul a ships bottom and affect its sailing capability, as an anti fouling device.

The specification for these sheaths was laid down very precisely by the admiralty as to size and number and pattern of nails to be used. This was because copper was a very precious material and unless specific numbers were given there was the danger that platers would skimp and pocket the nails to weigh in for cash perhaps putting ships, (and sailors) in jeopardy.

Andrew King, arguably the world's greatest living authority on John Harrison's wooden clocks made the liner with a wide hole covered by a plate that screws down on to it and located in the 4 inch deep recess in the crown by 3 lugs to enable the whole to be screwed into recesses in the rim of the crown. Access can then be easily gained from the bottom of the crown without disturbing it from its mounting.

We were very conscious that we were using part of this wonderful ship and of its history, bearing this in mind we decided to simply flatten the nail holes and accept them as part of the finished article and not to mess around too much with it.

This liner is made from a copper sheath from HMS Victory and we wanted it to look as though it was. If we had wanted a pristine liner then new copper would have done the job better. Also, this liner is not seen at all it being secreted inside. The finish was left exactly as it came from the soldering with little tidying here and there. It would have been easy to pickle the whole thing but we thought that the decision as to how far to take it was to be with Jim Frecklington at a later date and hope that he agrees with our conclusions.

On the corner of the sheath we found the makers name and the weight of the material stamped on it. It was a little battered but the corner was cut off, hammered flattish and soldered onto the lid of the liner for interest and historical link.

The orb was the last thing to be done; again making a pattern from the master it was taken to Roy Smith to turn which despite problems with the timber was done successfully and as usual, exactly.

The crosses and pearls were carved in and this revealed more long gone worm which was not apparent at all until the wood was opened up, filling will deal with that. The orb and its bands were carved back and the whole was ready to be fitted to the junction of the bridges. There was some tweaking necessary to achieve the specified height of 12 inches, when this was right the orb was glued into place and when dry dowels were added for mechanical strength and peace of mind.

The crown was now ready to finally glue down the bridges into place after carefully sanding the undersides and the awkwardly reached areas of the velvet under. This was done absolutely at the last ditch before I had a three hour drive to meet Jim down at my in-laws house in Essex, a good half way point for us both.

I did hope to persuade Jim to let me keep the crown for another 2 days so that I could properly sand, fill and tweak the crown to my satisfaction and then send it on by special courier but he wasn't having any of that and I reluctantly had to leave that part of the job to him, leaving me with a feeling of incompletion.

The standard of finish was always a doubt because the crown is to be gold leafed, part of this process is the gessoing of the surface which tends to fill as it goes and form fillets too, so perhaps that was better left to the gilders in case I did something wrong and irreversible.

So the crown is now in Australia and I can say that it was a great honour to be part of such a wonderful and romantic venture. The crown will be to me the centre piece of the coach in that it does surmount the whole thing and is a very visible symbol.

Little did I think that when I was a small boy at the coronation of Her Majesty some 50 odd years ago that the crown we drew and coloured in school would one day be a subject that I would have the chance to carve for the nation.

The fact that it is timber, a piece of *HMS Victory* is so significant, especially in this year, 2005, the 200th anniversary of the Battle of Trafalgar and that when the coach travels down the Mall as it has to on virtually every outing, a piece of Victory will glide past lampposts that contain representations of all the ships that were at the Battle of Trafalgar, in effect, the flagship reviewing the fleet. It cannot get to be more romantic or significant than that.

Copyright OH Boyd
25th February 2005